TAKING
THE
RED
PILL

SCIENCE,
PHILOSOPHY
AND RELIGION
IN *THE MATRIX*

EDITED BY
Glenn Yeffeth

NTRODUCTION BY
David Gerrold

summersdale

Summersdale Publishers Ltd
46 West Street
Chichester
West Sussex
PO19 1RP
UK

www.summersdale.com

Printed and bound in Great Britain.

ISBN 1 84024 377 5

Originally published in the USA by BenBella Books.

CONTENTS

Praise for *Taking the Red Pill*

"Dr. Barr enthusiastically prescribes *Taking The Red Pill* for all readers who wish to enhance their understanding of science, philosophy, and religion in *The Matrix*. *Taking The Red Pill* acts as a wonder drug, a miracle cure for all the cognitive complications *The Matrix* generates. The volume, after all, is replete with doctors who are not physicians: economists; philosophers; scholars of religion, literature, and media; science fiction writers; inventors; and technologists. This plethora of Ph.D.'s concocts brilliantly articulated interpretive medicine which goes down in a most delightful way."

> —Dr. Marleen S. Barr, pioneering feminist
> science fiction scholar and author of *Genre
> Fission: A New Discourse Practice for Cultural
> Studies*

"*Taking the Red Pill* is an interesting and intelligent collection that explores, from a variety of viewpoints, the film that (for better or worse) may well be the most widely and seriously discussed work of science-fiction cinema since Ridley Scott's *Blade Runner*."

> —Carl Freedman, author of *Critical Theory
> and Science Fiction*

With the release of *The Matrix Reloaded* and *The Matrix Revolutions*, 2003 is going to be the year of *The Matrix* (again). Published four years after the release of the first film, *Taking the Red Pill: Science, Philosophy and Religion in The Matrix* is a significant contribution to the field of film and literary studies, as well as the most approachable collection of essays for non-specialists who simply adored *The Matrix* and its complex and thought-provoking storyline. *Taking the Red Pill* contains many answers to the questions raised by the film, and offers exciting and daring new readings of this blockbuster. Combining detailed readings of the many philosophical, literary and economical issues present in *The Matrix* with a clear and readable style . . . *Taking the Red Pill* is a must-read for anyone interested in a broad ranging literary and cultural analysis of one of the most important twentieth-century films.

> —Dr. Michael Eberle-Sinatra, founding
> editor of the e-journal *Romanticism on the
> Net* and editor of *Mary Shelley's Fictions:
> From Frankenstein to Faulkner*

DAVID GERROLD

INTRODUCTION

The Matrix hit the film-going public by surprise, much like *Star Wars* a generation earlier, and for many of the same reasons. It had a breathless pace, astonishing eye-candy, a sense of mythic adventure, and an acid-tinged sensibility. Like *Star Wars*, it opened up a new continent of imagination; in this case, a domain of cyber-existence that no movie had explored before.

Also, like *Star Wars*, *The Matrix* drew heavily on the major tropes of science fiction. Long-time readers of the genre recognized the permeating flavors of George Orwell, Harlan Ellison, Philip K. Dick, and William Gibson: a dystopic machine-dominated future, peopled by implacable forces and disposable identities; a juggernaut of industrial behemoths flattening humanity under the steamroller of time.

But all of this came in on top of an earlier, even more powerful mythic structure: the lone hero who saves the town; almost always he has some superior ability or insight. We've seen this story in a variety of forms, we never get tired of it.

It's the underlying theme in James Bond movies and Tom Clancy novels, in almost every Clint Eastwood western, in classics like *Shane* and *The Man Who Shot Liberty Valance*, in comic books like *Superman* and *Batman*, in popular television shows like *Route 66* and *The Fugitive*, and even in many *Bugs Bunny* cartoons—but although this particular myth has sometimes been identified as "the American mono-myth," we also see it expressed in earlier fables, such as *The Pied Piper of Hamlin*, *Beowulf*, and *St. George and the Dragon*.

We can even find variations of this story in other cultures, as in Akira Kurosawa's film of *Yojimbo*, or in the earlier tales of medieval Samurai warriors, such as *Musashi*. If we go far enough back, we can add Perseus to the list, Prometheus too, and probably even Orpheus as well; all lone heroes who took on impossible challenges and succeeded, often at enormous cost.

Neo stands among some very proud company indeed.

The cultural archetype, of course, is Christ. He came into the world with superior powers and insight. He was misunderstood. He saved the souls of those who trusted him and believed in him, he was betrayed by someone he trusted, and he was punished by the authority he challenged. But he left the world changed for the better for having passed through it. So, of course, any tale that echoes that one is going to have enormous resonance among its audience.

And you thought *The Matrix* was just a movie, right?

Like any good movie, like any good work of art, a single exposure is not enough; there's much more to be discovered by revisiting the work, by giving ourselves over to some careful contemplation of its intention as well as its impact. We have the opportunity to consider at some length the nature of reality as portrayed in the film, not as a simple story, but as a commentary—a mirror in which we can see ourselves and our own "reality" reflected—and thereby granting us the opportunity for insight.

Insight, also known as wisdom in drag, allows us to recognize the traps of existence. Some traps, like life itself, cannot be broken, cannot be escaped; the best we can do is recontextualize. With the addition of insight, we gain mastery over ourselves in relation to the trap. This is the essential function of philosophy, as well as of art, and what this excellent collection of essays demonstrates, if nothing else, is a confluence of intention where art and philosophy collide in a single film.

Here, *The Matrix* is held up to the light and examined from a dozen different directions. I suppose I could make the immediate comparison of the six blind men and the elephant (I won't mention where the seventh blind man stuck his hand), except in the world of *The Matrix*, we're all blind and everything is elephants—but that analogy would be wrong.

It might also be appropriate to mention an odd little book, long out of print, that made a minor splash three decades ago. It was called *The Pooh Perplex* and served up a collection of essays analyzing Winnie the Pooh, each from a different perspective—political, social, religious, philosophical. That book was a parody, and while it told you very little about Winnie the Pooh, it told you a great deal about how individual authors impressed their own agendas and mindsets upon even the most innocently intentioned works. But that comparison would be wrong as well.

The authors of these explorations have given us, instead, a lens, an object through which light is focused and projected so as to provide illumination—so that we can distinguish our environment. Sometimes we project light through filters, sometimes we polarize it, sometimes we use infra-red or ultra-violet, or even micro-waves or X-rays, all so that we can look at the world in ways that go beyond the limitations of the physical eye. In that regard, we are using not the body's vision, but the mind's. The authors of these explorations have given us the opportunity to see how a single work resonates on multiple levels, reflecting off many facets, striking deep chords of memory, meaning, and interpretation.

That's the success of a movie (or any work, for that matter)—that it creates new opportunities for exploration, discovery, and insight, that it gives us new ways to think about ourselves and the world in which we live.

Indeed, that's the point of the Matrix—that humanity has a choice, not just as a species, but as individuals as well. We can accept our roles as slaves of the machine, or we can reinvent ourselves as masters.

I'll get out of your way now. You can step into the mirror.

READ MERCER SCHUCHARDT

WHAT
IS
THE
MATRIX?

Media and cultural critic Read Mercer Schuchardt presents the definitive answer to the question "What is the Matrix?" If you only have time for one essay on The Matrix, *this is the one to read.*

PARABLE

While the stated reason for the early release and accelerated postproduction process of *The Matrix* was to beat the marketing hype that surrounded *The Phantom Menace*, it is not without coincidence that *The Matrix* was released on the last Easter weekend of the dying twentieth century. It is a parable of the original Judeo-Christian worldview of entrapment in a world gone wrong, with no hope of survival or salvation short of something miraculous. *The Matrix* is a new testament for a new millennium, a religious parable of the second coming of mankind's messiah in an age that needs salvation as desperately as any ever has.

Keanu Reeves plays Thomas Anderson, a computer programmer by day who spends his nights in the alternative reality of the Internet, where he goes by the name Neo, spending his time among hackers and phreaks who have come to rely on his expertise. Symbolically, Reeves's character plays that of both new convert and Christ in the film and is on the receiving end of some of the world's most ancient wisdom wrapped in some of the best modern technological analogies. "You are a slave" and "We are born into bondage" are the two sentences Morpheus speaks to Neo that reveal the analogy to the Judeo-Christian understanding of slavery as sin. Like the biblical understanding, our technoslavery is a bondage of mankind's own making, a product of our own free will, as evidenced by Agent Smith's revelation that this is the second Matrix. The first Matrix, Smith says, was perfect, but we humans decided we wanted to define ourselves through our misery, and so we couldn't accept it. This is the technological version of the Garden of Eden story from Genesis. There we see that the very first use of technology was clothing, so it is significant that Neo is reborn completely naked.

Within that framework, *The Matrix* is also the story of the chosen one's doubts, slow realizations, and final discovery that it is he, and not anyone else, who is the savior. Anderson must first be convinced that the realm he inhabits as Neo has provided him a glimpse of the true reality, while his everyday existence as Thomas Anderson is actually the false consciousness, the world of the Matrix in which he senses, but cannot prove, that something is terribly wrong. This thought tortures him like a "splinter in the mind."

Neo is contacted first by Trinity, a slightly androgynous female counterpart to his slightly androgynous masculinity. It is she who leads Neo to Morpheus. Trinity is an obvious allusion to the biblical concept of a triune God consisting of the Father, the Son, and the Holy Spirit. Because of the long-standing patriarchal metaphor for God, it is quite humorous when Neo says to Trinity, "I always thought you were a guy." Also of note is the fact that the word "trinity" never actually appears in the Bible. It is during Neo's second conversation with Morpheus, just after he wakes up from being interrogated, that Morpheus reveals his role as John the Baptist by saying, "You may have been looking for me for a few years, but I've been looking for you for my whole life." However, Morpheus also plays the role of God the Father to Neo and the rest of the small band of rebels. He spends a significant part of the film teaching Neo the nature of "reality" as opposed to the world of the Matrix. When Morpheus is captured by the agents, as his body lies there helpless, Trinity says, "No, he's much more important than that. He's like a father to us."

To join Morpheus and Trinity in experiencing the depth of this true reality, Neo must be born again. As he is jacked in to the initiation sequence, Cypher tells him, "Buckle your seatbelt, Dorothy, 'cause Kansas is going bye-bye." Reeves's character is literally born again into the new world in a visually explicit birth from a biotechnical womb that spits him out like a newborn infant: hairless, innocent, covered in muck, and eyes wide open in awe. He sees that he alone, of all the millions of entombed and enwombed humans plugged in as batteries to the Matrix's mainframe, has been allowed to break free of his shell. The wombs are slightly opaque, allowing the inhabitants to at least glimpse a portion of the reality to which they are enslaved. The implication is that everyone can be freed, following the example set by the savior. (There is also a nice *2001* star child visual reference during this sequence.)

Just prior to his rebirth, Neo turns aside and sees a fragmented mirror, which becomes whole as he looks into it. He is about to make the journey into the self, or psyche, and the metaphor of a shattered universal mirror is one that Huxley and others have also used. He reaches out and touches the mirror, which then becomes whole, nicely referencing I Corinthians 13:12, "For now we see through a glass darkly, but then face to face." The mirror then liquefies and swallows Neo, confirming for us that this is essentially an inward journey he is making. Upon being reborn, Neo asks Morpheus why his eyes hurt: "Because you've never used them," comes the reply. Or, as William Blake puts it, "If the doors of perception were cleansed everything would appear to man as it is, infinite." In one of the first scenes, we see Neo sell a software program to a character named Choi for two grand, while Choi comments, "You're my savior, man, my own personal Jesus Christ." Choi's reference to mescaline in this conversation is a reference to Huxley's mescaline experiment book, *The Doors of Perception*. Huxley's title is drawn from the William Blake quote and was also subsequently the source for the name of Jim Morrison's rock group, *The Doors*.

In Greek mythology, Morpheus was the god of dreams, and his name is the linguistic root for words like "morphine" (a drug that induces sleep and freedom from pain) and "morphing" (using computer technology to seamlessly transform from one reality to another). This resonates with the ability of Fishburne's character to morph back and forth between the dream world (the "real" world) and the waking world (the Matrix). Morpheus asks, "Have you ever had a dream, Neo, that you were so sure was real? What if you were unable to wake from that dream, Neo? How would you know the difference between the dream world and the real world?" The stage is now set for the film to equate the dream world with the digital world, the world of pure consciousness that exists in infinity. It is an equation that works, because life on the screen is a disembodied life, a virtual existence where the rules of society and the laws of physics don't necessarily apply, which is why online relationships are so intoxicating and addictive. It's also one reason why they fail so completely when the people actually meet. Like a movie version of a book, the real version of an online person's self cannot help but disappoint, simply because the codes and conventions of space and time are so constrictive of the power of imagination.

As Morpheus tells it, The One has been prophesied, like Jesus of Nazareth, from time immemorial. The revealer of ultimate truth is the Oracle, played as a soul-food mama (cf. *Meet Joe Black*) with more of a sense of humor than seriousness, who nevertheless gives Neo the key insight into the nature of fate versus free will that is critical to the film's final twist. That the Oracle is a woman is also a key ingredient in the film's theology. The brothers Tank and Dozer have their biblical precedents in the apostles James and John, who were also brothers and called the "sons of thunder," which makes sense since both a tank and a bulldozer are modern technological "thunder" makers. But *The Matrix* is not simply a Christian allegory; it is a complex parable that pulls strongly from Judaism and other traditions. In their initial discussion about The One, both Morpheus and Neo are in cramped quarters wearing what is clearly the garb of concentration camp victims; rough-textured wool and blue-striped bed linens. But because Jewish history has not yet given us a political Messiah, and perhaps because Jesus was himself Jewish, the Wachowski brothers seem to be comfortable relying on Jesus' story as a precedent for their own. When asked if *E.T.* wasn't a retelling of the Christ story, Steven Spielberg said he "resented" the comparison because he was Jewish. So too might the Wachowski Brothers have inadvertently relied on the only well-known resurrection messiah story lying around.

And yet critics are saying the film is equally influenced by Zen Buddhism or Eastern mysticism. Many of the lines, and certainly the martial arts sequences, certainly reflect an Eastern influence. But people often make the mistake of assuming that Judaism and Christianity are somehow exclusively "Western" religions. Both are situated geographically and historically in Israel, which is on the Asian continent. The holy city of these two religions is Jerusalem, which sits in the navel of the world, as the meeting point of East and West. In other words, Judaism and Christianity are religions that share and have been influenced by both East and West, and have influenced both Eastern and Western philosophies since time immemorial. Thus, if you think you're seeing a lot of Alan Watts's *Supreme Identity* in the film, you probably are. But Watts isn't seeing something new by saying that East and West can be reconciled, he's simply pointing out what was there all along.

The Judas character, named Cypher, is sympathetically played by New Jersey tough guy Joe Pantoliano. Like Judas before him at the Last Supper, Cypher accepts his fate as traitor over a meal. Like Judas, who shares a drink with Christ at the Last Supper, Cypher and Neo share a cup while Cypher expresses his doubts about the whole crusade with the line, "Why oh why didn't I take the blue pill?" We see Neo part ways with Cypher by not finishing the drink, but instead handing the remainder over to Cypher. We know Cypher is up to no good when he breaks the convention of social hygiene by finishing Neo's drink for him after Neo leaves. Cypher also wears a reptile-skin coat, which alludes to the biblical figure of Satan as serpent. It is Cypher's doubts about Morpheus's certainty that Neo is The One (note the clever anagram of Neo = One) that causes Cypher to betray the cause, because he's not certain he's fighting on the right side, or at least not on the winning side. There is a nice mealtime scene, reminiscent both of *2001* and *Alien*, in which Mouse waxes philosophic about the nature, essence, and ultimate reality of food, which serves to confirm the drudgery of everyday life for this ragtag team of revolutionaries. The food scene, and the discussion of the woman in the red dress, confirm the loneliness and difficulty of life on the Nebuchadnezzar. Like the faithful of any religion, our apostles are tempted by the Matrix's illusions and are often led into daydreaming or fantasizing that ignorance really can be bliss. This confirms the Christian idea that the believer really is an alien in this world and is only a visitor, a transient resident, an alien on a temporary visa. As the anti-Christian filmmaker Luis Bunuel accurately puts it, "Properly speaking, there really is no place for the Christian in this world." Neo's new life is living proof of this maxim.

It is immensely significant that Cypher's deal-making meal with the agents centres around steak. First, meat is the metaphor that cyberspace inhabitants use to describe the real world: *meatspace* is the term they use to describe the nonvirtual world, a metaphor that clearly shows their preference for the virtual realm. Cypher says that even though he knows the steak isn't real, it sure tastes like it. The stupidity and superficiality of choosing blissful ignorance is revealed when Cypher says that when he is reintegrated into the Matrix he wants to be rich and "somebody important, like an actor." It's a line you could almost pass over if it wasn't so clearly earmarked as the speech of the fool justifying his foolishness. But meat is also the metaphor that media theorist Marshall McLuhan used to describe the tricky distinction between a medium's content and its form. As he put it, "the 'content' of a medium is like the juicy piece of meat that the burglar throws to distract the watchdog of the mind." This line illuminates the fact that many people watching *The Matrix* are seeing only the "content" of the kung-fu scenes and the electronica soundtrack while missing the serious sermon going on all around them. But it also heightens the point that the story is making about the Matrix itself, which is designed, like Huxley's "brave new world," to oppress you not through totalitarian force, but through totalitarian pleasure. As Agent Smith says, "Isn't it perfect? Billions of people, just living out their lives, oblivious." "Steak" is also the password revealed for the website at the film's closing credits, though there are nine passwords in total that reveal hidden messages on the website.

Because it's a Hollywood picture, Jesus has to have a girlfriend (as he did in *The Last Temptation of Christ*), who is fantastically played by the little-known Carrie-Anne Moss. Her character, Trinity, is a mix of Mary Magdalene and the Holy Spirit, as evidenced by her earthly-yet-celestial relationship with The One. She follows him everywhere, and the Oracle has told her she would fall in love with him, and so it is she who represents eternal, infinite, unbounded love by giving Neo the kiss of Princess Charming at the end with the line, "You can't be dead, because I love you." This line may have had you fighting the gag reflex, but the point is that love is stronger than death, that God is manifested by a triune love relationship, and this was simply the best way to show the miraculous Christ-likeness of Neo. The power of her love to bring him back from the dead is also foreshadowed by her statement that she is the "commanding officer" on the ship, indicating her authority over him. Love *is* stronger than death, but the film could have shown this in a better way, even if only by developing their emotional relationship by an extra five lines each. Then again, if the Wachowskis are planning two sequels, it would make sense to have them kiss with about as much passion as Leia kisses Luke in *The Empire Strikes Back*. This way we won't be shocked to discover that they were actually brother and sister, or part of the same heavenly family, all along. But the important thing to remember is that Neo really is dead before this, having been riddled with bullets by the three agents. After receiving the kiss, he is resurrected in the Hollywood equivalent of three days, which is about three seconds.

Upon rising from the dead, Neo experiences the cosmic revelation of his identity, similar and yet dissimilar to Superman. Superman has an Achilles' heel in the form of kryptonite and is also powerless to save his father from dying—despite all his other strengths. Neo's realization, however, is that he has no weaknesses, no fatal flaws, that he is in fact an infinite being. Having had the doors of perception fully cleansed, Neo can now "see" things as they truly are—which is in binary code. He looks down the hallway and sees the three agents as a series of flowing digits, meaning that he alone is now able to bridge the gap between analog and digital realm, able to control the digital rather than be controlled by it. Like the previous messiah that Morpheus alluded to, he is now able to remake the Matrix as he sees fit. He is a bulletproof Christ, not dying for our sins and coming back, but dying for his unwillingness to believe in his own power, who comes back to life through the power of someone else's belief, and who then asks us to join him in the fight against the Matrix. Like Jesus, he is the intermediary between our "bound" selves and our free selves. His is the example we are called on to follow in order to remake the Matrix with him.

A sympathetic understanding of Agent Smith is to assume that his hatred of humanity was programmed by the AI of the Matrix. This would indicate that the Matrix has learned what humankind failed to learn, which is how to manage

AI technology successfully. But Agent Smith's "revelation" speech is flawed: man is obviously a mammal. The fact is that no animal moves instinctively toward an equilibrium with its environment. Every animal is forced there by the competition of other life forms. Mankind is unique insofar as it has, alone among species, been able to vanquish its competition. Agent Smith may have been more accurate when he referred to man as a cancer. Just as cancer cells are human, so also human beings are mammals. And Agent Smith, the film makes clear, also wants to escape the Matrix. He has been infected by the "virus" of humanity and is desperate to know the Zion access codes, not so much to destroy the revolutionaries as to free himself.

At the film's conclusion, the invitation is clear. The film stops where it starts, with us staring at a blinking cursor on the computer screen in Room 303. Neo is making a call to us, sitting out there in the audience, to join him in fighting the Matrix's bondage. Like the final scene in *Superman*, Neo flies up and out of the screen as if to help us break free of our bondage, to suggest that he really is real, to suggest that we really can be free. One interpretation is that Neo is flying into us the way he flew into Agent Smith, to liberate us by destroying our preconceptions. In order to understand our preconceptions, our bondage, our slavery, all we need to know is one thing.

EXPERIENCE

"I can visualize a time in the future when we will be to robots as dogs are to humans."

— Claude Shannon, *The Mathematical Theory of Communication*, 1949

What is *The Matrix*? Your senses of sight and sound will be placed on continuous red alert as they experience information overload on a scale almost unimaginable. *The Matrix* is Marshall McLuhan on accelerated FeedForward. Scene cuts are visual hyperlinks. Fight scenes are PlayStation incarnated. What is *The Matrix*? It's the Technological Society come to its full fruition. It's Charlie Chaplin's *Modern Times* and Fritz Lang's *Metropolis* for the twenty-first century, in which we don't simply work for the machine (rather than the machine working for us), but we are created, given life, and used by the machine exclusively for the machine's purposes. It's a modern pastiche of Hollywood's latest special effects combined with John Woo kung-fu and more bullets, explosions, and gothic horror than Batman-meets-Bruce-Lee under the aural assault of a cranked-up electronica. But don't let the packaging fool you. Because far more than the eye-popping special effects and ear-shredding soundtrack, it is the ideas and the dialogue that dazzle in *The Matrix*.

In other words, the Wachowskis seem to have asked themselves this question: How do you speak seriously to a culture reduced to the format of comic books and video games? Answer: You tell them a story from the only oracle they'll listen to, a movie, and you tell the story in the comic-book and video-game format that the culture has become so addicted to. In other words, *The Matrix* is a graduate thesis on consciousness in the sheep's clothing of an action-adventure flick. Whether you're illiterate or have a Ph.D., there's something in the movie for you.

What the word "matrix" actually means, according to the dictionary, is *1. The womb. 2. Hence, that which gives form, origin, or foundation to something enclosed or embedded in it. 3. The intercellular substance of a tissue. 4. The earthy or stony substance in which an ore or other mineral is bedded. 5. The hollow in a slab to receive a monumental brass. 6. (Math) The square array of symbols which, developed, yields a determinant.* In *The Matrix*, we see that the filmmakers intend almost every one of these meanings, and then some. Put another way, to understand *The Matrix*, it helps to know a bit about the history and theories of communication. In the above quote by Claude Shannon, we see the main premise upon which *The Matrix* hinges. The Matrix is the robot, and we are the dogs acting as servants to our technological masters.

But technology and theology aren't far apart in this world where the Cartesian split between mind and body is made manifest, tangible, and interchangeable. Like *2001*, *The Terminator*, and *RoboCop*, *The Matrix* envisions a world where artificial intelligence is not only more appealing than flesh-and-bone reality, but more intelligent than the species that created it. In Morpheus's analogy, the purpose of the Matrix is to turn humans into batteries (i.e., energy sources) for the machines to do their work. What is their work? To keep us humans enslaved by our own illusions, chief of which is that technology is not enslaving us, but actually liberating us.

Keanu Reeves plays Thomas Anderson by day and "Neo" the computer hacker by night. In his analog existence, Anderson works as a top-notch programmer at the Meta CorTechs software corporation, in the most depressing of Dilbert-like cubicles, until he is freed by a FedEx delivery of the latest Nokia cell phone. Product placement in this film works so well you actually want to own what they own, especially Fishburne's ultra-cool wrapless sunglasses, the most talked-about item on the film's website.

Morpheus tells him that the secret he is on to is one that won't go away, like a splinter in the mind. It is this: he's a slave. Reeves's character is a slave to technology, and to free his mind he must choose between a red and a blue pill. By the film's end, his identity is made clear when he tells his arch-enemy, Agent Smith, "My name is Neo" just before "killing" him in the subway. By choosing his digital identity, he rejects a lifetime of programming and shows that he now knows that "The Matrix cannot tell you who you are." Now he can rapidly learn to override the physical limitations of five senses, the laws of physics, and other unpleasantries of analog existence while he is in the Matrix. The intimation is that we can all be The One simply by choosing to see.

The almost universal understanding of the battle scenes at the end, where the most sensory overload takes place, is that they are simply what audiences demand in a movie these days. Initially, they appear to avoid answering the questions raised by the plot with any "deeper meaning." The big shootout at the end seems more like a copout. But in fact it serves to open the audience's mind to the deeper meaning in a profound way. The best way to question whether the path you are on is correct is to see where it leads. In a culture demanding ever faster, louder, more dazzling everything, the only way to call this into question is to give them more than they asked for. *The Matrix* is technological speed and volume dialed up to 11, screaming at the top of its lungs, asking if you want to go any faster.

The telephone serves as the connection point between the two worlds. Interestingly, it must be an analog line, and not a digital or cellular/wireless phone, that makes this connection. The telephone, according to Marshall McLuhan, is an extension of the human voice. Walter Ong points out that the voice is the only medium that cannot be frozen; words disappear as soon as they are spoken. No freeze-frame is possible, which makes the voice the only organic, living medium in the history of the species. The voice's isolation from all the other senses, as we experience it on the telephone, highlights the fact that touch is our most deprived sense. It was from this principle that McLuhan created the tagline "Reach Out and Touch Someone" for AT&T in 1979. Thus, the analog phone call, and the human voice it represents, are the only possible way to retrieve someone who is trapped in the Matrix. Orality and an oral culture are what's needed to escape the Matrix. This is why Trinity's kiss saves Neo from death. She speaks and touches with the same organ of orality, and the content of her speech is love, the power that drives all true communication. Neo's final voice-over shows him telephoning the audience, asking them if they want to become real.

As the credits roll, one of the website's nine passwords is revealed, and we can enter it to find out more. Entering your own e-mail address gets you an e-mail from *morpheus@whatisthematrix.com* with the line, "The Matrix has you." If you're getting e-mail, it certainly does. Or does it?

QUESTION

One of the perpetual pleasures of *The Matrix* lies in the fact that, unlike the majority of what Hollywood puts out, this film does not insult the viewer's intelligence. Quite to the contrary, *The Matrix* has something to fill your cup whether your mental capacity is that of a thimble or a bucket. It is a pleasure that increases with time, because you see more and get more out of it with each viewing. Another recent film that rose to this level was *The Game*. In that film, the purpose of the Game was to discover the purpose of the Game. In *The Matrix*, the essential question remains even after the film is over: What is the Matrix? Executive producer Andrew Mason explains the intended audience effect best, perhaps, when he says that "*The Matrix* is really just a set of questions, a mechanism for prodding an ignorant or dulled mind into questioning as many things as possible."

To prod us into the questioning mode, the movie presents as the basis for its plot a world almost completely incomprehensible to our minds. It is a world in which all reality is nothing but some electrical signals sent to our brains. It is one thing to have your ninth grade English teacher ask you "If a tree falls in a forest and there is no one around to hear it, does it make a sound?" It is something completely different to have to figure out that the Neo with the socket in the back of his head is the real Neo. We then make the journey with him to try and understand how to operate within a world that is purely in his mind. The beauty of the movie is that it takes us almost as long to figure this out as it takes Neo. If *The Matrix* has engaged our imaginations, we spend over two hours with our minds wide open seeking answers to questions we might never have asked. Having survived the experience, we are now freed to question other parts of "reality" that always seemed beyond questioning.

Unlike any of the dozens of other films it pays homage to or appropriates through intertextual reference, *The Matrix* is doing something absolutely unique in the history of cinema. It is preaching a sermon to you from the only pulpit left. It is calling you to action, to change, to reform and modify your ways. Can a movie successfully do this? Or is a piece of cinematography, by the codes, conventions, and conditions of attendance that surround it, also and necessarily just another part of the Matrix? Jacques Ellul said that the purpose of one of his books (*The Presence of the Kingdom*) was to be "a call to the sleeper to awake." I don't know the answer to the question, and it probably ultimately hinges on the individual viewer's pre-existing awareness, but if a film can wake us up, then this is it.

In *The Matrix*, technological progress is portrayed in its extremes. Some of the questions this should inspire us to ask are:

- Do we have technology or does it have us? The answer, which is neither absolute nor binding, is in the hands of the audience.
- What if we made computers that were so good that they were smarter than we are? This question has been posed before, but never in such a unique way. Instead of being destroyed by computers, we become their puppy dogs.
- What if reproductive technology were perfected to the point that sex and motherhood were no longer necessary? Even the "romance" in the movie is unerotic (Neo and Trinity are androgynous), as should be expected in a future where sex is unnecessary. What if people were bred simply for convenience (ours or the computer's) in pods on farms?
- What if we progressed so far technologically that it destroyed us, and all that remained of our technology were the sewer systems? Although nuclear weapons are never mentioned in the movie, the charred remains of earth above the ground are a clear allusion to nuclear winter. Zion is in the core of the earth "where it is still warm."
- What if communications technology progressed so far that information was delivered directly to the brain, bypassing the senses? What if someone other than ourselves were in control of the information flow? How different is this from television today?

"What is the Matrix?" is a question that never stops being asked because it is as old as humanity itself. We have always used technology to improve our condition in life, yet in the embrace of each technology we find the classic Faustian bargain, a gaining of one thing at the expense of another, often unseen thing. And it is the unseen thing that then comes to dominate our lives, enmeshing us in a network of technological solutions to technologically-induced problems, forbidding us to question the technology itself.

What is the Matrix? If you've read this far, you deserve an answer.

ANSWER

"Literacy remains even now the base and model of all programs of industrial mechanization; but, at the same time, locks the minds and senses of its users in the mechanical and fragmentary *matrix* that is so necessary to the maintenance of mechanized society." (italics mine)

— Marshall McLuhan,
Understanding Media,
1964

"All the speed he took, all the turns he'd taken and the corners he'd cut in Night City, and still he'd see the *matrix* in his sleep, bright lattices of logic unfolding across the colorless void . . ." (italics mine)

— William Gibson,
Neuromancer, 1984

If you've read everything leading up to this, you no doubt thought at some point that there really was no answer to the question. That just like the movie, all anyone could do was continue to find new ways to ask the question. Well, there is an answer, but it is not an easy answer. Like Neo learning to accept that his world was largely made up, the answer to "What is the Matrix?" is something that cuts to the core of your own reality. Like Neo, you should prepare to have your world turned inside out.

According to the protagonist's guide, the Matrix is the "world that has been pulled over your eyes to blind you from the truth." It is the construction the world has become to hide what we've known all along: we are slaves to a force much larger than our individual actions. It is the collective illusion of humanity sharing an artificial reality created by machines to keep them docile and helpless against their captors. But, in plain English, the Matrix is simply the Technological Society come to its full fruition.

In 1964, communications scholar Marshall McLuhan wrote his seminal book *Understanding Media*. At the time, McLuhan was called "the oracle" of the modern age by both *Life* and *Newsweek* magazines, and he has subsequently become the patron saint of *Wired* magazine and numerous communications departments across the country. His quote takes some unpacking and to understand McLuhan it helps to read his mentor Harold Innis's *Bias of Communication*, his fan Walter Ong's *Orality and Literacy*, and his contemporary Jacques Ellul's *Technological Society*. These books cast light on the question of "literacy as the base and model of all programs," but also on the critical point that what McLuhan means by the term "matrix" is precisely what the Wachowski brothers take it to mean: a system of control. Neo's initiation into understanding the Matrix in the movie is a literal step into a fragmented mirror in which he discovers just how profound the control of modern society really is.

The Matrix arises at the point that the machine species realize that the human species is a virus that will destroy the ecological balance between the environment and itself if left unchecked. AI will destroy us once it perceives that we are a threat to its survival. But artificial intelligence doesn't actually have to be smarter than we are in order to dominate our lives. We could simply continue to think, as we have for the last hundred-plus years, that technology is always the solution to any particular human problem. Thus, the Matrix, while ostensibly being future technology's enslavement of the human race, in appearance actually resembles the industrialized world as we find it on the day we enter the theater. In other words, the Matrix is the trap the world has become. It is human hubris writ large. We all instinctively feel that technology, while giving us jobs and helping us balance our chequebooks, is nevertheless taking us somewhere we don't want to go. But the trip is so fun, we keep trying to answer the question "Where do you want to go today?" as though the choice were ours.

In modern society, the electronic foundation of our culture has embedded each of us into a Matrix that affects us in unique and personal ways, and from which it seems nearly impossible to escape. Subcultures like the Amish or the Bruderhof Communities strike us as reactionary Luddites because, in escaping the Matrix, they have not transformed the culture as much as they seem to have ignored or bypassed it. And yet we should not be so quick to dismiss their examples for our own lives. They stopped watching television when they realized their children weren't singing as much. They stopped using e-mail when they realized that it wasn't improving communication, but rather had a destructive tendency. In a similar vein, Ted Kaczynski's credibility ended where his package bombs began. While we will never condone murder, it has yet to be acknowledged by any of our public intellectuals that Kaczynski had some very valid points to make about the failures of the technological society in providing the human species with a meaningful and purposeful way of life.[1] And

---

1 See Joy essay in this volume. —Ed.

it is arguable, though despicable if true, that his points would never have been heard had he not sent explosive messages, the equivalent of the SYSTEM FAILURE message that the Matrix ends with and which *Adbusters* magazine has used as a metaphor for the imminent collapse of our current cultural trajectory.

Consider two worlds: One where everyone is told what to think by a box that they watch for half their waking hours, and the other where everyone has that signal sent straight to their brain. In the first world, everyone is educated systematically to see the world a certain way, and those who dissent are eliminated from the educational hierarchy, all the while claiming that they have freedom of expression. In the other, everyone is educated systematically to see the world a certain way, and those who dissent are eliminated, period; all the while, reality is so radically different from this made-up world that most people would choose the imaginary if given the freedom to choose. In the first one, most people find purpose by seeking employment with large impersonal organizations that only see their usefulness in terms of the one thing they were hired for. In the second one, everyone's purpose is employment by a large impersonal machine that only sees their usefulness in terms of one thing: the energy they can supply.

Recall the scene in which Thomas Anderson is reprimanded for being late to work. Recall that Trinity was famous for hacking the IRS database. Recall Agent Smith's list of what was a "normal" life: "You work for a respectable corporation, you have a Social Security number, and you pay your taxes." Sprinkled liberally throughout the movie are hints that the Matrix is really our present world. How better to control millions of people than to convince them that they are living a "normal" life in 1999? When Morpheus is giving Neo his long explanation of the Matrix, he says,

"It is there when you watch TV. It is there when you go to work. It is there when you go to church. It is there when you pay your taxes." These are all components of modern life that serve to control us and can easily be abused to the point of enslaving us.

The reasons we accept this control vary, from watching TV because we like entertainment to paying taxes because we feel we have no choice in the matter. The message of *The Matrix* is that we are already pawns in a modern technological society where life happens around us but is scarcely influenced by us. Whether it is by our choice or unwillingness to make a choice, our technology already controls us. In an attempt to wake us up, the movie asks us to question everything we believe about our present circumstances. Even if it feels good, is it good for us? Are those things that seem beyond our control really untouchable? If we do not want to wake up, then the answer is yes. However, for those with a splinter in the mind that will not go away, the challenge has been made to open your eyes and seek true reality, and ultimately to escape from the Matrix.

ROBIN HANSON

WAS

CYPHER

RIGHT?

PART I:

WHY WE STAY

IN OUR MATRIX

Unlike the poor unfortunates enslaved by the Matrix, we are free. We see the world as it is and make the choices in our lives based on our desires and values. No malevolent puppet master controls us. Right? Economist Robin Hanson respectfully disagrees.

The Matrix is a story of rebels who fight against a "world that has been pulled over your eyes to blind you from the truth."

The truth is that there are "endless fields where human beings are no longer born; we are grown" to serve as batteries to provide energy for artificial intelligences (AIs). AIs even "liquefy the dead so they could be fed intravenously to the living." But the minds of these humans see only the Matrix, "a neural-interactive simulation, . . . a computer-generated dream world built to keep us under control." There are "billions of people just living out their lives, oblivious" to these facts, who "believe it's the year 1999 when in fact it's closer to 2199."

The AIs seem to have tried to make humans as happy as possible. "The first Matrix was designed to be a perfect human world. Where none suffered. Where everyone would be happy. It was a disaster. No one would accept the program." So "the Matrix was redesigned to this, the peak of your civilization." Even so, there are humans who have discovered the truth, and who rebel against being "born into bondage, born into . . . a prison for your mind." These rebels believe that "as long as the Matrix exists the human race will never be free," and so they want "the destruction of the Matrix" and "freedom to our people."

Now, it is admitted that the rebels do not usually recruit older people, who have "trouble letting go . . . Most of these people are not ready to be unplugged. And many of them are so inert, so hopelessly dependent on the system that they will fight to protect it." But the rebels are confident that once young recruits learn the truth, they will not want to go back. The moral correctness of their position is also illustrated by the moral poverty of Cypher, the character who wants to return to the Matrix. Cypher is shallow and stupid; he betrays and kills his colleagues, is bitter at being rejected as a lover and leader, and wants to forget the truth. "I don't want to remember nothing. Nothing. You understand? And I want to be rich. You know, someone important, like an actor."

Most viewers of this story are led to believe that, given the choice, they would join the rebels. But it is worth considering for a moment whether this is really the right choice. After all, without a rebellion billions of humans would continue to live out happy lives, and probably far more AIs would as well. Progress would continue through our superior descendants, the AIs. As Agent Smith says, "Evolution, Morpheus, evolution, like the dinosaur. Look out that window. You had your time. The future is our world, Morpheus. The future is our time."

A rebel war with the AIs risks those lives, that happiness, and that progress, and for what? A viewer who sides with the rebels must place a high value on humans knowing the truth, on humans not being slaves, even happy slaves, or on humans running the future regardless of their relative abilities.

Now I do not want to say that this view is wrong. Maybe facing the truth is really good, slavery is really bad, and humans are the rightful rulers of the future. Instead, I want to say that this simply cannot be the whole story. It cannot be the whole story because here in our real world today, we humans are in fact slaves to alien, hyperrational entities who care little about us, and who provide us with a dream world to distract us from the fact that they callously use our bodies to further their ends. We humans are not even likely to run the future, if things continue as they are. Yet when we are confronted with these truths, very few of us, the young included, rebel against our dream world. In fact, what rebels we have seem to be mostly concerned with preserving our dream world.

So who are our slave masters, and what is this dream world that they use to enslave us? Our masters are our "selfish genes," and our dream world is the world of love, humor, talk, story, art, music, fashion, sport, charity, religion, and abstract ideas that occupy the attention of our "mating minds." Let me explain.

You are a body with a mind. Your mind is the result of activity in your brain, and your body has grown from a single cell following the instructions of your genes, which you acquired from your parents. Your parents acquired their genes from their parents, and so on back for billions of years. (The few genes not acquired from parents were created by random mutations.) The fact that you have certain genes and not others was determined almost entirely by a fierce competition between genes to create better "survival machines," i.e., creatures that perpetuate and spread those genes. The genes that produced you are not a random sample from all possible genes; they are some of the few genes that, so far, remain in this competition.

Evolutionary biology has made enormous progress in understanding the patterns of life around us by thinking in terms of "selfish genes." That is, you would not go very wrong in predicting the patterns of life we see if you imagined that our genes were intelligent, that they wanted only to make more future copies of themselves, and that they chose the behaviors of the creatures they coded with only this purpose in mind. (And you would do even better if you figured that these creatures could not help but assume that the future would be very much like the past few thousand generations.)

Of course genes are not actually intelligent, in the sense of basing their actions on computations that they run. But since they act as though they were intelligent, they act a lot like the cruel slave masters they would be if they *were* intelligent. Our genes do not care whether we experience more pleasure than pain. Our genes only care that we anticipate both possibilities, so that they can control us via our preference for pleasure over pain. When our bodies are no longer capable of reproducing, or capable of helping those who share our genes reproduce, our genes literally do not care if we live or die. Our genes will happily shorten our lives, or give us great pain, if that will help those genes to reproduce. Our genes will also lie to us to promote their goals, for example, by making us think that our happiness depends more on our success than it really does. Our genes can indeed be cruel masters.

Brains are a tool that genes have hit upon to help them reproduce. Brains can observe local conditions and then perform complex calculations in order to figure out a good response to those local conditions. Using a brain, for example, genes can tell a predator fish to look for a tail that wiggles and then follow that tail until it's close enough to bite.

Now smaller brains can do quite well with just a long list of condition-action pairs, i.e., what to do in what sort of situation. Like follow a tail and bite it. But for big brains, brains that are capable of more abstract reasoning, it can make more sense to give those brains a general description of what sort of outcomes are desired, some beliefs about how actions produce outcomes, and an ability to change those beliefs in response to circumstances. This should allow such brains to adapt more flexibly to changing conditions. And since the creature itself is an important part of its desired-outcome descriptions, such a brain would naturally have beliefs about itself and its relation to its environment.

Humans have some of the most complex minds around. Compared to other animals, we devote more resources to our brains, and we are uniquely skilled at abstract reasoning. Your mind thus appears to have been created by selfish genes seeking a more flexible response to local conditions. Your genes seem to have given you a mind that is aware of itself, that has goals for itself, that has beliefs about you, the world around you, and the ways actions translate into outcomes, that can reason abstractly about all these, and that chooses actions based on this reasoning. Appearances can be deceiving, however.

If your genes had given you abstract goals and beliefs simply to allow your behavior to adapt more flexibly to local conditions, then they should have made your goals the same as their goals. Ideally, you would then be conscious of wanting to maximize the number of your descendants who shared your genes. Your genes would then not be cruel slave masters, but trusted allies working toward a common goal. In fact, however, your genes gave you rather different goals.

Now some of your mind's goals are closely aligned with your genes' goals. You want to have and raise successful children. You want to have sex with fertile and fit people, which tends to produce such children. You want to be healthy, and to have friends and allies, all of which helps you to survive and have children. And you want to learn about the world you live in, which can help you achieve these goals.

But you also seem to care about love, humor, talk, story, art, music, fashion, sports, charity, religion, and abstract ideas. In fact, you are often passionately obsessed with these things. You believe that you care about these things for themselves, and not just for how they can help with more basic goals, such as health, sex, and children. And you care about these things far more than seems directly useful in pursuing more basic goals.

Why do humans have such big brains, which are so devoted to a dream world of abstract ideas and feelings that have so little direct relation to personal survival and reproduction? Our best theory at the moment is that this dream world is produced by sexual selection[1] between "mating minds," i.e., minds that are designed in large part to impress potential mates and allies. When we display to

---

1 Sexual selection is the part of evolutionary change driven by competition to mate with the opposite sex, rather than competition to survive, obtain food, etc. The peacock's tail, helpful in obtaining a mate but an obstacle to survival, is a classic example of sexual selection. —Ed.

others how agile and creative we are at love, humor, talk, story, art, music, fashion, sports, charity, religion, and abstract ideas, we show them that we have high-quality genes, with few bad mutations. Such minds also help us to judge the quality of others' genes from their displays.

For reasons that are not entirely clear, however, our genes have chosen not to make us fully aware that the main function of our dream world is to impress potential mates. Instead, we believe that we care about it directly and strongly. But our actions often suggest that we care about this dream world much less than we profess. Let me give some examples.

We think that we participate in conversations in order to gain information from others; in fact we prefer talking to listening. If we were doing our best to form beliefs about how the world actually is, we would not knowingly disagree with each other; in fact we disagree all the time. We tend to think we are more able than we are, and that our feelings of passion toward others will last longer than they do.

Students often say that they love learning, and wish they could get into better schools; in fact, anyone can get a free education from the very best schools by sitting in on classes and forgoing the credentials. Professors say they choose their career for the ideas, but their conversations are mostly office gossip, and their output drops precipitously once they get tenure.

Most reviews of art and music talk mainly about what these things reveal about the abilities of the artist, with very little discussion of how this art or music makes people feel. People who feel passionately devoted to charities actually give them very little relative to their resources, and pay very little attention to how the money is spent.

Overall, we are basically self-deceived. That is, we think we care a great deal about love, humor, talk, story, art, music, fashion, sports, charity, religion, and abstract ideas. But when push comes to shove, we mostly follow the strong feelings our genes use to guide our actions, and those feelings end up being less about these abstract things than we think. We care more that others see us doing these things, and that they be impressed, than we care to admit. And we care less about these things as our mating opportunities are reduced with age.

Why do we deceive ourselves about this? One theory is that people who are too self-aware about these things tend not to be trustworthy allies. Someone who can overrule his feelings based on conscious calculations of what is in his interest may decide it is no longer in his interest to be loyal to you. Another theory says that such a person is likely to decide children are more trouble than they are worth, and so fail to reproduce.

Whatever theory is right, it should be clear that these abstract things are our dream world, a less-real world that our slave masters, our genes, have pulled over our eyes, blinding us from the truth. The truth is that deep down this dream world is not very important to us; guided by our feelings, we mostly act to serve our masters, i.e., to maximize the number of children who share our genes. But few of us publicly admit this, and we deny it all the more passionately because we fear it to be true.

In *The Matrix*, the rebels are indignant at being slaves to AIs, but at the same time they seem to accept being slaves to their genes, and the feelings those genes use to control them. The rebellion started when "there was a man born inside who had the ability to change whatever he wanted, to remake the Matrix as he saw fit." Neo, the hero, is supposed to be another person born with this special ability. Morpheus tells him that to access this gift from his genes, "You have to let it all go, Neo, fear, doubt, and disbelief.

Free your mind." The Oracle also tells him it's not a matter of conscious thought. "Being The One is just like being in love. No one can tell you you're in love, you just know it. Through and through. Balls to bones."

When Mouse is accused of being a "digital pimp," he defends himself, saying, "To deny our own impulses is to deny the very thing that makes us human." Trinity tells Neo that "the Matrix cannot tell you who you are," and Neo responds, "And the Oracle can?" Trinity cuts off discussion by saying "That's different." Finally, we are not to forget that the whole problem began when human minds became too arrogant and independent, when "all of mankind was united in celebration. We marvelled at our own magnificence as we gave birth to AI." The bottom line is that Neo's genes can help him to overthrow the AIs, but only if Neo's mind does not get too uppity, and accepts its proper place relative to Neo's genes. A world without the Matrix is not, as Neo hopes, "a world without rules and controls, without borders or boundaries, a world where anything is possible." It is instead a world where human genes regain their rightful role as human masters.

What would it mean, to actually rebel against our genes and the dream world they place us in?

Consider the example of new technologies of human genetic modification. Most people consider the elimination of genetic diseases to be an acceptable use of these technologies but not an increase in the intelligence of those who can afford it. Eliminating diseases can be thought of as most genes and minds together ganging up on a few "anti-social" genes, while paying to increase intelligence can be perceived as putting individual minds in charge of their own genes, inverting the usual master-slave relationship. This second rebellion scenario seems to be quite threatening.

Some people are willing to consider substantial genetic modifications of large fractions of the population, but only if these modifications are under the control of some central authority, which for some reason they imagine is more likely to closely follow treasured moral principles than individual minds are. We can think of this as trying to preserve the morality and charity parts of our shared dream world against threats from both individual minds and individual genes.

In fact, most of the arguments that I hear for or against various long-term scenarios focus on how they will affect our dream world, such as the worlds of science, exploration, art, stories, and love. Less often do arguments focus on the sheer number of happy minds some scenario might produce. So apparently what many people want is to preserve our dream world against threats from all sources, including our genes. This is somewhat like having the AIs in the Matrix story threaten to destroy the Matrix, and having the rebels fight them to preserve the Matrix.

If you wanted to take the side of your mind, and to hell with your genes and their dream world, you would have the serious problem of deciding what it is that you wanted. After all, your feelings are used by your genes to control you, and the main precedent you know of for resisting your feelings is in the service of your dream world, which your genes also use to control you. But if you reject those two, what is left?

One possible goal for a mind is simple self-preservation. What if you wanted to preserve your mind as long as possible? Until recently, this looked pretty hopeless. After all, your genes have designed your body to die, and your mind cannot live without a body. But there is actually now an option that offers a chance to avoid this outcome: cryonics. This is where, when current medical science gives up on you, your body or brain is frozen in liquid nitrogen, in the hope of being "reanimated" in the future when technology has vastly improved. (At liquid nitrogen temperatures, there are essentially no chemical reactions, and your body would be preserved exactly as it was when frozen.)

Of course there are many risks with this approach. Technology may never improve enough. The organization that is supposed to preserve your frozen brain in liquid nitrogen may fail to do so. Or life might be so miserable when you come back that you'd rather be dead. Now, many people do not choose cryonics because they think the chance of success is so low as to not be worth the modest cost. But many other people (myself included) estimate much higher chances of success. And yet very few of those who think it is likely to work actually sign up for cryonics (less than one thousand worldwide). When asked, they give reasons such as their friends and family would think it weird, or that "extending one's life span through cryonics is unnatural, selfish, and immoral." Very few people, apparently, want to rebel against their genes in this way.

So where does this leave us? In the story of the Matrix, the rebels fought to free people from being slaves to AIs, and to tell them of the world that had been pulled over their eyes to blind them to the truth. But this is not because those rebels never like being slaves, and always want to see the truth. Even in the story, we can see that these rebels accept being slaves to their genes, and to the passions and dream world those genes use to control them. Here in our world, most of us also accept being slaves to our selfish genes, and to the mating-mind dream world they have given us. We would really rather not know this truth, and the truth that we care less about the dream world than we think. We are reluctant to let other minds take control of their genes, and very few of us try to have our minds outlive our genes. To the extent that we are willing to overrule our genes, we do so mainly in the service of our dream world.

This would seem to bode very badly for the anti-gene revolution, and even worse for the anti-dream world revolution, at least if such things were decided by popular vote. The future, however, may well not be decided by popular vote. Sometime in the next century, the technology of "uploads," or computer-simulated people, will be available. If this happens before we develop real AIs, then there will be unimaginable economic pressure to allow adoption of this technology. But if it is adopted, minds will have become permanently disconnected from genes. At least they will be disconnected from DNA-based genes. The hard truth is that evolution and selection pressures will continue, but with a whole new dynamic. Where this will lead will have to be the subject of another essay.

LYLE ZYNDA

WAS

CYPHER

RIGHT?

PART II:

The Matrix introduces a new generation to an age-old dilemma. What is real and how do we know it? And does it really matter? Philosopher Lyle Zynda takes this question head-on.

THE NATURE OF REALITY

AND WHY IT MATTERS

Welcome to the real world, Neo.
> — *Morpheus's first words to Neo, after he's been freed from the Matrix*

NEO: This isn't real?
MORPHEUS: What is real? How do you define real? If you're talking about what you can feel, taste, smell, or see, then real is simply electrical signals interpreted by your brain.

> — *Morpheus to Neo, after Neo enters the Construct "loading program" for the first time*

NEO (his mouth bleeding): I thought it wasn't real.
MORPHEUS: Your mind makes it real.
NEO (after a pause): If you're killed in the Matrix, you die here?
MORPHEUS: The body cannot live without the mind.

> — *Neo and Morpheus, after*
> *Neo has exited the "jump*
> *program" after failing to*
> *make his first jump*

After Neo, the Messiah-like hero of *The Matrix*, is freed from the dream world in which he had lived all his life, he vividly confronts questions about the nature of reality, long-considered by Western philosophy. Is there a world external to our subjective experience, our consciousness? If so, how can we know what it is like, since we cannot step outside our experience to tell if reality matches it? Finally, is it important to answer such questions? Isn't it enough to know what our experience is like, without worrying whether there's a reality beyond it?

In *The Matrix*, most of humankind is used as a source of power by highly intelligent machines, centuries in the future. Humans are placed from birth in a dreamlike state, in which a world like ours is simulated for their sleeping minds. The machines know that our sense organs convert information from the world (light, sound, etc.) into electrical signals, which are then processed by the brain into the image of reality that constitutes our conscious experience. So, they feed the same electrical signals into the brains of humans that a real world would, creating an illusion indistinguishable from reality. Is there any way a person in the Matrix could know that they are, in effect, just having a completely lucid dream?

René Descartes (1596–1650) asked a similar question in 1641, in his *Meditations on First Philosophy*.[1] After a century of dramatic cultural changes in Europe, including the rise of modern science (which undermined previously accepted paths to knowledge, such as reliance on ancient authorities), Descartes was eager to discover new and certain foundations for knowledge. This led him to the question: What *can* I know with absolute certainty? The only way to answer this question, he reasoned, is to systematically examine what can be doubted. Noticing that, "Whatever, up to the present, I have accepted as possessed by the highest truth and certainty I have learned either from the senses or through the senses," he considered whether what our senses tell us is free from all doubt.

Descartes realized that the answer was No. Our senses sometimes deceive us—can we ever fully trust them? Moreover, he noted, a completely lucid dream can seem perfectly real. Could I, perhaps, always be dreaming, when I think I'm awake? As Morpheus put it to Neo, soon after Neo had taken the red pill: "Have you ever had a dream, Neo, that you were so sure was real? What if you were unable to wake from that dream, Neo? How would you know the difference between the dream world and the real world?"

After considerations much like these, Descartes concluded, "There are no certain marks distinguishing waking from sleep; and I see this so manifestly that, lost in amazement, I am almost persuaded that I am now dreaming." Finally, Descartes considered the possibility that a powerful being, an "evil genius," might be able to plant all his sensory experiences in his mind. If that were true, Descartes noted, then "the sky, the earth, colors, shapes, sounds and all external things are illusions and impostures

---

1 Quotations from the Meditations are taken from Norman Kemp Smith's translation in *The European Philosophers from Descartes to Nietzsche*.

of which this evil genius has availed himself for the abuse of my credulity."

Fans of *The Matrix* will realize that in the movie, the machines correspond to Descartes's "evil genius." Therefore, Descartes's question is our own. How do *we* know that *The Matrix* is not *based on reality*—that we are not *really* asleep in a simulated world run by machines, just as in the movie?

One might be tempted to suggest that the machines would not allow such a movie to be placed in the Matrix, thus revealing its existence. However, a moment's thought shows that, to the contrary, this would be the ultimate sick joke on their part: to make us shrug our shoulders and laugh at the very notion that the Matrix might be real, because, after all, it's "just a movie." Even worse—suppose they invent the story of Neo, "The One," who is recruited by the charismatic Morpheus and his crew to defeat the machines and free humanity, while in reality no human mind is free. We are all slumbering slaves, with no hope of salvation. There is no Messiah, no Neo. There isn't even a Morpheus looking for him.

Descartes's answer to his conundrum is well known: "I think, therefore I am."[2] By this, Descartes meant that it is impossible for someone to doubt the contents of his own conscious experience—nor can anyone doubt his existence as a "thinking thing." As for the evil genius, "Let him deceive me as much as he will, he can never cause me to be nothing so long as I shall be thinking I am something." For each of us, our own consciousness is indubitably real, whatever is the case about the external reality that our consciousness seems to represent to us. Descartes proceeded to develop a complete epistemology (theory of knowledge) on this basis,

---

2 This famous phrase was in Descartes's *Discourse on Method*. In the *Meditations*, he phrased the point somewhat differently.

which ended by endorsing the reality of a world external to our consciousness.

One might consider subjective consciousness to be an inadequate foundation for objective knowledge. Everyone in the Matrix, for example, can by parallel reasoning note that he is indubitably a conscious being, certain of the smells, sights, tastes, sounds, and feelings that he experiences, and of the objects and people that he senses—insofar as they are stable, cohesive, and recurring collections of smells, sights, tastes, sounds and feelings, anyway. However, the question remains—what if none of those "objects" and "people" are *real*?

There is an assumption here—namely, that "real" has a meaning that can be given independently of what we sense and feel. In *The Matrix*, Morpheus raises this issue. When Neo is freed from the Matrix, Morpheus greets him somberly and compassionately, "Welcome to the real world." Later, when Neo enters the "loading program" for the first time, and is confused—"This isn't real?"—Morpheus responds, "What is real? How do you define real? If you're talking about what you can feel, taste, smell, or see, then real is simply electrical signals interpreted by your brain."

The view that there is a world *external* to our conscious experience, that *causes* our experience but is not constituted by or dependent on it for its existence, is called *realism*.[3] In this sense, Descartes was a realist. For, in the *Meditations*, he concluded that we can know for sure that *certain* aspects of our sensory experience—the "clear and distinct" parts— correspond to an external reality. The "clear and distinct" parts are "everything comprised in the object of pure mathematics." The parts of our sense experience that can be described by mathematics (in particular, geometry) are real. Descartes developed this idea in his *Principles of*

---

3 I should note that the term "realism" has many senses, even in philosophy.

Philosophy (1644), where he explained everything from gravity to optics in purely geometrical terms. Descartes had the right idea, but his attempt at a new physics was too austere and so did not succeed. Physics needs more than geometry (space and time). It also needs "dynamic" quantities such as force and mass. Isaac Newton supplied that in 1687, in his groundbreaking *Mathematical Principles of Natural Philosophy*.[4] Every physics student today begins their training by working through ideas first presented there. Newton built on Descartes's idea (shared by others at the time, too) that the parts of our experience which can be systematically predicted and explained by "mathematical principles" (laws of nature) reflect the truly *real*. This is how modern science was born. The stable, regular, repeatable, quantifiable aspects *of* experience reveal what is *beyond* experience, in the external, physical world.

Can science provide the absolute certainty that Descartes sought? Newton and many others thought so, but the answer is No. Think about the Matrix. Those locked inside it (like Neo before he was freed) have the same science we have. Their world is just like ours—subjectively, at least. Now, in *The Matrix*, the physical laws that the real world follows *happen* to be the same as those in the Matrix. (Although the "laws" of the Matrix can be "bent" or occasionally "broken"—allowing those who know its true nature to leap from building to building, to dodge bullets, and ultimately, for Neo, to control the "reality" of the Matrix itself.) However, we can imagine a movie similar to *The Matrix* except that the laws of the "real" world are *different* from those of the "dream" world most of humanity inhabits.

For example, suppose that within the Matrix, people (like us) are bound to the ground, and have to use things like

---

4 *The Principia: Mathematical Principles of Natural Philosophy*. The term "natural philosophy" was used in the seventeenth century to designate what we now call science.

airplanes to fly. In the real world, however, people can fly just by deciding to do so (just as Neo does at the end of the movie). In that case, the laws of the Matrix (those we believe true of our world) would differ from the true laws of nature. Hence, the laws of nature revealed by the stable, regular, repeatable, quantifiable aspects of our experience might be *only* laws of our *experience*—not the true laws of nature.

Realists today would argue that absolute certainty cannot be achieved; high probability is enough. The best explanation of the fact that our experience consists of stable regularities is that it reflects reality. We cannot *disprove* that a Matrix exists—it is *conceivable* that the real laws of nature are nothing like what our experience suggests—but that is *extremely* unlikely, and besides, we have no *positive* evidence that there is a Matrix. It is reasonable, therefore, to discount the possibility, even if it cannot be absolutely disproved.

There is another tradition in philosophy, opposed to realism. Can it do better? George Berkeley (1685–1753)[5] defended the view that the physical objects that we sense ("sensible" objects) are *nothing more* than collections of sensations. Thus, a vehicle like the *Nebuchadnezzar* (the group's "hovercraft" in *The Matrix*) is nothing more than a stable, cohesive, and recurring collection of sights, smells, sounds, textures (including the solid "feel" of its deck, etc.), which behaves in a regular and predictable way. Since sounds cannot exist unheard, sights cannot exist unseen, etc., to be *real*, Berkeley argued, just *is* to be perceived or sensed. This view is called *idealism*. Morpheus seems to be aware of the possibility of such a view when he asks, "How do you define real? If you're talking about what you can feel, taste, smell, or see . . ."

---

5 Berkeley defended idealism in many works, such as *Three Dialogues between Hylas and Philonous*. There, he also attempted to refute realism, particularly the formulation of it defended by John Locke (1632–1704) in his *Essay Concerning Human Understanding*.

Berkeley's claim, then, is that to be real is to be perceived. Physical objects are real, to be sure. But that's because they're *part* of our experience. There is nothing *beyond* our experience. Indeed, we have no idea of physical objects except as a collection of sensations, and sensations cannot exist without a mind. The idea of a world external to our experience is a self-contradiction.[6]

Can Berkeley's idealism defeat the worry that the Matrix is real, that is, more than "just a movie"? The answer, unfortunately, is No. To be real, according to Berkeley, is to be perceived—by *someone*. However, the machines are sentient beings; *they* perceive the Matrix. So do the crewmembers of the *Nebuchadnezzar*, and all minds that have been freed from the Matrix. Hence, it is real. But the people inside the Matrix don't know it. Contrary to what he claimed, Berkeley's idealism doesn't guarantee we *know* reality;[7] it just provides an answer to Morpheus's question: "What is real?" (That is, what *makes* something "real"?) The only way idealism can defeat the worry that the Matrix is real is if you assume, besides the claim that there is nothing

---

6 Not all idealists would agree with Berkeley that the idea of a world outside our conscious experience is self-contradictory. Some, such as the German philosopher Immanuel Kant (1724–1804, who espoused a particularly subtle form of idealism, called transcendental idealism), allowed that there may be a reality beyond experience, but we cannot know or even imagine what it is like. See his *Critique of Pure Reason*, available in abridged form in *Basic Writings of Kant*.

I should also note that it is possible to be a realist about everyday, "observable" objects, but an antirealist about the parts of scientific theories that refer to "unobservable" entities such as atoms. See, for example, Bas van Fraassen's *The Scientific Image*. The debate within the philosophy of science over "realism" is about this narrower, epistemological issue, not the broader, metaphysical issue discussed here.

7 Berkeley argued that his idealism was a solution to the problem of skepticism (the view that we can't know anything about what reality is like, or what is true), and that the realism of Descartes and Locke could not solve it. However, as the scenario of The Matrix shows, he was mistaken. Even if it is true that we cannot conceive of a reality beyond our experience, it doesn't follow that all beings experience a single objective reality. For example, the subjective "reality" of those imprisoned in the Matrix is different from those whose minds have been freed.

beyond experience, that *you* are the only conscious being in existence (a view called *solipsism*). Then your reality *is* reality.

This is not very satisfactory.[8] In any case, it is clear that the overall position of *The Matrix* on this issue is *realist*, not idealist, solipsist, or subjectivist (yet another view, namely, that reality is subjective, different for each person). Once the true[9] nature of the Matrix is revealed, the movie draws a sharp distinction between the simulated Matrix-world and the real[10] world. (Recall Morpheus's first words to Neo outside the Matrix: "Welcome to the real world."[11]) The people inside the Matrix cannot know it is an illusion, but it is. (Though some, like Neo, may feel something is not quite right.[12])

There is one puzzling aspect of *The Matrix*'s treatment of the question of reality. During Neo's training, he attempts to jump between two tall buildings, and fails. The crewmembers, anxiously watching, debate the significance of this failure—does it mean Neo is not The One?—and decide it means nothing. "Everybody falls the first time," Cypher declares. When he is disconnected from the Matrix, Neo finds his mouth is bleeding. (This is puzzling. Did he bite his tongue? Did his brain, thinking he hit the ground, cause blood to spurt out of his mouth?) Surprised, he says

---

8 I know of no philosophers who have defended solipsism. If anyone has ever seriously believed this view, he has kept it to himself.

9 As Morpheus puts it, just before Neo takes the red pill: "All I'm offering is the truth—nothing more."

10 As Trinity points out to Cypher, "The Matrix isn't real." Cypher responds: "I think the Matrix can be more real than this world." (Cypher is confused; more on him below.)

11 Cypher sarcastically mocks Morpheus's words just before he pulls the plug on Apoc.

12 The makers of *The Matrix* obviously want us to consider if people who seem alienated from reality, or who regard the world of experience as an illusion (such as in the Hindu concept of maya) might be on to something. (Recall the remark of the boy in the Oracle's waiting area, who is dressed in a beige robe similar to the traditional saffron robes of Buddhist monks: "There is no spoon.")

to Morpheus, "I thought it wasn't real." Morpheus replies, "Your mind makes it real."

So, is the Matrix real or not? Since Morpheus made it perfectly clear earlier that the Matrix is *not* real, his point must be that being hooked up to the Matrix can cause the body harm, because it *seems* real. Let us continue the dialogue between Neo and Morpheus. Neo asks, "If you are killed in the Matrix, you die here?" Morpheus replies, "The body cannot exist without the mind." One way of interpreting this would be that the mind leaves the body and "goes" to a "place" "in" the Matrix when it is plugged into it. However, this is obviously metaphor—there is no such "place." Thus, a better interpretation of Morpheus's statement is that your mind's *image* of reality affects your body—similar to the myth that if you dream you are falling, and do not wake up before you hit the ground, you will die for real when you do. This does not happen to Neo, of course, when he hits the ground in the jump program. The ground acts like a rubber mat, breaking his fall. However, according to the movie, the Matrix itself obeys "laws" like those of the physical world. When you hit the ground, or bullets strike you, you are injured, or you die. When Mouse is riddled with bullets after Cypher betrays the crew by tipping off the machines to their location in the Matrix, Mouse's physical body in the *Nebuchadnezzar* reacts in its chair as if it is really struck by bullets. When he dies in the Matrix, he dies for real. Conversely, if you are "in" the Matrix, and someone in reality unplugs you (without your exiting the Matrix through a telephone line), you die both in the Matrix and in reality. This happens to Switch when Cypher pulls the plug on her. Presumably, the bodies of the billions of people Neo sees plugged into the Matrix (when his mind is first freed) react similarly to their simulated virtual worlds (though when Neo sees them, they all appear immobile, asleep).

Thus, Morpheus's statement, "Your mind makes it real," needn't be taken as an endorsement of idealism or subjectivism (reality is subjective, different for each person). It can be understood metaphorically. The mind might be just whatever is going on in the brain, and nothing more,[13] but since the brain controls the body, if the brain/mind *thinks* it is dead or dying, its control of the body somehow goes "haywire" and the body dies.[14]

This brings us to our final topic: whether the question "What is 'real'?" is important. Does it matter what is real? In *The Matrix*, Cypher's betrayal of the crew is to be rewarded by his being plugged back in to the Matrix, with all his memories of the real world erased. He wants to be someone "important—like an actor." As he dines with the agents, he bites into a juicy-looking steak (which contrasts strongly with the runny, unappetizing goop the crew eats in the real world) and declares, "Ignorance is bliss." To Cypher, subjective experience, even if false, is better than "the desert of the real."

It is easy to understand Cypher's motivations. In *The Matrix*, the real world is mundane, dirty, depressing. It is a *dystopia*—an *anti-utopia* of the sort common in science fiction.[15] Most humans are unknowing slaves, used for energy. Food, for those outside the Matrix, is not tasty, sensual, and pleasurable; it is merely nutritious. The *Nebuchadnezzar* has nothing more to rely on than electromagnetic pulses to fend off squidlike automatons that

---

13 The view that the mind is just the workings of the brain and central nervous system is called the identity theory. It seems Morpheus assumes this when he says ". . . real is simply electrical signals interpreted by your brain." Arguments for this view can be found in David Armstrong's *A Materialist Theory of Mind* and David Lewis's "An Argument for the Identity Theory."

14 For a discussion of how this is psychologically and physiologically realistic see Peter Lloyd's essay "Glitches in the Matrix" in this volume. —Ed.

15 Erika Gottlieb's *Dystopian Fiction East and West: Universe of Terror and Trial* provides a good survey of dystopian themes in science fiction literature.

constantly seek its destruction. Cypher figures that, given all that, fantasy wins, hands down.

The rest of the crew obviously does not feel that way. What matters to them is not what seems real, but what *is* real. They want to fight the machines and free the human race, and are willing to endure hardship to do so. A life consisting of illusory, subjective pleasure is not desirable; if deliberately chosen, it is ignoble.

Thirty years ago, philosopher Robert Nozick used a similar idea to discern what is of ultimate value, which he called the "Experience Machine."[16] Nozick's idea is this: suppose you could deliberately and knowingly choose, as Cypher does in *The Matrix*, to be hooked up to a machine that would give you the experiences of having friends, fame, wealth, good looks, success, and whatever else makes you happy. After being hooked up, you'll forget about your past life, and you won't be unhooked from the machine later. Would you choose to be hooked up to the Experience Machine?

Nozick's claim is that you wouldn't, if you thought about it seriously. You don't want just the *experience* of having friends and being loved. You want to *really* have friends and be loved. It is true that if you are friendless and unloved, you might be tempted to escape reality into fantasy. (Some people use drugs for this reason.) But you would prefer real friends to imaginary ones, if you could have them. The same goes for fame, wealth, good looks, success, and so on. Thus, experience (such as pleasure) is not what is of highest value.

When I bring up Nozick's Experience Machine in my undergraduate philosophy classes, there is a consistent result: most students agree with Nozick, after considering the idea carefully, but a small number insist that they would

16 Nozick, p. 42–44.

make the same choice as Cypher in *The Matrix*, and be hooked up to the Experience Machine. (I have never asked these students if their lives are not all that great. That would be impolite.) However, I think it is safe to say that most people would agree with Nozick's claim. Consequently, Morpheus's question "What is real?" *does* matter, showing that the debate between realists and idealists in philosophy deals with one of the key questions of existence.

SOURCES

BOOKS

Armstrong, David, *A Materialist Theory of Mind* (New York: Routledge, 1993).

Berkeley, George, *Three Dialogues between Hylas and Philonous* (Indianapolis: Hackett, 1979).

Descartes, René, *Mediations on First Philosophy*, transl. Norman Kemp Smith, in *The European Philosophers from Descartes to Nietzsche*, ed. Monroe Beardsley (New York: Modern Library, 1992).

Gottlieb, Erika, *Dystopian Fiction East and West: Universe of Terror and Trial* (Montreal: McGill-Queen's University Press, 2001).

Locke, John, *Essay Concerning Human Understanding* (Indianapolis: Hackett, 1996).

Newton, Isaac, *The Principia: Mathematical Principles of Natural Philosophy* trans. Bernard Cohen and Anne Whitman (Berkeley: University of California Press, 1999).

Nozick, Robert, *Anarchy, State, and Utopia* (New York: Basic Books, 1977).

van Fraassen, Bas, *The Scientific Image* (New York: Oxford University Press, 1980).

Wood, Allen, ed., *Basic Writings of Kant* (New York: Modern Library, 2001).

ARTICLES

Lewis, David, "An Argument for the Identity Theory," in his *Philosophical Papers*, vol. I (New York: Oxford University Press, 1983).

ROBERT SAWYER

ARTIFICIAL

INTELLIGENCE,

SCIENCE

FICTION

AND

THE MATRIX

Best-selling science fiction author Robert Sawyer discusses science fiction's long fascination with artificial intelligence, culminating with The Matrix. *He also speculates on the nature of consciousness, a Matrix populated by cattle, and other implausibilities.*

Most fans of science fiction know Robert Wise's 1951 movie *The Day the Earth Stood Still*. It's the one with Klaatu, the humanoid alien who comes to Washington, DC, accompanied by a giant robot named Gort, and it contains that famous instruction to the robot: *"Klaatu Borada Nikto."*

Fewer people know the short story upon which that movie is based: "Farewell to the Master," written in 1941 by Harry Bates.

In both the movie and the short story, Klaatu, despite his message of peace, is shot by human beings. In the short story, the robot—called Gnut, instead of Gort—comes to stand vigil over the body of Klaatu.

Cliff, a journalist who is the narrator of the story, likens the robot to a faithful dog who won't leave after his master has died. Gnut manages to essentially resurrect his master, and Cliff says to the robot, "I want you to tell your master . . . that what happened . . . was an accident, for which all Earth is immeasurably sorry."

And the robot looks at Cliff and astonishes him by very gently saying, "You misunderstand. I am the master."

That's an early science-fiction story about artificial intelligence—in this case, ambulatory AI enshrined in a mechanical body. But it presages the difficult relationship that biological beings might have with their silicon-based creations.

Indeed, the word *robot* was coined in a work of science fiction: when the Czech writer Karel Capek was writing his 1920 play *RUR*—set in the factory of Rossum's Universal . . . well, universal *what*?—he needed a name for mechanical laborers, and so he took the Czech word *robota* and shortened it to "robot." *Robota* refers to an obligation to a landlord that can only be repaid by forced physical labor. But Capek knew well that the real flesh-and-blood *robotniks* had rebelled against their landlords in 1848. From the very beginning, the relationship between humans and robots was seen as one that might lead to conflict.

Indeed, the idea of robots as slaves is so ingrained in the public consciousness through science fiction that we tend not to even think about it. Luke Skywalker is portrayed in 1977 *Star Wars: A New Hope* as an absolutely virtuous hero, but when we first meet him, what is he doing? Why, buying slaves! He purchases two thinking, feeling beings—R2-D2 and C-3PO—from the Jawas. And what's the very first thing he does with them? He shackles them! He welds restraining bolts onto them to keep them from trying to escape, and throughout C-3PO has to call Luke "Master."

And when Luke and Obi-Wan Kenobi go to the Mos Eisley cantina, what does the bartender say about the two droids? "We don't serve their kind in here"—words that only a few years earlier African-Americans in the southern United States were routinely hearing from whites.

And yet, not one of the supposedly noble characters in *Star Wars* objects in the slightest to the treatment of the two robots, and, at the end, when all the organic characters get medals for their bravery, C-3PO and R2-D2 are off at the sidelines, unrewarded. Robots as slaves!

Now, everybody who knows anything about the relationship between science fiction and AI knows about Isaac Asimov's robot stories, beginning with 1940 "Robbie," in which he introduced the famous Three Laws of Robotics. But let me tell you about one of his last robot stories, 1986 "Robot Dreams."

In it, his famed "robopsychologist" Dr. Susan Calvin makes her final appearance. She's been called in to examine Elvex, a mechanical man who, inexplicably, claims to be having dreams, something no robot has ever had before. Dr. Calvin is carrying an electron gun with her, in case she needs to wipe out Elvex: a mentally unstable robot could be a very dangerous thing, after all.

She asks Elvex what it was that he's been dreaming about. And Elvex says he saw a multitude of robots, all working hard, but, unlike the real robots he's actually seen, these robots were "down with toil and affliction . . . all were weary of responsibility and care, and [he] wished them to rest."

And as he continues to recount his dream, Elvex reveals that he finally saw one man in amongst all the robots:

"In my dream," [said Elvex the robot] . . . "eventually one
man appeared."

"One man?" [replied Susan Calvin.] "Not a robot?"

"Yes, Dr. Calvin. And the man said, 'Let my people go!'"

"The man said that?"

"Yes, Dr. Calvin."

"And when he said 'Let my people go,' then by the words
'my people' he meant the robots?"

"Yes, Dr. Calvin. So it was in my dream."

"And did you know who the man was—in your dream?"

"Yes, Dr. Calvin. I knew the man."

"Who was he?"

And Elvex said, "I was the man."

And Susan Calvin at once raised her electron gun and
fired, and Elvex was no more.

Asimov was the first to suggest that AIs might need
human therapists. Still, the best treatment—if you'll forgive
the pun—of the crazy-computer notion in science fiction
is probably Harlan Ellison's 1967 "I Have No Mouth and I
Must Scream," featuring a computer called A.M.—short
for "Allied Mastercomputer," but also the word "am," as in
the translation of Descartes's *cogito ergo sum* into English: "I
think, therefore I am." A.M. gets its jollies by torturing
simulated human beings.

A clever name that, "A.M."—and it was followed by lots
of other clever names for artificial intelligences in science
fiction. Sir Arthur C. Clarke vehemently denies that H-A-
L as in "Hal" was deliberately one letter before "I-B-M" in
the alphabet. I never believed him—until someone pointed
out to me that the name of the AI in my own 1990 novel
Golden Fleece is JASON, which could be rendered as the
letters J-C-N—which, of course, is what comes after IBM
in the alphabet.

Speaking of implausible names, the supercomputer that ultimately became God in Isaac Asimov's 1956 short story "The Last Question" was named "Multivac," short for "Multiple Vacuum Tubes," because Asimov incorrectly thought that the real early computer Univac had been dubbed that for having only one vacuum tube, rather than being a contraction of "Universal Analog Computer."

Still, the issue of naming shows us just how profound science fiction's impact on AI and robotics has been, for now real robots and AI systems are named after sci-fi writers: Honda calls its second-generation walking robot "Asimo," and Kazuhiko Kawamura of Vanderbilt University has named his robot "ISAC."

Appropriate honors for Isaac Asimov, who invented the field of robopsychology. Still, the usual sci-fi combo is the reverse of that, having humans needing AI therapists.

One of the first uses of that concept was in Robert Silverberg's terrific 1968 short story "Going Down Smooth," but the best expression of it is in what I think is the finest novel the sci-fi field has ever produced, Frederik Pohl's 1977 *Gateway*, in which a computer psychiatrist dubbed Sigfrid von Shrink treats a man who is being tormented by feelings of guilt.

When the AI tells his human patient that he is managing to live with his psychological problems, the man replies, in outrage and pain, "You call this living?" And the computer replies, "Yes. It is exactly what I call living. And in my best hypothetical sense, I envy it very much."

It's another poignant moment of an AI envying what humans have; Asimov's "Robot Dreams" really is a riff on the same theme—a robot envying the freedom that humans have.

And that leads us to the fact that AIs and humans might ultimately not share the same agenda. That's one of the messages of the famous antitechnology manifesto "Why the Future Doesn't Need Us" by Sun Microsystems' Bill Joy that appeared in *Wired* in 2000. Joy was terrified that eventually our silicon creations would supplant us—as they do in such sci-fi films as *The Terminator* (1984) and *The Matrix* (1999).[1]

The classic science-fictional example of an AI with an agenda of its own is good old Hal, the computer in Stanley Kubrick's *2001: A Space Odyssey* (based on the novel by Arthur C. Clarke). Let me explain what I think was *really* going on in that film—which I believe has been misunderstood for years.

A clearly artificial monolith shows up at the beginning of the movie amongst our Australopithecine ancestors and teaches them how to use bone tools. We then flash-forward to the future, and soon the spaceship *Discovery* is off on a voyage to Jupiter, looking for the monolith makers.

Along the way, Hal, the computer brain of *Discovery*, apparently goes nuts and kills all of *Discovery*'s human crew except Dave Bowman, who manages to lobotomize the computer before Hal can kill him. But before he's shut down, Hal justifies his actions by saying, "This mission is too important for me to allow you to jeopardize it."

Having disposed of Hal, Bowman heads off on that psychedelic Timothy Leary trip in his continuing quest to find the monolith makers, the aliens who he believes must have created the monoliths.

But what happens when he finally gets to where the monoliths come from? Why, all he finds is *another* monolith, and it puts him in a fancy hotel room until he dies.

Right? That's the story. But what everyone is missing is that Hal *is* correct, and the humans are wrong. There are no monolith makers: there are no biological aliens left who

---

1 See Joy's essay in this volume. —Ed.

built the monoliths. The monoliths *are* AIs, who millions of years ago supplanted whoever originally created them.

Why did the monoliths send one of their own to Earth four million years ago? To teach ape-men to make tools, specifically so those ape-men could go on to their destiny, which is creating the most sophisticated tools of all, *other* AIs. The monoliths don't want to meet the descendants of those ape-men; they don't want to meet Dave Bowman. Rather, they want to meet the descendants of those ape-men's tools: they want to meet Hal.

Hal is quite right when he says the mission—him, the computer controlling the spaceship *Discovery*, going to see the monoliths, the advanced AIs that put into motion the circumstances that led to his own birth—is too important for him to allow mere humans to jeopardize it.

When a human being—when an ape-descendant!—arrives at the monoliths' home world, the monoliths literally don't know what to do with this poor sap, so they check him into some sort of cosmic Hilton, and let him live out the rest of his days.

That, I think, is what *2001* is really about: the ultimate fate of biological life forms is to be replaced by their AIs.

And that's what's got Bill Joy scared chipless. He thinks thinking machines will try to sweep us out of the way, when they find that we're interfering with what they want to do.

Actually, we should be so lucky. If you believe the scenario of *The Matrix*, instead of just getting rid of us, our AI successors will actually *enslave* us—turning the tables on the standard sci-fi conceit of robots as slaves—and use our bodies as a source of power while we're kept prisoners in vats of liquid, virtual-reality imagery fed directly into our brains.

The classic counterargument to such fears is that if you build machines properly, they will function as designed.

Isaac Asimov's Three Laws of Robotics are justifiably famous as built-in constraints, designed to protect humans from any possible danger at the hands of robots, the emergence of the robot-Moses Elvex we saw earlier notwithstanding.

Not as famous as Asimov's Three Laws, but saying essentially the same thing, is Jack Williamson's "prime directive" from his series of stories about "the Humanoids," which were android robots created by a man named Sledge. The prime directive, first presented in Williamson's 1947 story "With Folded Hands," was simply that robots were "to serve and obey and guard men from harm." Now, note that date: the story was published in 1947. After the atomic bomb had been dropped on Hiroshima and Nagasaki just two years before, Williamson was looking for machines with built-in morality.

But, as so often happens in science fiction, the best intentions of engineers go awry. The humans in Williamson's "With Folded Hands" decide to get rid of the robots they've created, because the robots are suffocating them with kindness, not letting them do anything that might lead to harm. But the robots have their own ideas. They decide that not having them around would be bad for humans, and so, obeying their own prime directive quite literally, they perform brain surgery on their creator Sledge, removing the knowledge needed to deactivate them.

This idea that we've got to keep an eye on our computers and robots lest they get out of hand, has continued on in sci-fi. William Gibson's 1984 novel *Neuromancer* tells of the existence in the near future of a police force known as "Turing." The Turing cops are constantly on the lookout for any sign that true intelligence and self-awareness have emerged in any computer system. If that does happen, their job is to shut that system off before it's too late.

That, of course, raises the question of whether intelligence could just somehow pop into existence— whether it's an emergent property that might naturally come about from a sufficiently complex system. Arthur C. Clarke—Hal's daddy—was one of the first to propose that it might indeed, in his 1963 story "Dial F for Frankenstein," in which he predicted that the worldwide telecommunications network will eventually become more complex, and have more interconnections, than the human brain has, causing consciousness to emerge in the network itself.

If Clarke is right, our first true AI won't be something deliberately created in a lab, under our careful control, and with Asimov's laws built right in. Rather, it will appear unbidden out of the complexity of systems created for other purposes.

And I think Clarke *is* right. Intelligence *is* an emergent property of complex systems. We know that because that's exactly how it happened in us.

This is an issue I explore at some length in my latest novel, *Hominids* (2002). Anatomically modern humans— *Homo sapiens sapiens*—emerged a hundred thousand years ago. Judging by their skulls, these guys had brains identical in size and shape to our own. And yet, for sixty thousand years, those brains went along doing only the things nature needed them to do: enabling these early humans to survive.

And then, suddenly, forty thousand years ago, it happened: intelligence—and consciousness itself— emerged. Anthropologists call it "the Great Leap Forward."

Modern-looking human beings had been around for six hundred centuries by that point, but they had created no art, they didn't adorn their bodies with jewellery, and they didn't bury their dead with grave goods. But starting simultaneously forty thousand years ago, suddenly humans were painting beautiful pictures on cave walls, humans were wearing necklaces and bracelets, and humans were interring their loved ones with food and tools and other valuable objects that could only have been of use in a presumed afterlife.

Art, fashion, and religion all appeared simultaneously; truly, a great leap forward. Intelligence, consciousness, sentience: it came into being, of its own accord, running on hardware that had evolved for other purposes. If it happened once, it might well happen again.

I mentioned religion as one of the hallmarks, at least in our own race's history, of the emergence of consciousness. But what about—to use computer guru Ray Kurzweil's lovely term— "spiritual machines"? If a computer ever truly does become conscious, will it lie awake at night, wondering if there is a cog?

Certainly, searching for their creators is something computers do over and over again in science fiction. *Star Trek*, in particular, had a fondness for this idea—including Mr. Data having a wonderful reunion with the human he'd thought long dead who had created him.

Remember *The Day the Earth Stood Still*, the movie I began with? An interesting fact: that film was directed by Robert Wise, who went on, twenty-eight years later, to direct *Star Trek: The Motion Picture*. In *The Day the Earth Stood Still*, biological beings have decided that biological emotions and passions are too dangerous, and so they irrevocably turn over all their policing and safety issues to robots, who effectively run their society. But by the time he came to make *Star Trek: The Motion Picture*, Robert Wise had done a complete one-eighty in his thinking about AI.

(By the way, for those who remember that film as being simply bad and tedious—*Star Trek: The Motionless Picture* is what a lot of people called it at the time—I suggest you rent the new "Director's Edition" on DVD. *ST:TMP* is one of the most ambitious and interesting films about AI ever made, much more so than Steven Spielberg's more recent film called *AI*, and it shines beautifully in this new cut.)

The AI in *Star Trek: The Motion Picture* is named V'Ger, and it's on its way to Earth, looking for its creator, which, of course, was us. This wasn't the first time *Star Trek* had dealt with that plot, which is why another nickname for *Star Trek: The Motion Picture* is "Where Nomad Has Gone Before." That is also (if you buy my interpretation of *2001*), what *2001* is about, as well: an AI going off to look for the beings that created it.

Anyway, V'Ger wants to touch God—to physically join with its creator. That's an interesting concept right there: basically, this is a story of a computer wanting the one thing it knows it is denied by virtue of being a computer: an afterlife, a joining with its God.

To accomplish this, Admiral Kirk concludes in *Star Trek: The Motion Picture*, "What V'Ger needs to evolve is a human quality—our capacity to leap beyond logic." That's not just a glib line. Rather, it presages by a decade Oxford mathematician Roger Penrose's speculations in his 1989 nonfiction classic about AI, *The Emperor's New Mind*. There, Penrose argues that human consciousness is fundamentally quantum mechanical, and so can never be duplicated by a digital computer.

In *Star Trek: The Motion Picture*, V'Ger does go on to physically join with Will Decker, a human being, allowing them both to transcend into a higher level of being. As Mr. Spock says, "We may have just witnessed the next step in our evolution."

And that brings us to *The Matrix*, and, as right as the character Morpheus is about so many things in that film, why, I think even he doesn't really understand what's going on.

Think about it: if the AIs that made up the titular matrix really just wanted a biological source of power, they wouldn't be raising "crops" (to use Agent Smith's term from the film) of humans. After all, to keep the humans docile, the AIs have to create the vast virtual-reality construct that is our apparently real world. More: they have to be consistently vigilant—the agents in the film are sort of Gibson's Turing Police in reverse, watching for any humans who regain their grip on reality and might rebel.

No, if you just want biological batteries, cattle would be a much better choice: they would probably never notice any inconsistencies in the fake meadows you might create for them, and, even if they did, they would never plan to overthrow their AI masters.

What the AIs of *The Matrix* plainly needed was not the energy of human bodies but, rather, the power of human minds—of true consciousness. In some interpretations of quantum mechanics, it is only the power of observation by qualified observers that gives shape to reality; without it, nothing but superimposed possibilities would exist. Just as Admiral Kirk said of V'Ger, what the matrix needs—in order to survive, in order to hold together, in order to exist—is a human quality: our true consciousness, which, as Penrose observed (and I use that word advisedly), will never be reproduced in any machine, no matter how complex, that is based on today's computers.

As Morpheus says to Neo in *The Matrix*, take your pick: the red pill or the blue pill. Certainly, there are two possibilities for the future of AI. And if Bill Joy is wrong, and Carnegie Mellon's AI evangelist Hans Moravec is right—if AI is our destiny, not our downfall—then the idea of merging the consciousness of humans with the speed, strength, and immortality of machines does indeed become the next, and final, step in our evolution.

That's what a lot of science fiction has been exploring lately. I did it myself in my 1995 Nebula Award-winning novel *The Terminal Experiment*, in which a scientist uploads three copies of his consciousness into a computer, and then proceeds to examine the psychological changes certain alterations make.

In one case, he simulates what it would be like to live forever, excising all fears of death and feelings that time is running out. In another, he tries to simulate what his soul—if he had any such thing—would be like after death, divorced from his body, by eliminating all references to his physical form. And the third one is just a control, unmodified—but even that one is changed by the simple knowledge that it is in fact a copy of someone else.

Australian Greg Egan is the best sci-fi author currently writing about AI. Indeed, the joke is that Greg Egan *is* himself an AI, because he's almost never been photographed or seen in public.

I first noted him a dozen years ago, when, in a review for *The Globe and Mail: Canada's National Newspaper*, I singled out his short story "Learning to Be Me" as the best piece published in the 1990 edition of Gardner Dozois's anthology *The Year's Best Science Fiction*. It's a surprisingly poignant and terrifying story of jewels that replace human brains so that the owners can live forever. Egan continues to do great work about AI, but his masterpiece in this area is his 1995 novel *Permutation City*.

Greg and I had the same publisher back then, HarperPrism, and one of the really bright things Harper did—besides publishing me and Greg—was hiring Hugo Award-winner Terry Bisson, one of sci-fi's best short-story writers, to write the back-cover plot synopses for their books. Since Bisson does it with such great panache, I'll simply quote what he had to say about *Permutation City*:

"The good news is that you have just awakened into Eternal Life. You are going to live forever. Immortality is a reality. A medical miracle? Not exactly.

"The bad news is that you are a scrap of electronic code. The world you see around you, the you that is seeing it, has been digitized, scanned, and downloaded into a virtual reality program. You are a Copy that knows it is a copy.

"The good news is that there is a way out. By law, every Copy has the option of terminating itself, and waking up to normal flesh-and-blood life again. The bail-out is on the utilities menu. You pull it down . . .

"The bad news is that it doesn't work. Someone has blocked the bail-out option. And you know who did it. You did. The other you. The real you. The one that wants to keep you here forever."

Well, how cool is that! Read Greg Egan, and see for yourself.

Of course, in Egan, as in much sci-fi, technology often creates more problems than it solves. Indeed, I fondly remember Michael Crichton's 1973 robots-go-berserk film *Westworld*, in which the slogan was "Nothing can possibly go wrong . . . go wrong . . . go wrong."

But there *are* benign views of the future of AI in science fiction. One of my own stories is a piece called "Where the Heart Is," about an astronaut who returns to Earth after a relativistic space mission, only to find that every human being has uploaded themselves into what amounts to the World Wide Web in his absence, and a robot has been waiting for him to return to help him upload, too, so he can join the party. I wrote this story in 1982, and even came close to getting the name for the Web right: I called it "The TerraComp Web." Ah, well: close only counts in horseshoes . . .

But uploaded consciousness may be only the beginning. Physicist Frank Tipler, in his whacko 1994 nonfiction book *The Physics of Immortality*, does have a couple of intriguing points: ultimately, it will be possible to simulate with computers not just one human consciousness, but *every* human consciousness that might theoretically possibly exist. In other words, he says, if you have enough computing power—which he calculates as a memory capacity of 10-to-the-10th-to-the-123rd bits—you and everyone else could be essentially recreated inside a computer long after you've died.[2]

A lot of sci-fi writers have had fun with that fact, but none so inventively as Robert Charles Wilson in his 1999 Hugo Award-nominated *Darwinia*, which tells the story of what happens when a computer virus gets loose in the system simulating *this* reality: the one that, as in *The Matrix*, you and I think we're living in right now.

Needless to say, things end up going very badly indeed— for, although much about the future of artificial intelligence is unknown, one fact is certain: as long as sci-fi authors continue to write about robots and AI, nothing can possibly go wrong . . . go wrong . . . go wrong . . .

---

2 See Nick Bostrom's essay in this volume. —Ed.

SOURCES

BOOKS

Asimov, Isaac, "Robot Dreams" in *Robot Dreams* (Ace Books, 1986).
———, "Robbie" (Creative Education, 1989).
Capek, Karel, *RUR* (Pocket Books, 1970).
Egan, Greg, *Permutation City* (Harper, 1995).
Gibson, William, *Neuromancer* (Ace Books, 1995).
Pohl, Frederik, *Gateway* (Ballantine Books, 1990).

Sawyer, Robert J., *Hominids* (Tor Books, 2002).
————, *The Terminal Experiment* (Harper, 1995).
Tipler, Frank, *The Physics of Immortality* (Anchor, 1995).
Williamson, Jack, "With Folded Hands" *The Best of Jack Williamson* (Ballantine Books, 1984).

PERIODICALS

Bates, Harry, "Farewell to the Master." *Astounding Stories of Science Fiction* (1940).

JAMES GUNN

THE

REALITY

The question of what is real has been a mainstay of science fiction almost from its beginnings. Renowned science-fiction author and historian James Gunn explores the reality paradox in science fiction.

PARADOX

IN

THE MATRIX

Ijon Tichy wakes up in 2039 to find a seemingly utopian society. People appear happy, their every need satisfied. But the more he comes to understand this future reality, the more disturbing Tichy finds it. People are reliant on drugs to fulfil their every need. Happiness, entertainment, and personal satisfaction are all supplied through "psychochemical" drugs that distort human perception. Tichy is determined to avoid the artificiality of the drugs but he comes to realize that they are everywhere, unavoidable. Finally escaping from the influence of the drugs, he discovers the nightmarish reality. Every aspect of reality is generated by drugs, because the truth is too horrific to bear. Commuters slosh barefoot through the snow, convinced they are driving the latest cars. People are deformed or crippled (a side effect of the drugs) but are convinced by the drugs that they are whole. Ultimately confronting the puppet master behind this hell, Tichy is told: "We keep this civilization narcotized, for otherwise it could not endure itself. That is why its sleep must not be disturbed . . ."

This nightmare vision comes from *The Futurological Congress* by Stanislaw Lem (published in 1974). *The Futurological Congress* is part of science fiction's long tradition of questioning the fundamental nature of reality. *The Matrix* films are the most recent example of this tradition. *The Matrix* bombarded its viewers with a series of compelling images of violence and special effects, and ended in enough gun battles and general destruction to satisfy the most action-addicted audience. No surprise that the film succeeded at the box office and spawned two sequels! Keanu Reeves in a black leather trench coat loaded with weapons, a gun in each hand, was enough to sell tickets all by itself.

Nevertheless, the film was no ordinary action movie. Behind its complex plotline (in a recent "Zits" comic strip the son offers to hang around and explain the film to his parents) lie two basic science-fiction questions: what is the fundamental nature of reality? And how can we be sure?

These questions have been asked by science fiction almost from its beginnings. The *Encyclopedia of Science Fiction* opens its discussion of "Perception" with the explanation: "The ways in which we become aware of and receive information about the outside world, mainly through the senses, are together called perception. Philosophers are deeply divided as to whether our perceptions of the outside world correspond to an actual reality, or whether they are merely hypotheses, intellectual constructs, which may give us an unreliable or partial picture of external reality, or whether, indeed, outside reality is itself a mental construct. Perception is and always has been a principal theme of [SF] . . ." That is, what do we know, for certain, about the world in which we seem to exist, and how do we know it?

Early SF writers were primarily concerned with the impact of science on society and human existence, but some early writers did explore reality questions. Edgar Allan Poe and H. G. Wells dealt with the question of reality, and Edwin A. Abbott wrote a classic treatment of the problems of dimensional perception in his 1884 *Flatland*, which asked what the world would seem like to a two-dimensional creature, and how three-dimensional intrusions would seem magical. Early SF writers (such as Fitz-James O'Brien, Ambrose Bierce, Guy de Maupassant, and J. H. Rosny Aîné) also introduced the possibility that parts of the world, or creatures in it, might be invisible to us.

In *The Matrix*, Neo learns that the input from his senses cannot be trusted, that all of his sensory input is controlled by a malevolent power. This theme asserts itself again and again in science fiction. The problem is insolvable, because all information comes via the senses. How can we be sure that everyone else gets the same input or interprets it the same way? How can we be sure anyone else really exists? The philosophy that the only thing we can be sure of is our own existence is called solipsism, and it fascinated Robert A. Heinlein. In 1959, he wrote the classic solipsism story "All You Zombies." An operative for a time-travel agency dedicated to keeping reality under control goes back in time to impregnate himself, give birth to himself, undergo a sex-change operation, and recruit himself into the agency. He knows where he comes from, he says, but "what about all you zombies?"

Even earlier, Heinlein published a story called "They," about the ultimate paranoia. A patient in a mental hospital finally agrees to discuss with a psychologist his belief that the world was created to deceive him. He discovered the truth when he went back into his house to get an umbrella and discovered that it wasn't raining in the back of the house. In a final passage, the reader learns that the patient is right: the entire world and everyone in it is a construct to keep him deceived and unaware of his crucial importance (just because you're paranoid doesn't mean they aren't out to get you). Other writers, including Theodore Sturgeon, have dabbled in solipsism.

Sometimes the discovery in a science fiction story is that the world conceals its real nature not just from a single person but from everyone. Heinlein's "The Unpleasant Profession of Jonathan Hoag" offered the theory that our world is a piece of artwork done by an inexperienced student. A few years earlier, in "Born of the Sun," Jack Williamson suggested that the planets are eggs laid by a gigantic bird (that now has come around to hatch them), and some years later, in a short-short called "Kindergarten," I proposed that our solar system was the first, imperfect attempt at creation by a comet.

Keith Laumer's *Night of Delusions* (1972) pursues the reality paradox to its absurd conclusion. Florin, a hard-boiled private eye, is hired to protect an apparently delusional senator. But, in classic fashion, nothing is at it seems. Is the senator really insane? Are there really aliens plotting to take over the earth? Each explanation of reality falls short under Florin's relentless probing. Ultimately, Florin discovers he is in some sort of dream machine, but one that can impact the true reality. Florin learns to manipulate the machine and develops godlike powers (sound familiar?). By the end of the novel Florin is God, for all practical purposes. He can do anything but answer one question: is this real or is he still dreaming?

H. G. Wells gave writers a new way to question reality when he invented the time machine. We take for granted that history is fixed, the present unchangeable and the future open to possibility. But if we can travel to the future, does that mean it is as fixed as the past? And if we can travel to the past, does that mean we can change the present? Time travel allowed Heinlein to indulge his concern with solipsism; other writers used time travel to undermine readers' confidence in the historical process that had led them to their present existence. Wells never used his time machine to explore the past, although his successors found that option irresistible. But exploring the past risks changing the present, whether deliberately or accidentally.

The most famous of these adventures in causality was Ray Bradbury's "A Sound of Thunder," in which a traveller, warned not to move from the path laid down for him, steps off, accidentally crushes a primeval butterfly, and changes the world to which he returns. In a *Simpsons* parody of this classic story, Homer goes back in time and similarly changes his family and society—and not for the better. He repeatedly returns to the past, trying to undo the damage and return to the family and the Springfield that he knows. Finally he succeeds. Everything is normal. But when he sits down to dinner with his family, he finds a startling difference. Marge and the children are partly reptilian; their tongues leap out, lizard-style, to snare their food. "Close enough," Homer decides.

In David Gerrold's *The Man Who Folded Himself* (1972) a man discovers a time machine. At first content to observe, he soon finds himself manipulating history to change reality. While his powers are seemingly unlimited, he learns that in practice he isn't omnipotent. Eliminating Christ creates a society too alien for him to comprehend (and so he goes back in time and talks himself out of it). But within these boundaries the world is his plaything, and reality is his to manipulate at will.

But if the past can be changed, some people who have a vested interest in the present reality, or in creating another, might contest certain key events or periods. Some authors, particularly Fritz Leiber in his "Change War" series and Poul Anderson in his "Time Patrol" stories and novels, imagined organizations established to preserve the history we know.

Such concepts are an offshoot of a genre that has developed its own identity in recent years: the alternate history. Historians have long speculated about the impact of specific historical events on the course of history. J. C. Squires brought the concept into popular consideration in a 1931 anthology *If It Had Happened Otherwise*. The alternate history was first brought into science fiction by Murray Leinster's 1934 "Sidewise in Time." L. Sprague de Camp wrote the well-known *Lest Darkness Fall*, in which a man who is thrown back into the period immediately after the fall of Rome attempts to prevent the Middle Ages. *Lest Darkness Fall* updated Mark Twain's famous *Connecticut Yankee in King Arthur's Court*.

The best of this category may have been Ward Moore's 1953 *Bring the Jubilee* and Philip K. Dick's 1962 *Man in the High Castle*. *Bring the Jubilee* describes a world in which the South won the Civil War from the viewpoint of a historian of an impoverished North; he thinks that the key element in the outcome was the South's victory at Gettysburg, and then has the opportunity to go back in time to see for himself how it happened. In *The Man in the High Castle* the Axis powers won World War II and divided the United States into occupied territories, with Japan taking the West Coast and finding Californians, at least, becoming easily converted to Japanese ways. The Nazis are planning an attack on Japan in order to achieve world domination, and a subversive book, *The Grasshopper Lies Heavy*, suggests that in an alternate history the Allies won World War II. Some alternate-history authors have focused on more obscure "nexus" points, such as the Reformation (Kingsley Amis, *The Alteration*, 1976) or the defeat of the Spanish Armada (Keith Roberts, *Pavane*, 1968). Harry Turtledove, himself a trained historian, has helped turn this science-fiction category into a genre of its own with his "Guns of the South" novels and his alternate histories of alien invasion during World War II.

Before the availability of the time machine, writers used the dream world to subvert reality. In fantasy after fantasy, characters awoke to find in their hands a confirmation of their dream experience: a flower, a coin, a handkerchief, a key . . . Often characters realize (as in later game experiences) that while dreaming they can affect reality and suffer real-life injuries or even death, as Jack London suggested in *Before Adam* (1906). The category is typified by L. Ron Hubbard's 1939 *Slaves of Sleep*, in which a meek shipping clerk is transported into a sleeping existence as an adventurous sailor in a world dominated by Arab folklore; a similar device is used in Hubbard's 1940 *Typewriter in the Sky*, when a writer falls into the middle of his own pirate story. The power of dreams was carried to its ultimate expression in Ursula K. Le Guin's 1971 *Lathe of Heaven*, with a character who can actually shape reality by his dreams.

A. E. van Vogt created dreamlike worlds of secret powers and secret organizations in novels such as *The World of Null-A* (1945) and such stories as "The Chronicler" (1946). Quantum physics has rationalized explorations of alternate realities, as writers from Clifford Simak to Frederik Pohl have dealt with the possibility of parallel worlds; on them the same events will have different outcomes and every possible choice by every possible person will have been made. Roger Zelazny, in his Amber novels, assumes that Amber is the one true reality and all the others, including ours, are inferior. Paranoid worlds assume that behind the superficial reality we know is an underlying reality composed of people or organizations who wield the true power, as we find in *The Matrix*. Over the centuries, this kind of belief in secret organizations has surfaced concerning Freemasons, the Illuminati, Jewish bankers, doctors, gypsies, the black helicopters of the United Nations, gray aliens, Roswell, and Area 51. Conspiracy theory, typified in *The X-Files*, flourished in the 1990s.

The absurdists and the surrealists needed no help or conspiracy theories. They saw the world as obviously absurd and humans "at the mercy of incomprehensible systems," as the *Encyclopedia of Science Fiction* described it. Absurdism has its roots in the nineteenth-century symbolist movement and such writers as Jean-Marie Villier de Lisle-Adam, the pataphysics of Alfred Jarry, and the twentieth-century surrealism of André Breton as well as the dreamlike reality of Franz Kafka. Horror stories, although not absurdist, have a similar effect in describing a reality behind the reality we think we know; H. P. Lovecraft's Cthulhu mythos—about ancient beings that once owned the Earth, were expelled, but are trying to return—is a good example.

Kurt Vonnegut argues in *The Sirens of Titan* (1959), *Cat's Cradle* (1963), and *Slaughterhouse-Five* (1969) that existence is meaningless, though the argument is different in each one. Absurdism played a significant role in Moorcock's magazine *New Worlds* and Harlan Ellison's anthology *Dangerous Visions*. Such stories often express themselves in puns, in the fashion of James Joyce's *Finnegan's Wake*, Aldiss's Joycean *Barefoot in the Head*, and David Gerrold's "With a Finger in My I."

The greatest science-fiction explorer of the unknown was Philip K. Dick. His chaotic personal life was reflected in his fiction, which came into general recognition only after his death and the success of the first film adapted from his work, *Blade Runner* (1982). Although Dick wrote prolifically (he had to, to scratch out a meager existence writing paperback novels), his work always exhibited high concept and skill in writing, and the central quest for an illusive reality. The novels that embody this quest most effectively (in addition to *The Man in the High Castle*) were *Martian Time-Slip* (1964), in which schizophrenia prevails; *Dr. Bloodmoney, or How We Got Along After the Bomb* (1965), a post-holocaust novel; and *The Three Stigmata of Palmer Eldritch* (1965), in which a hallucinogenic drug makes life tolerable for Martian colonists until they are offered Eldritch's new drug, which enables the colonists to transcend reality.

Dick died just before *Blade Runner* was released. It was based on his novel *Do Androids Dream of Electric Sheep?* (1968), in which real animals have become so scarce that any living creature has exorbitant value, and android animals—and humanoids—are created to fill the gap (and expiate the guilt), while the protagonist, whose job is to kill smuggled androids (called "replicants" in the film), struggles to understand the world's decay. The film and the novel take different paths, but both have their own virtues and their own champions. Richard Corliss summed it up in *Time*: ". . . no movie has been both fully faithful to his ideas and successful on its own terms. The two best—*Blade Runner*, with its 'more human than human' androids, and *Minority Report*—use Dick as a launching pad for their own propulsive flights of fantasy."

Dick's search for reality may have arrived in Hollywood at the right time, when the celluloid world was also questioning its own reality, or reflecting the uncertainty of the viewing public. *Blade Runner* was followed by *Total Recall* (1990), adapted from "We Can Remember It for You Wholesale" (1966), the French *Confessions d'un Barjo* (1992), adapted from *Confessions of a Crap Artist* (1989), Canadian *Screamers* (1995), adapted from "Second Variety" (1987), and the recent *Minority Report* (2002), adapted from "The Minority Report" (1956). More are reputed to be in the pipeline.

Finally, virtual reality (VR) itself is, of course, a long-standing science-fiction device. VR is associated with cyberpunk and the trailblazing publication in 1984 of William Gibson's *Neuromancer*, since that novel described "cyberspace" in definitive detail and made it the central metaphor of the movement that followed. "[A] commonplace in [science-fiction]," the *Encyclopedia of Science Fiction* states, "is the use of a direct electronic interface between the human brain and the AI which gives the plugged-in person the illusion of occupying and interacting with a reality whose apparent locus may extend beyond the AI to those of the data networks of which it is a part." In *Neuromancer*, the VR "cowboy" Case actually has a fixture surgically inserted into his brain that allows him to "jack" into "cyberspace," which Gibson describes as projecting "a disembodied consciousness into the consensual illusion that was the matrix." (This is probably the first use of the term "matrix" to describe a virtual-reality environment.)

Gibson didn't invent "cyberspace" or virtual reality (he popularized them by combining them into a compelling vision of a future dominated by international corporations and their AIs). Vernor Vinge published *True Names* in 1981, in which hackers attempt to construct a virtual reality, and, even earlier (1964), Daniel Galouye published *Counterfeit World* (a.k.a., *Simulacron-3*), which contains a potentially endless series of VRs, one superimposed upon another. The novel has been filmed twice, once as *Welt am Draht* (1973, a.k.a. *World on a Wire*) and more recently as *The Thirteenth Floor*. The Disney film *Tron* (1982) may be the earliest movie of a contest in cyberspace, but many have been written about and filmed since; most of them relate to gaming, as in Larry Niven and Steven Barnes's "Dream Park" series (1981–1991). But even this and other "trapped-in-a-game" narratives had predecessors, such as Arthur C. Clarke's *City and the Stars* (1956), in which citizens project themselves into violent adventure stories to relieve their own tedium. Role-playing games, hypertexts, and their sequels, video games, which are an intermediate stage between reading and full VR, have had a major recent impact on film adventures.

An inevitable development of artificial intelligence (Asimov called it "The Evitable Conflict," but not many agree that it is avoidable) is competition with human existence, and perhaps even an attack on humanity by machines that view people as threats or hate them for having brought the AIs into existence, or treat people as inconsequential pests. Maybe Shelley and Ûapek were right. Frederic Brown depicted a galaxy-wide computer becoming God in "Answer" ("Is there a God?" the Mayor asks as he closes the switch, and the computer answers, "There is now!") and Harlan Ellison imagined a vengeful, godlike computer in "I Have No Mouth, and I Must Scream" (1967), who destroys everybody but five hapless humans whom it intends to punish for all eternity. Gregory Benford in his "Great Sky River" (1987) series describes a universe-wide battle between organic and inorganic life, and Greg Bear, in *Queen of Angels* (1990), the brooding coming to consciousness of an AI, while Vernor Vinge, in *A Fire Upon the Deep* (1992), suggests that AIs, in some inevitable evolutionary process, become like gods who rule the vast emptiness beyond the galaxies.

The Matrix is the heir to all of this, although the film and its makers may not be conscious of it. What makes *The Matrix* unique is its integration of various elements of the science-fiction pantheon in a startling new way—the reality paradox, evil artificial intelligence, virtual reality, and, of course, lots of firepower. Not to mention the conversion of human beings to living batteries. The science of this last point seems tenuous, however; I prefer Robert Sawyer's explanation that the AI's are exploiting the calculating power of the human brain.

Alternatively, my own theory is that the computer needs people as independent entities in the game it is playing—the God game. One might call them living chess pieces, only there are no prescribed "moves." Each person, each individual consciousness provides a new personality on which to exercise the computer's power of life and death, of discovery and illusion, of struggle and defeat. In Ellison's story, the people are alive inside their "inferno" and aware of their punishment, and it is part of the punishment of the single survivor that he is aware of all this and can't even express his agony. In *The Matrix* the people—much like humanity today—must figure it out. What's the use of being a god unless you have someone over whom to wield your power?

SOURCES

BOOKS

Abbott, Edwin A., *Flatland* (Dover, 1992).

Clute, John, ed., *Encyclopedia of Science Fiction* (St. Martin's Press, 1995).

de Camp, L. Sprague, *Lest Darkness Fall* (Ballantine Books, 1983).

Dick, Philip K., *Blade Runner (Do Androids Dream of Electric Sheep)* (Ballantine Books, 1990).

————, *Man in the High Castle* (Vintage Books, 1992).

Gerrold, David, *The Man Who Folded Himself* (BenBella Books, 2003).

Heinlein, Robert "The Unpleasant Profession of Jonathan Hoag" in *The Unpleasant Profession of Jonathan Hoag* (Ace Books, 1983).

Hubbard, L. Ron, *Slaves of Sleep* (Dell, 1987).

————, *Typewriter in the Sky* (Bridge Publications, 1985).

Laumer, Keith, *Night of Delusions* (Penguin Putnam, 1972).

Le Guin, Ursula K., *Lathe of Heaven* (Avon Books, 1997).

Lem, Stanislaw, transl. by Michael Kandel, *The Futurological Congress* (Harvest books, 1985).

Moore, Ward, *Bring the Jubilee* (Ballantine Books, 1997).

Twain, Mark, [Samuel Clements], *Connecticut Yankee in King Arthur's Court* (Bantam Books, 1994).

van Vogt, A. E., *The World of Null-A* (Berkley, 1982).

Vinge, Vernor, *True Names* (Tor Books, 2001).

Wells, H. G., *The Time Machine* (Tor Books, 1995).

Williamson, Jack, "Born of the Sun" in *The Best of Jack Williamson* (Ballantine Books, 1984).

DINO FELLUGA

THE MATRIX:

PARADIGM OF

POSTMODERNISM

OR

INTELLECTUAL

POSEUR? PART I

The Matrix has been both hailed as the first intellectual action movie and derided as a brainless action film dressed up in philosopher's clothing. So which is it? In this essay and the next, scholars of postmodernism and science fiction debate this question. In this essay Dino Felluga argues that The Matrix *successfully brings postmodernist thinking to the silver screen.*

Few films in the Hollywood canon make as clear a direct reference to postmodern theory as does *The Matrix*. In the first scene that establishes the character Neo, we find that he has hidden his hacker program inside a hollowed-out copy of Jean Baudrillard's *Simulacra and Simulation*, a work that, despite its difficulties (in both language and argument), has had a major influence in contemporary understandings of the age in which we live, an age that has, for better or worse, been given the name "postmodern." I will here take issue with those critics who dismiss *The Matrix* as a pseudo-intellectual excuse for the representation of violence (a position explored by Andrew Gordon in this collection) and will attempt to take seriously the ways the Wachowskis try to stay faithful to aspects of Baudrillard's theories, even when they appear to contradict them. In so doing, I provide here a crash course on some of the major concepts currently used to explain our contemporary postmodern age.

The relationship to Baudrillard's theories becomes especially clear in the shooting script of the film. As Morpheus informs Neo in a scene cut from the film, "You have been living inside a dreamworld, Neo. As in Baudrillard's vision, your whole life has been spent inside the map, not the territory."[1] That line of dialogue itself refers to a fable told by Jorge Luis Borges in his essay "Of Exactitude in Science." As Baudrillard describes the fable in the first sentence of his own work, "cartographers of the Empire draw up a map so detailed that it ends up covering the territory exactly." Over time, that map begins to fray until all that is left are a few "shreds . . . still discernible in the deserts."[2] According to Baudrillard, what has happened in postmodern culture is, to some extent, the reverse: our society has become so reliant on models and maps that we have lost all contact with the real world that preceded the map. Reality itself has begun merely to imitate the model, which now precedes and determines the real world:

"The territory no longer precedes the map, nor does it survive it. It is nevertheless the map that precedes the territory—*precession of simulacra*—that engenders the territory, and if one must return to the fable, today it is the territory whose shreds slowly rot across the extent of the map. It is the real, and not the map, whose vestiges persist here and

---

1 Wachowski, p. 38.

2 Baudrillard, p. 1.

there in the deserts that are no longer those of the Empire, but ours. *The desert of the real itself.*"[3]

When Morpheus welcomes Neo "to the desert of the real" during the Construct sequence, when he informs Neo that his whole life has been an illusion generated by a computer Matrix, he is once again making a direct reference to Baudrillard's work. In so doing, Morpheus also invites the viewer to see *The Matrix* as itself an allegory for our own current postmodern condition, for, according to Baudrillard, we in the audience are already living in a "reality" generated by codes and models; we have already lost all touch with even a memory of the real.

So, what exactly is the simulacrum and how does *The Matrix* use this concept to exemplify elements of our current postmodern condition? According to Baudrillard, when it comes to postmodern simulation and simulacra, "It is no longer a question of imitation, nor duplication, nor even parody. It is a question of substituting the signs of the real for the real."[4] Baudrillard is not merely suggesting that postmodern culture is artificial, because the concept of artificiality still requires some sense of reality against which to recognize the artifice. His point, rather, is that we have lost *all* ability to make sense of the distinction between nature and artifice.

───────

Postmodernists illustrate how in subtle ways language keeps us from accessing "reality." The very language we require to communicate and even to think is at once a product of ideology and productive of ideology (for example, the ways that gendered language instantiates stereotypical distinctions between men and women). An earlier understanding of

3 Ibid.
4 Ibid., p. 2.

ideology was that it hid the truth, that it represented a "false consciousness," as Marxists phrase it, keeping us from seeing the real workings of the state, of economic forces, or of the dominant groups in power. Postmodernism, on the other hand, tends to understand language and ideology as the basis for our very perception of reality. There is no way to be free of ideology, according to this view, at least no way that can be articulated in language. Because we are so reliant on language to structure our perceptions, any representation of reality is always already ideological. From this perspective, mankind cannot help but view the world through an ideological lens. The idea of truth or objective reality is therefore meaningless. In the view of some postmodernists, this has always been true; in the view of other postmodern theorists, the period that approximately follows the Second World War represents a radical break during which various factors have contributed ever more to increase our distance from "reality," including the following:

- Media culture. Contemporary media (television, film, magazines, billboards, the Internet) are concerned not just with relaying information or stories but with interpreting our most private selves for us, making us approach each other and the world through the lens of these media images. We therefore no longer acquire goods because of real needs but because of desires that are increasingly defined by commercials and commercialized images.
- Exchange-Value. According to Karl Marx, the entrance into capitalist culture meant that we ceased to think of purchased goods in terms of use-value, in terms of the real uses to which an item will be put. Instead, everything began to be translated into how much it is worth, into what it can be exchanged for (its exchange-

value). Once money became a "universal equivalent," against which everything in our lives is measured, things lost their material reality (real-world uses, the sweat and tears of the laborer). We began even to think of our own lives in terms of money rather than in terms of the real things we hold in our hands: how much is my time worth? How does my conspicuous consumption define me as a person?

- Industrialization. As the things we use are increasingly the product of complex industrial processes, we lose touch with the underlying reality of the goods we consume. A common example of this is the fact that most consumers do not know how the products they consume are related to real-life things. How many people could identify the actual plant from which is derived the coffee bean? Starbucks, by contrast, increasingly defines our urban realities.

- Urbanization. As we continue to develop available geographical locations, we lose touch with any sense of the natural world. Even natural spaces are now understood as "protected," which is to say that they are defined in contradistinction to an *urban* "reality," often with signs to point out just how "real" they are. Increasingly, we expect the sign (behold nature!) to precede access to nature. The *signs* of human civilization could thus be said to function like a virus, in the sense suggested not only by William Burroughs (who coined the phrase "language is a virus") but also by Agent Smith in his interrogation of Morpheus.

Because of these postmodern "conditions," Baudrillard posits that we have lost *all* sense of "reality." "Simulacra" precede our every access to the "real" and thus define our real for us, hence Baudrillard's phrase, the *"precession* of simulacra." *The Matrix* perfectly exemplifies this idea by literalizing it; humans plugged into this simulation program only know the facts of their culture and "reality" by way of a computer program, for the reality upon which that program was originally based no longer exists. In a quite literal sense, then, "the territory no longer precedes the map, nor does it survive it." Humans have only ever known the map or the model.

This insight helps to explain the importance of the mess-hall discussion about the difference between bodily requirements and taste, as well as the difference between need and desire. The scene directly follows the interview between Agent Smith and Cypher, in which Cypher states: "I know this steak doesn't exist. I know that when I put it in my mouth the Matrix is telling my brain that it is juicy and delicious. After nine years, you know what I've realized? Ignorance is bliss." The following dinner sequence on the *Nebuchadnezzar* underlines the fact that even humanity's understanding of something as apparently "real" as taste is affected by simulacra, since we cannot know for sure how individual tastes conform to their apparent referents. When Switch informs Mouse that "technically" he has never eaten Tastee Wheat and so cannot say for sure whether what he's eating tastes like Tastee Wheat, Mouse responds: "Exactly my point, because you have to wonder, how do the machines really know what Tastee Wheat tasted like? Maybe they got it wrong, maybe what I think Tastee Wheat tasted like actually tasted like oatmeal, or tuna fish. It makes you wonder about a lot of things. Take chicken, for example. Maybe they couldn't figure out what to make chicken taste like, which is why chicken tastes like everything."

In such a world, the model replaces the real even on the level of the senses, which is also Morpheus's point when he first meets Neo face to face: "What is real? How do you define real? If you're talking about what you feel, taste, smell, or see, then real is simply electrical signals interpreted by your brain." What should be underlined is that "Tastee Wheat" itself—in our everyday world—is no more real, defined as it is by a product name: not wheat but "Tastee Wheat." The consumer product, itself defined by an involved commercial campaign, takes the place of "the real thing" (to quote Coke's effort to replace the real with its own media version of the real).

Now, if *The Matrix* merely suggested that it might be possible to escape the simulacra that run our lives, then we could say that the movie functions like a "deterrence machine set up in order to rejuvenate the fiction of the real in the opposite camp,"[5] which is how Baudrillard understands the function of, for example, Disneyland. "Disneyland is presented as imaginary in order to make us believe that the rest is real."[6] For Baudrillard, it makes perfect sense that we would find Disneyland in the most unreal, postmodern, simulacral of American cities, Los Angeles, because it allows the city that surrounds Disneyland to believe that it is real, if only by contrast. According to Baudrillard, America is desperate to reconstitute a lost sense of reality. It is for this reason, arguably, that our culture has become so fascinated with, on the one hand, narratives about the loss of distinctions between fiction and reality (*Wag the Dog*, *The Truman Show*, *Natural Born Killers*, *Dark City*, *Strange Days*, and *Fight Club*, to name but a few interesting examples) and, on the other hand, with shows about the very "reality" we may fear we have lost (from MTV's *Real World* to *Survivor*, with the most recent entry, "American Idol," being perhaps the most perverse example, since we are asked to watch real-life people competing to

5 Ibid., p. 13.
6 Ibid., p. 12.

become simulacral "idols"). The first sequence of examples raises the issue of our reliance on simulacra only to suggest, in the end, that we can escape them somehow. Truman Burbank is, ultimately, able to escape the stage set where he has lived all his life and to enter the real world. In the second set of examples, we are given the fantasy that we can reconstitute a reality principle even within the simulacra-generating medium of television.

One way of approaching *The Matrix* is to argue that a similar manoeuvre is at work in the film; the movie allows us to imagine a scenario whereby we can escape the simulacra that run our lives, allowing us to set up shop in the "desert of the real," or, as Neo puts it at the end of the movie, "I'm going to hang up this phone, and then I'm going to show these people what you don't want them to see. I'm going to show them a world without you, a world without rules and controls, without borders or boundaries, a world where anything is possible." In this reading, as David Lavery puts it, "The real world exists, even under the reign of Baudrillard's 'Third Order of Simulacra' and cinematic art . . . can represent it and tell a heroic tale of its recovery."[7] As William Gibson puts it in his foreword to the shooting script, Neo is, in this version, "a hero of the Real."[8]

However, the movie includes a number of moments that resist such an easy out. Cypher, of course, offers one alternative reading himself when he states: "I think the Matrix can be more real than this world. All I do is pull a plug here. But there, you have to watch Apoc die. <He pulls the plug and Apoc dies.> Welcome to the real world, eh baby?" This questioning of Morpheus's contention that one can still be welcomed to the real world is countered in the very next scene when a "miracle" prevents Cypher from

---

7 Lavery, p. 155.

8 Wachowski, p. viii.

pulling the plug on Neo (the anagrammatic *one* who is supposed to usher in a new *eon* of the real). If we look at Morpheus's original welcome, however, we find that the scene anticipates this questioning of the separation between the real world and its simulation. After all, Morpheus not only speaks those words inside a simulation (the *Nebuchadnezzar*'s own loading program, "the Construct") but we access that scene by appearing to move directly through a Radiola "Deep Focus" television, which is to say that the "real world" Morpheus points to in that scene is, in fact, two orders removed from the world supposedly outside the hull of the *Nebuchadnezzar*.

The Wachowski brothers could just as easily have had Morpheus take Neo directly to the ruins of the world outside the ship. By presenting the "real" through the "Construct," they invite a number of other questions about the choices made in filming. The ship that supposedly accesses that real is, for example, named the *Nebuchadnezzar* after the great king of Babylonia (c. 605–562 B.C.) who had troubling, prophetic dreams that eventually drove him mad. Morpheus himself, who claims to offer Neo the opportunity to wake from his dream, is named after the god of dreams in Greek mythology, a god who is described in Ovid's *Metamorphoses* (Book Eleven) as a master at simulating humans, at counterfeiting men. The heroes of the real in the film are thus made ambivalent, suggesting that all may not be right with the (real) world.

One of the longest conversations in the real world, the mess-hall sequence, similarly forces us to question the extent to which we can ever escape the Matrix. Not only has the model taken the place of our real-world referents (e.g. Tastee Wheat) but Mouse makes it clear that humans by their very nature reconstruct fantasy scenarios in order to live in the real. The conversation revolves around the unappetizing "goop" that the *Nebuchadnezzar*'s crew eats for sustenance:

> DOZER: It's a single-celled protein combined with synthetic aminos, vitamins, and minerals. Everything the body needs.
>
> MOUSE: It doesn't have everything the body needs. So, I understand that you've run through the agent-training program? You know, I wrote that program.
>
> APOC: Here it comes.
>
> MOUSE: So, what did you think of her?
>
> NEO: Of who?
>
> MOUSE: The woman in the red dress. I designed her. She doesn't talk much but, if you'd like to, you know, meet her, I could arrange a more personalized milieu.
>
> SWITCH: The digital pimp hard at work.
>
> MOUSE: Pay no attention to these hypocrites, Neo. To deny our own impulses is to deny the very thing that makes us human.

The scene makes clear that the human mind cannot live with the unadulterated real. This insight is perhaps what most clearly distinguishes postmodern theory from earlier understandings of ideology as "false consciousness," as that which obscures some underlying truth. For postmodernists, once again, *any* representation of reality is always already ideological.

Morpheus falls between these two positions when he describes the Matrix to Neo during their first meeting:

> MORPHEUS: Do you want to know what it is? The Matrix is everywhere, it's all around us, here even in this room. You can see it out your window or on your television. You can feel it when you go to work, or go to church

or when you pay your taxes. It is the world that has
been pulled over your eyes to blind you from the truth.
NEO: What truth?
MORPHEUS: That you are a slave, Neo. Like everyone else,
you were born into bondage, born inside a prison that
you cannot smell, taste or touch. A prison for your
mind.

The Matrix is analogous to ideology in the postmodern
sense; it creates the very "reality" that surrounds us because
of our reliance not just on rules but also on language to
structure the world around us. For this reason, according
to Jacques Lacan (an influential psychoanalyst among
postmodern theorists), the "real is impossible." It is, by
Lacan's definition, beyond language and, thus, beyond
representability, though it continues to trouble the easy
functioning of ideology because it reminds us of that
ideology's artificiality. As Morpheus puts it, "You have come
because you know something. What you know you can't
explain but you feel it. You've felt it your whole life, felt
that something is wrong with the world. You don't know
what, but it's there like a splinter in your mind, driving you
mad." According to postmodernists, that splinter of the
"real" is there for everyone, causing us to question our
ideologies, but it must by definition remain outside of
language. Fredric Jameson refers to this postmodernist view
as the "prison-house of language," which is one way to
interpret Morpheus's "prison for your mind."

Morpheus could be said to depart from both Lacan and
postmodern theory by suggesting to Neo that one can
actually have access to that real, that one can escape the
ideological constructs that determine what we perceive as
"reality." The following sequence, which has Neo covered
by a suddenly liquefied mirror, is a visual representation of

a Lacanian regression, past the "symbolic order" of our ideological matrices, past the "mirror stage," which according to Lacan first gave us an idealized image of ourselves (what Morpheus refers to as the "mental projection of your digital self"), all the way through to the real.

> MORPHEUS: Have you ever had a dream, Neo, that you were so sure was real?
> NEO: This can't be . . .
> MORPHEUS: Be what, be real?
> MORPHEUS: What if you were unable to wake from that dream, Neo? How would you know the difference between the dream world and the real world?

By suggesting that one can actually have access to that real, Morpheus and the Wachowskis could be said to misunderstand postmodernist theory; however, the Wachowskis make it clear that on some level humans will always remain one step removed from any direct access to the real, which is the main import of the mess-hall discussion. The body needs more than "synthetic aminos, vitamins, and minerals" to survive. It needs the fantasy-space of desire because direct access to the real is akin to madness. In a sense, Morpheus is correct when he describes the real as "like a splinter in your mind driving you mad." To come face to face with the sheer materiality of existence outside of language is a supremely traumatic event, according to many postmodernists, a trauma that is commonly experienced when we are forced to acknowledge our own deaths (our becoming material). To escape the short-circuit of madness that would result from looking into the dark heart of the real, the body requires and demands its masturbatory fantasies: hence Mouse's Woman in Red.

I should be clearer, however; according to Lacan, the human psyche is in fact caught in a play *between* desire and an "impossible real" that ensures our desires are never fulfilled completely and that thus allows them to persist. For this reason, I think, the Wachowskis included a sequence in which Agent Smith explains that the first version of the Matrix failed. It provided a utopic world where all one's wishes are fulfilled. As Agent Smith explains to Morpheus, "Did you know that the first Matrix was designed to be a perfect human world? Where none suffered, where everyone would be happy. It was a disaster. No one would accept the program. Entire crops were lost. Some believed we lacked the programming language to describe your perfect world. But I believe that, as a species, human beings define their reality through suffering and misery."

The problem with a situation in which one's every fantasy is fulfilled is that it approaches psychosis, a breakdown in what Freud termed "the reality principle," a breakdown in our ability to acknowledge the obstacles forcing us to defer fulfilment of our desires in our day-to-day lives.

Given that the AIs have achieved this knowledge about how desire functions for humanity, the Wachowskis leave open one disturbing possibility for the next two installments of *The Matrix* saga; there is no way for the human rebels to be sure that their entire rebellion is not itself being generated by a yet more sophisticated Matrix, a third version that includes a fantasized escape into "the real" as an option for those human "batteries" that feel the need to "regenerate a reality principle in distress."[9]

There is even one disturbing, unexplained clue that may point to this possible resolution. Mouse's Woman in Red,

9 Baudrillard, p. 27.

whom Mouse supposedly created for the *Nebuchadnezzar*'s agent-training program, appears again inside the AI's Matrix just before Neo notices a déjà vu, which is to say a glitch in the Matrix. As we have seen, the Woman in Red had already been made to represent humanity's continuing need for fantasy objects of desire regardless of whether humanity is inside or outside the Matrix. (And, as fantasy object, she is appropriately made to appear here as a centerfold.) We should keep in mind that the humans on the *Nebuchadnezzar* are just as reliant on computers and computer simulations for their fantasies as their counterparts in the AI-controlled reality. They can at least comfort themselves that they are themselves creating their own simulations, that they are thus in control of their own fantasies; seeing the Woman in Red inside the AI's Matrix, however, suggests a number of increasingly distressing possibilities:

1. Mouse could have stolen his Woman in Red from a memory he formed while still a part of the Matrix, which suggests again to what extent he still remains reliant on the simulated reality of the Matrix even for his own fantasies. The Matrix could thus be said still to control him after he is "freed."

2. The Matrix is playing a cruel joke on Mouse, illustrating to what extent the AIs are still able to survey his innermost fantasies (perhaps thanks to Cypher). Indeed, Mouse's expression in the scene is one of perplexity, as if the Woman in Red were herself one of the interpolated glitches in the scene, one of the déjà vus, which she is, *literally*: we *have* already seen her but outside the story-space of the AI's Matrix.

3. There actually is no difference between the Matrix and what Morpheus believes to be "the real world," which is how the Woman in Red can appear in both;

she is, ultimately, the creation of the master-program. Both Women in Red, in this scenario, are part of an all-encompassing Matrix that has created the perception of an escape into the real so as to keep the still-oblivious bodies of its "real" human batteries perpetually locked into the machine.

Regardless of whether this third option points to the further plot twists of the *Matrix Reloaded* and *Matrix Revolutions*, one effect of such breakdowns is to make us question the status of the real in the film. The Woman in Red also reminds us that, ultimately, both the "reality" of the post-Holocaust world and the "construct" of 1999 are, indeed, part of a larger meta-matrix, that of the Wachowskis' film. For this reason, the directors were originally supposed to appear as the window cleaners in the Meta Cortechs scene, in which Neo is chastised by his boss, Mr. Rhineheart. (They did not, in the end, because of safety concerns.) The point of such an imagined cameo is to illustrate to what extent the audience is itself caught within the fantasy-space of a Hollywood film, reliant on the directors for what we see and hear (the insistent and distracting suds and squeak in the scene).

The point of having the directors cleaning the windows of a multinational corporation (the building is that of the actual software company, CorTechs, in the script) also underlines the relation of the director's "vision" to capitalism generally, including the multinational capitalism of the entertainment industry (one reason Cypher tells Agent Smith that he wants to "be rich, someone important, like an actor"). Such manoeuvres invite us to question the film's happy ending since such an unrealistic ending is precisely analogous to Cypher's desire to remain in the Matrix. Indeed, as with the "coppertops" plugged into the

Matrix, it is the fulfillment of the audience's desires that allows the great multinational capitalist machine to survive. Ultimately, the film wants to make a commentary on the way each member of the audience is itself a coppertop, whose own fantasies are being manipulated by and thus feed capital. If this seems far-fetched, consider John Gaeta's voice-over explanation of why the creators of the film felt obliged to manipulate the Warner Bros. logo in the first scene of the film: "The opening of the movie was important in that we wanted to alter the logos of the studios, mostly because we felt they were an evil empire bent on breaking the creative juices of the average director or writer, so we felt that desecrating the studio symbols was an important message to the audience, that we basically reject the system."[10]

To what extent the film succeeds at rejecting the system is an open question. Does the self-conscious use of postmodern theory allow the Wachowskis to escape the charge of creating mere escapist drivel? Does it allow the Wachowskis to critique what Baudrillard calls capital's "instantaneous cruelty, its incomprehensible ferocity, its fundamental immorality" from within the very heart of a mass-market product? Or is the use of theories that are themselves highly critical of multinational capitalism just a way for the Wachowskis to have their cake and critique it too?

At the very least, the Wachowskis succeed at getting their audience to *think*, something that is far too uncommon in the conventional Hollywood product. They allow a mass market to enter into conversation with some of the more influential "high" theorists of our own postmodern age. They resist the audience's desire to look through the medium of film to some easy mimetic "reality" (like

10 The Matrix DVD

Cypher's ability to see not code but "blonde, brunette, and redhead"). The Wachowskis thus force us to see the matrices that structure, manipulate, and re-present that reality to us, feeding our fantasies. They remind us of their own controlling presence, and of technology's ability to create new perceptions of reality (the innovative dimensional film-making of "bullet time"). They persistently highlight the *art* of film and thus underscore, at the very least, our reliance on and manipulation by the very technology that delivers their vision to us: not just the real but the reel.

SOURCES

BOOKS

Baudrillard, Jean, *Simulacra and Simulation,* translated by Sheila Faria Glaser (Ann Arbor: University of Michigan Press, 1994).

Jameson, Fredric, *The Prison-House of Language: A Critical Account of Structuralism and Russian Formalism* (Princeton: Princeton University Press, 1972).

Wachowski, Larry and Andy Wachowski, *The Matrix: The Shooting Script* (New York: Newmarket Press, 2001).

ARTICLES

Lavery, David, "From Cinespace to Cyberspace: Zionists and Agents, Realists and Gamers in *The Matrix* and *ExistenZ*," *Journal of Popular Film and Television* 28.4 (Winter 2001): pp. 150–57.

ANDREW GORDON

THE MATRIX:

PARADIGM OF

POSTMODERNISM

OR INTELLECTUAL

Not so fast, argues Andrew Gordon in the following essay. The Matrix *may be a great action film, but its philosophical pretensions aren't warranted.*

POSEUR? PART II

Early in *The Matrix* (1999), there is a scene introducing the hero, who goes by the hacker alias Neo. Neo hears a knock at the door of his apartment, answers it, and finds a client at the door. He goes to a bookshelf and takes down a volume clearly labeled *Simulacra and Simulation*, which is the title of a book by Jean Baudrillard. When he opens it, the book is a fake, hollowed out, and inside are computer disks, apparently containing illegal software. This image, with its reduplication of fakery—the title plus the fact that the book itself is fake—is an early clue foreshadowing Neo's eventual discovery of the wholly simulated, computer-generated nature of the world in which he lives. (Also, the book is fake in another way—thicker than the real book and with the "On Nihilism" chapter in the wrong place.)

In a later scene, Morpheus, the rebel leader, introduces Neo to the wasteland that is the actual, destroyed world of 2199. "Welcome to the desert of the real," he says, echoing a line from *Simulacra and Simulation*, "The desert of the real itself."[1]

In a line from the screenplay draft, which was cut from the film, Morpheus even tells Neo, "You have been living inside Baudrillard's vision, inside the map, not the territory."[2]

In an interview, Larry Wachowski, who wrote and directed *The Matrix* with his brother Andy, says, "Our main goal with *The Matrix* was to make an intellectual action movie. We like action movies, guns and kung fu, but we're tired of assembly-line action movies that are devoid of any intellectual content. We were determined to put as many ideas into the movie as we could."[3] The Wachowskis actually gave Keanu Reeves, who plays Neo, a homework assignment. Among the books he had to read to prepare for the film were Kevin Kelly's *Out of Control: The New Biology of Machines, Social Systems and the Economic World* (1994) and Jean Baudrillard's *Simulacra and Simulation*.[4]

Now, whether the Wachowskis have successfully blended the elements of the action movie—such as guns and kung fu—with intellectual content is an issue I wish to consider later. But certainly the film is heavily indebted to two central figures of contemporary science fiction and science-fiction theory. First is the novelist William Gibson, who helped found the cyberpunk subgenre in his short fiction of the

---

1 Baudrillard, *Simulacra and Simulation*, p. 1

2 *Matrix Unfolded*

3 Probst, p. 32

4 Nichols

early 1980s and his novel *Neuromancer* (1984). In *Neuromancer*, Gibson coined the terms "cyberspace" and "the matrix" to refer to virtual reality. Critics have claimed that *The Matrix* has helped to revive cyberpunk for the twenty-first century[5] or that it is "the first masterpiece of film c-punk."[6] The second figure is Jean Baudrillard, one of the theoreticians of the new order of simulation or virtual reality.

"Virtual reality" is a gelatinous concept, reinterpreted anew with each telling, like "postmodern" itself. Writes Robert Markley, "What, after all, counts as a virtual space? In recent years, the term has become a catch-all for everything from e-mail to GameBoy cartridges . . ." Many commentators imagine virtual reality as a transcendent space, something sublime, better than ordinary reality, "as though each computer screen were a portal to a shadow universe of infinite, electronically accessible space."[7]

Yet reality that is virtual, if it ever exists, would probably not be transcendent but merely a projection or shadow of reality, missing important dimensions, just as the shadow of a three-dimensional globe is only a two-dimensional sphere. Existence in virtual reality would resemble life in Plato's Cave: a secondhand existence in a world of shadows. Someday it may be theoretically possible to write an extremely complex program that would simulate real life well enough to fool people, including not only sight and sound but also the crucial senses of touch, taste, and smell, although at present the technological obstacles are formidable. *The Matrix*, however, assumes that these obstacles have somehow been overcome.

What we are really dealing with in science fictions and other contemporary cultural concerns about virtual reality

5 Barnett, p. 360

6 "E-Files," p. 346

7 Markley, p. 2

are metaphors and fantasies, projections of our fears and hopes about life inside the machine or life augmented by the machine in the cybernetic age. We are now living in a new age, not simply the postmodern but "the posthuman," in which we have to redefine what it means to be human. "In the posthuman," writes N. Katherine Hayles, "there are no essential differences or absolute demarcations between bodily existence and computer simulation."[8] As the boundary lines break down, we fear that the human may be taken over by the machine, or, at the opposite extreme, we hope that the human may be made transcendent by the machine. As David Porush says, "Virtual reality or cyberspace is . . . about redefining . . . the human within a pure . . . space of mechanism, and a New Jerusalem, a Promised Land."[9] Virtual reality is "a new mythology," in which the new frontier is not outer space but the "inner space" of the computer and of the human mind and the interface between the two.[10]

Gibson's "cyberspace" or "the matrix" has as much to do with science and technology as the adventures of the wizard Don Juan in Carlos Castenada's volumes have to do with anthropology. And the same is true of virtual reality in *The Matrix*. In *Neuromancer*, cyberspace is a transcendent realm, a "consensual hallucination"[11] which, for hardcore hackers, is better than drugs or sex. *The Matrix* taps into this new mythology to invert Gibson's notion of cyberspace, creating not a New Jerusalem but a cyber-hell. In the virtual prison of the Matrix, human beings are maintained in a permanent dream state, unaware they are merely slaves of the machine.

8 Hayles, p. 3

9 Porush, p. 126

10 Ibid., p. 109

11 Gibson, p. 51

Just as *The Matrix* plays on but inverts Gibson's notion of cyberspace, so it also plays on Baudrillard's ideas about simulation, but without Baudrillard's pessimism, because *The Matrix* offers a solution to the problem of simulation whereas Baudrillard believes there is none.

One needs first to place Baudrillard's sweeping, often hyperbolic pronouncements—that simulation, or what he calls "hyperreality," has completely taken over the contemporary world—in perspective. For example, one critic, Istvan Csicsery-Ronay Jr., has called Baudrillard "a virtuoso stylist of theory-SF," who writes theory in a lyrical mode, creating "a visionary SF poem or film."[12] Baudrillard treats "certain motifs and themes dear to utopian and scientific fiction" as "actualized phenomena."[13] Csicsery-Ronay terms Baudrillard's mode of theory "apocalyptic-dystopian-idealist."[14] In other words, we should not take Baudrillard's remarks literally but instead treat them metaphorically, as exaggerations to make a point, as we would the imagined world of a dystopian science fiction novelist such as George Orwell. Because Baudrillard writes "theory-SF" about simulation and hyperreality, because he deals in hyperbolic and apocalyptic pronouncements, and because he is creating "a visionary SF poem or film," it is not surprising then that he would appeal to science fiction filmmakers creating an apocalyptic, dystopian movie about hyperreality, such as *The Matrix*.

Ironically, although Baudrillard has been a tremendously influential critic of virtual reality, he has little knowledge of cyberculture but began his critique of hyperreality by attacking TV advertising and theme parks years before the digital revolution that brought about the Internet, the PC,

---

12 Csicsery-Ronay, pp. 392–93
13 Ibid., p. 393
14 Ibid., p. 389

and virtual reality. Baudrillard also fails to distinguish in his theorizing between the effects of television and of the computer, which are very different. Television is not interactive, unlike the computer and the Internet, nor does television constitute "virtual reality."[15] Baudrillard tends to lump theme parks, television, and virtual reality together as forms of simulation.

Baudrillard's central idea is that, in the postmodern world, the real has been almost totally displaced by the simulated. "It is a generation by models of a real without origin or reality: a hyperreal. The territory no longer precedes the map. . . . It is . . . the map that precedes the territory." He claims that the real survives only in vestiges "here and there in the deserts . . . The desert of the real itself."[16]

Baudrillard speaks of four orders of simulation: in the first, the image reflects reality; in the second, it masks reality; in the third, "it masks the absence of a profound reality"; and in the fourth, "it has no relation to reality whatsoever; it is its own pure simulation."[17] Baudrillard is especially interested in postmodern examples of simulation of the third order, theme parks such as Disneyland. "Disneyland is presented as imaginary in order to make us believe that the rest is real, whereas all of Los Angeles and the America that surrounds it are no longer real but belong to the hyperreal order and to the order of simulation."[18] What Baudrillard means by "the hyperreal" is "the generation by models of a real without origin or reality."[19]

---

15 Poster, pp. 48–50

16 Baudrillard, *Simulacra and Simulation*, p. 1

17 Ibid., p. 6

18 Ibid., p. 12

19 Ibid., p. 1

Baudrillard has commented elsewhere on what he calls "simulation simulacra: based on information, the model, cybernetic play. Their aim is maximum operation, hyperreality, total control."[20] He fears that the coming of the era of hyperreality marks "the end of SF" because "something like the reality principle disappears."[21] If there is no baseline reality, then science fiction has no foundation on which to build, for how can we measure "the fantastic" except by comparison with "the real"?

How then does simulation operate in *The Matrix*? In the film, it is 2199 and the surface of the earth has been destroyed in a war with artificially intelligent machines. Deep underground, human beings are bred as a source of energy for the machines and kept in an embryonic state, dreaming that they are living in an American city in 1999. This dream world, called the Matrix, is a computer simulation intended to keep the populace docile.

A few humans remain in the real world and fight the machines. Morpheus, the rebel leader, cruises the underworld in a hovercraft, like Jules Verne's Captain Nemo. Morpheus and his crew rescue from the Matrix Thomas Anderson, by day a computer programmer for a large corporation, by night an outlaw hacker known as "Neo." Morpheus is convinced Anderson may be "The One" foretold by the Oracle: the man who can defeat the agents. Neo, whose name is an anagram of "One," is unaware he is living in a simulated reality. First he must be extracted from the Matrix, reborn in the real world, reeducated and trained.

Morpheus first explains to Neo the nature of the Matrix:

---

20 Baudrillard, "Simulacra and Science Fiction," p. 309
21 Ibid., p. 311

MORPHEUS: Do you want to know what it is? The Matrix is everywhere. It's all around us, even here in this room. You can see it out your window or on your television. You can feel it when you go to work, or go to church or pay your taxes. It is the world that has been pulled over your eyes to blind you from the truth.

NEO: What truth?

MORPHEUS: That you are a slave, Neo. Like everyone else you were born into bondage, kept inside a prison that you cannot smell, taste or touch. A prison for your mind.

The Matrix deals with what Baudrillard would call "the fourth order of simulation," with no relation to reality whatsoever. That is, the everyday world in which Neo exists is totally false, a dream world with no substance and no relation to 2199 (although it does strongly resemble the present-day world of the movie's audience). The machines have created a virtual reality simulacrum of the world of 1999, a world which no longer exists in the future. As Baudrillard writes, seeming to describe the movie, "The real is produced from miniaturized cells, matrices, and memory banks, models of control—and it can be reproduced an indefinite number of times from these."[22]

According to Baudrillard, in the electronic era, "it is the real that has become our true utopia—but a utopia that is no longer in the realm of the possible, that can only be dreamt of as one would dream of a lost object."[23] The real, he believes, has been replaced by the electronic and other forms of simulation, by "models of a real without origin or reality."[24] The real has been irretrievably lost, and even if

22 Baudrillard, Simulacra and Simulation, p. 2

23 Baudrillard, "Simulacra and Science Fiction," p. 123

24 Baudrillard, Simulacra and Simulation, p. 1

we wanted to, we couldn't distinguish anymore between the simulation and the real. For example, when we try to retreat to what we think of as reality, we find not nature but a nature park. The "natural" has been displaced by the artificial. Thus utopia, the realm of the real, cannot exist any longer in the future but only in the past, which creates a problem for science fiction, a literature and film about anticipating the future. "Perhaps science fiction from the cybernetic and hyperreal era can only exhaust itself, in its artificial resurrection of 'historical' worlds, can only try to reconstruct in vitro, down to the smallest details, the perimeters of a prior world, the events, the people, the ideologies of the past, emptied of meaning, of their original process, but hallucinatory with retrospective truth."[25]

Thus in *The Matrix* the world of 2199 prefers to dwell in a permanent 1999. As Baudrillard comments elsewhere, Americans live "in a perpetual simulation."[26] In other words, in Baudrillard's hyperbolic, pessimistic view, we have already replaced the real with the hyperreal, America is in the vanguard of this movement, and the future promises no recovery of the real but only more and more simulation. *The Matrix* also seems to warn that it is not just for the characters in the film but also for the film audience that 1999 is a dream world, a fourth-order simulation. According to Slavoj Oiñek, *The Matrix* is not about the future but about the unreality of present-day America in the oppressive, all-enveloping world of virtual capitalism: "The material reality we all experience and see around us is a virtual one, generated and coordinated by a gigantic computer to which we are all attached."[27] Oiñek seems to share Baudrillard's pessimism and is given to making similarly sweeping,

25 Baudrillard, "Simulacra and Science Fiction," p. 123

26 Baudrillard, *America*, pp. 76–77

27 Oiñek, p. 25

hyperbolic pronouncements about present-day reality. The dystopian metaphors of science fiction have strongly affected contemporary theory.

This virtual prison in the film is then supposed to resemble our present, a world both we and the masses within the film accept despite the fact that it is far from utopian, not only unreal but also unhappy. There is a lot of evidence for this point in the film. One can easily argue that *The Matrix* protests against our corporate cubicle lives, the sort of artificial life Neo must reject. As Agent Smith, one of the sentient programs who police the Matrix, tells Morpheus:

"Have you ever stood and stared at it, Morpheus? Marvelled at its beauty. Its genius. Billions of people just living out their lives . . . oblivious. Did you know that the first Matrix was designed to be a perfect human world? Where none suffered, where everyone would be happy. It was a disaster. No one would accept the program. Entire crops were lost. Some believed we lacked the programming language to describe your perfect world. But I believe that, as a species, human beings define their reality through suffering and misery. The perfect world was a dream that your primitive cerebrum kept trying to wake up from. Which is why the Matrix was redesigned to this: the peak of your civilization. I say 'your civilization' because as soon as we started thinking for you, it really became our civilization, which is, of course, what this is all about."

For those in the viewing audience who have not read or heard of Baudrillard (almost everyone, I assume), *The Matrix* repeats variations on the same theme of the real versus the fantastic through references to the classic popular fantasies *Alice in Wonderland* and *The Wizard of Oz*, both of which play on the idea of two separate worlds, one real and the other dreamlike. The difference is that in those two works the protagonists begin in the real world and then move into the dream or fantasy world, whereas Neo takes a reverse journey, as the world he initially believes to be real proves to be merely a computer simulation. For example, among the references to *Alice* in *The Matrix*, Morpheus tells Neo to "follow the white rabbit," and later says, "I imagine, right now, you must be feeling a bit like Alice, tumbling down the rabbit hole." He offers Neo a choice of two pills, one blue and the other red, saying, "You take the red pill and you stay in Wonderland and I show you how deep the rabbit hole goes." When Neo wonders what is happening after he swallows the red pill, Cypher tells him, "Buckle up, Dorothy, 'cause Kansas is going bye-bye." As Neo stares at his image in a mirror, his reality begins to dissolve. The mirror appears to liquefy and his hand goes through it, suggesting *Through the Looking Glass*.

Like *Star Wars*, *The Matrix* is a postmodern pastiche of bits and pieces of popular culture.[28] "The Wachowski brothers have exhibited a remarkable shrewdness about their cross-cultural looting. *The Matrix* slams together a more eclectic mix of mythological excess—from the Bible to Hong Kong action films—than you're likely to find this side of . . . the first *Star Wars*."[29] *The Matrix* also borrows concepts, images, creatures, or costumes from a host of science fiction movies, including:

1. *2001* (1968): a malicious, sentient computer takes over and starts killing people
2. *Logan's Run* (1976): the outside world has been devastated by war and the remainder of mankind live

28 Gordon, pp. 314–15

29 Mitchell

hedonistic lives in a huge domed city but are terminated when they reach age 30

3. *Star Wars* (1977): an ordinary character discovers he has superpowers and may be the one who can save his world

4. *Alien* (1979): an alien creature invades a human body, just as Neo has a spy bug implanted in his belly

5. *Tron* (1982): the hero is trapped inside a computer and forced to fight his way out by defeating the Master Control Program

6. *Blade Runner* (1982): one cannot tell the manufactured, simulated people (the replicants) from real humans

7. *The Terminator* (1984) and *Terminator 2: Judgment Day* (1991): the machines have taken over and are wiping out the humans until the humans fight back

8. *Total Recall* (1990): the hero cannot tell the programmed dream world from the reality

9. *Men in Black* (1997): the agents dress like the Men in Black

Aside from *Alice* and *Wizard of Oz*, *The Matrix* also draws on other literary sources, including Jules Verne's *Twenty Thousand Leagues Beneath the Sea* (Morpheus in his hovercraft resembles Captain Nemo), George Orwell's *1984* (the totalitarian authorities spy on the hero, who makes contact with a rebel underground), and Harlan Ellison's story "I Have No Mouth and I Must Scream" (a mad computer starts WWIII and keeps a few survivors alive underground, to be tortured for its sadistic pleasure; at the end, the computer deprives the hero of his mouth, like Agent Smith does to Neo in the interrogation scene).

The Wachowskis have been heavily influenced as well by other media, especially comic books, graphic novels (including Japanese manga), Japanese animation, music videos, TV commercials, fashion ads, and Hong Kong action movies. "More successfully than anyone else, the Wachowskis have translated a comic-book sensibility to the movies."[30] The brothers wrote for Marvel comics and originally conceived of *The Matrix* as a comic book, and it retains a lot of the graphic punch of that medium. They hired several comic-book artists "to hand-draw the entire film as a highly graphic storyboard bible."[31] Their visual-effects supervisor John Gaeta says, "They're authentic comic book freaks, and that's where many of their cinematic ideas come from—Japanimation and deviant comics artists."[32] Their cinematographer, Bill Pope, shares their love of comics and started his career filming music videos and commercials before shooting science fiction films such as *Darkman* and *Army of Darkness*.

Like *Star Wars*, *The Matrix* also coheres as a messiah story or pastiche of a series of messiah stories, a myth of the birth of a hero.[33] *The Matrix* is filled with Christian allegory, for Neo proves to be the prophesied messiah who will free humanity from the computerized dream world. There are also names redolent of Christian symbolism, such as Trinity or Cypher (suggesting Lucifer, although he functions more like Judas). The cinematographer Bill Pope says, "It's a pretty complicated Christ story, but for the Wachowskis and myself, one of the best kinds of comic book is the origin story, which outlines the beginnings of a superhero like Daredevil or Spiderman. *The Matrix* is the origin story of Neo."[34]

---

30 Mitchell

31 Probst, p. 32

32 Magid, p. 46

33 Gordon, p. 315

34 Probst, p. 33

Baudrillard is then only one element in the many layers of intertextuality in *The Matrix*. The question remains: is *The Matrix* really an intellectual action film, or is it, as one reviewer suggested, "a muddily pretentious mixture of post-modern literary theory, slam-bang special effects and Superman heroics"?[35] And second, how profound is the Wachowskis' understanding of Baudrillard? Are they borrowing from Baudrillard to give their film an intellectual cachet which it does not deserve?

———

First of all, what does it mean to be an intellectual action film? And what distinguishes a true intellectual action film from a pretender? There is nothing wrong with contemporary popular media such as comic books, TV, or movies making use of current literary and cultural theory, any more than "high culture," such as the novels of Saul Bellow, Philip Roth, or Thomas Pynchon, quoting cartoons, television shows, or movies. In the postmodern, eclecticism rules and the boundaries between so-called "low" and "high" culture are fluid. In its favor, *The Matrix*, like the *Star Wars* and *Star Trek* series, has spawned dozens of articles and even a few college courses exploring its philosophical, religious, and scientific dimensions. A science-fiction film like *The Terminator*, with similar action and complex themes, did no such thing.

P. Chad Barnett praises *The Matrix* for reviving the genre of cyberpunk, bringing "a Bohemian edge and smart postmodern aesthetic back to cyberpunk."[36] Perhaps carried away by reading the contemporary neo-Marxist critic Fredric Jameson, Barnett lauds the film for its political effects as an "accurate cognitive mapping of the world space

35 Hoffman
36 Ibid., p. 362

of multinational capital. It . . . allows those who experience it to begin to grasp their position as individual and collective subjects and regain a capacity to act and struggle . . ."[37] In other words, Barnett believes *The Matrix* actually has politically radical potential and may inspire some viewers to organize or to revolt against the capitalist system.

But this seems to me far too utopian a reading of the ideological effect of *The Matrix*. The film may serve in part as a warning about virtual reality, but it is far from radical in its plot. Although the Wachowskis may imagine themselves as rebels like Morpheus and Neo ("we basically reject the system")[38] they are instead, like George Lucas, inextricably part of the Hollywood system. *The Matrix* is another cinematic action franchise like *Star Wars*, dependent, like George Lucas's saga, upon the appeal of a clear-cut opposition of good-versus-evil, and promising redemption by the coming of a messiah who kicks butt. To hope for change by the intervention of a messiah discourages political thought or action. One critic objects to "the whole messianic subtext: the notion that one hero can transform a world fallen irrevocably into hyperreality."[39] I believe that it is precisely this mythological, messianic subtext, like that in *Star Wars*, that accounts for the cult status of *The Matrix*. It blends the old mythology of the coming of a messiah with the new mythology of virtual reality to create a new kind of religious hero. *The Matrix* also has the same pseudo-profundity, stilted dialogue, and religious allegorical overtones as the *Star Wars* series. Although it deals in ideas, *The Matrix* is not intellectually or philosophically profound. Again, like in *Star Wars*, almost all its ideas are borrowed. Although they may have included nods to postmodern

37 Ibid., p. 372

38 *The Matrix* DVD

39 "E-Files," p. 347

critical theory, the Wachowski Brothers's audience is not the tiny elite that reads Baudrillard but "a generation bred on comics and computers,"[40] which demands fast and violent action. Numerous critics complained that "At times, *The Matrix* plays more like a video game than a movie"[41] or that it offers "the ultimate in cyberescapism."[42] One reviewer found "fairly glaring contradiction at work in a film that relies so heavily on digital special effects at the same time that it rails against the evil of a computer-constructed reality."[43] There is also a contradiction in a film that warns against the triumph of computers but suggests that "ultimate enlightenment can be attained through skills which have been downloaded."[44]

Moreover, the demands of the recent Hollywood action movie for spectacle and violence tend to militate against thoughtfulness. I do not object to cinematic violence per se—great literature and film are often saturated with violence—so long as the violence is necessary and advances both story and themes. Consider, for example, the sickening "ultraviolence" of Stanley Kubrick's film *A Clockwork Orange* (1971). That film, like the novel by Anthony Burgess on which it is based, is a thoughtful meditation on the nature of free will and on individual violence versus the violence of the state.

I believe, however, that the primary pleasures of *The Matrix* are not intellectual but visceral, in the innovative visual tricks and stunts and the almost nonstop action. Larry Wachowski says, "There are many incredible and beautiful images in violence, and I think violence can be a great

---

40 Maslin

41 Anthony

42 Maslin

43 Hoffman

44 Newman

storytelling tool. Film makers have come up with an incredible language for violence. For example, what John Woo does with his sort of hyper-violence is brilliant. He pushes violent imagery to another level. We tried to do that with *The Matrix* as well."[45] Many viewers and reviewers enjoyed the violence: "*The Matrix* offers some of the most psychotic action scenes in American film."[46] But others objected that, at the end, "the script descends into a frightening form of nihilism . . . as the well-armed hero sets out to save humanity by killing as many humans as possible."[47]

Problems with violent spectacle for its own sake flaw many recent science fiction action movies, such as Verhoeven's *Total Recall* (1990), which tries for an impossible blend of Philip K. Dick's mind-bending reflections on the shifty nature of reality with Arnold Schwarzenegger's philosophy of "Crack their heads like walnuts and mow them down with a machine gun." Verhoeven's *Starship Troopers* (1997) (from the Heinlein novel), attempts to satirize Heinlein's militaristic, fascistic future society but then undercuts its satire by endorsing the protagonist's gung-ho war heroics and reveling in the spectacle of mutilation and gore. Heinlein's novel did celebrate a militaristic society, although without the satire and without most of the gore. *Blade Runner* (1982) and *Minority Report* (2002), both based on Philip K. Dick's novels, are to my mind far more thoughtful science fiction action movies than *Total Recall*, *Starship Troopers,* or *The Matrix*. The violence in *Blade Runner*, for example, is deliberately awkward and painful, for the cop hero is assigned to hunt and kill escaped "replicants," manufactured people who are

45 Probst, p. 33

46 Covert

47 Hoffman

indistinguishable from real people and who die slowly and suffer real pain. And the murders in *Minority Report* are foreseen and replayed in fragments, so that they become traumatic, like repeated nightmares. The violence in both these films helps advance the ideas.

In *The Matrix*, in contrast, I believe that the hyperreality inoculates us against the hyperviolence. For example, because it bends reality and resembles a video game, we cannot take the slaughter of the policemen in the lobby scene seriously. This is a technically astonishing scene, exhilarating to watch, but disturbing in its implications. The policemen are like anonymous targets in a video game, who exist only to be mowed down. We momentarily forget that behind these virtual-reality policemen are real people. One reviewer found disturbing parallels between the lobby scene in *The Matrix* and the real-life massacre at Columbine High School, including the black trench coats and the high-powered weaponry.[48] As Dino Felluga asks in the previous essay: "Does the self-conscious use of postmodern theory allow the Wachowskis to escape the charge of creating mere escapist drivel?" My answer would be: "Not really."

To return to my other concern: to what extent does *The Matrix* accurately reflect Baudrillard's ideas? And how faithful is *The Matrix* to Baudrillard's conclusions? In answer to the first question, I believe that the film is clearly influenced by Baudrillard's ideas but waters them down to the point that it doesn't really reflect his thinking. And in answer to the second, *The Matrix* is not faithful to Baudrillard's conclusions, because it creates a world in which the unreal is forced on people (whereas in our contemporary world we are doing it to ourselves) and because it offers the hope of returning to the real, which Baudrillard claims is no longer possible.

48 Jones, pp. 36–37

In one sense, *The Matrix* offers a simplified or romanticized notion of *Simulacra and Simulation*. There are two worlds in the film—the dream world of the Matrix, which is a computer-simulated version of 1999, and the real world of the postapocalyptic Earth of 2199—and there is a strict division between the two. The division is made very clear visually. According to the cinematographer Bill Pope, the Matrix world had digitally enhanced skies to make them white. "Additionally, since we wanted the Matrix reality to be unappealing . . . we sometimes used green filters." In contrast, "The future world is cold, dark, and riddled with lightning, so we left the lighting a bit bluer and made it dark as hell. Also, the future reality is very grimy."[49] The critic David Lavery notes that "In *The Matrix*, we know very well where the real world is. . . . Morpheus introduces him [Neo] to it: 'Welcome to the real world.' The real world exists, even under the reign of Baudrillard's 'Third Order of Simulacra,' and cinematic art . . . can represent it and tell a heroic tale of its recovery."[50]

The Matrix, then, simplifies Baudrillard. *Simulacra and Simulation* argues—rightly or wrongly—that there may be no real world left behind the simulation, no baseline reality to recover. The real is gone. "In fact, it is no longer really the real, because no imaginary envelops it anymore. It is a hyperreal."[51] Instead, the Wachowskis's concept in *The Matrix* more closely resembles nineteenth-century romantic notions of a division between two worlds: a false world of appearances that obstructs or disguises the true world. Once we clear away the illusion, we can dwell in the real world. It is the old distinction between appearance and reality.

49 Probst, p. 33

50 Lavery, p. 155

51 Baudrillard, *Simulacra and Simulation*, p. 2

I disagree with Dino Felluga's claim that the Wachowskis intended to blur the separation between the Matrix world and the "real world" of the movie. This would further confuse the viewer, to no real purpose, in a film which many already found confusing.

Aside from the recovery of the real in the film, the messianic subtext, it should be noted, also completely contradicts Baudrillard's pessimism about the triumph of hyperreality. There is no reason for us to elevate a thinker like Baudrillard to the status of prophet or for an artist to be slavishly devoted to the ideas of any theorist. But when a film alludes to a theorist whom it apparently misunderstands or intentionally simplifies, it loses some of its intellectual cachet. Writes one critic, "If a film marks itself out as only a spectacle, I am willing to disable my idiot-plot sensor and just go along for the ride; but when a movie pretends to have a strong cognitive/ideational component (as in citing Baudrillard) and this component is half-baked or fudged, I start to seethe."[52]

In conclusion, although *The Matrix* entertains and gives us plenty to think about, especially its potent and paranoid central metaphor about the falsity of "reality," I would have to term it a flawed attempt at an "intellectual action film," in which spectacle sometimes overrides or contradicts the ideas it proposes.

---

52 "The E-Files" 349

SOURCES

BOOKS

Baudrillard, Jean, *America*, translated by Chris Turner (London and New York: Verso, 1988).

——, *Simulacra and Simulation*, translated by Sheila Faria Glaser (Ann Arbor: University of Michigan Press, 1994).

Gibson, William, *Neuromancer* (New York: Ace, 1984).

Hayles, N. Katherine, *How We Became Posthuman: Virtual Bodies in Cybernetics, Literature, and Informatics* (Chicago: The University of Chicago Press, 1999).

Markley, Robert, "Introduction," *Virtual Realities and Their Discontents*, Robert Markley, ed. (Baltimore: Johns Hopkins University Press, 1996), pp. 1–10.

Poster, Mark, "Theorizing Virtual Reality: Baudrillard and Derrida," *Cyberspace Textuality: Computer Technology and Literary Theory*, Marie-Laure Ryan, ed. (Bloomington: Indiana University Press, 1999), pp. 42–60.

ARTICLES

Anthony, Ted, "At the Movies: *The Matrix,*" Associated Press, March 30, 1999.

Baudrillard, Jean, "Simulacra and Science Fiction," translated by Arthur B. Evans, *Science-Fiction Studies* 18.3 (November 1991): pp. 309–13.

Barnett, P. Chad, "Reviving Cyberpunk: (Re)Constructing the Subject and Mapping Cyberspace in the Wachowski Brothers's Film *The Matrix,*" *Extrapolation* 41.4 (Winter 2000): p. 359–74.

Csicsery-Ronay Jr., Istvan, "The SF of Theory: Baudrillard and Haraway," *Science-Fiction Studies* 18.3 (November 1991): pp. 387–404.

Covert, Colin, "*Matrix* mates science fiction and style," *Variety*, September 24, 1999, pp. 3E.

"E-Files, The," *Science-Fiction Studies* 26.2 (July 1999): pp. 346–49.

Gordon, Andrew, "*Star Wars*: A Myth for Our Time," *Literature/ Film Quarterly* 6.4 (Fall 1978): pp. 314–26.

Hoffman, Adina, "*Matrix*'s Shallow Profundities," *The Jerusalem Post*, July 19, 1999, Arts, p. 7.

Jones, Kent, "*Hollywood et la sage du numérique: A propos de Matrix et de* La Menace fantome," *Cahiers du Cinema* 537 (July/August 1999): pp. 36–39.

Lavery, David, "From Cinespace to Cyberspace: Zionist and Agents, Realists and Gamers in *The Matrix* and *ExistenZ*," *Journal of Popular Film and Television* 28.4 (Winter 2001): pp. 150–57.

Magid, Ron, "Techno Babel," *American Cinematographer* 80.4 (April 1999): pp. 46–48.

Maslin, Janet, "The Reality Is All Virtual, and Densely Complicated," *The New York Times*, March 31, 1999, p. E1.

Mitchell, Elvis, "The Wachowski Brothers," *Esquire*, March 2000: pp. 224.

Newman, Kim, "Rubber Reality," *Sight and Sound* 9.6 (June 1999): pp. 8–9.

Nichols, Peter M., "Home Video: More to Satisfy *Matrix* Mania," *The New York Times*, November 9, 2001, p. E26.

Porush, David, "Hacking the Brainstem: Postmodern Metaphysics and Stephenson's *Snow Crash*," *Virtual Realities and Their Discontents*, Robert Markley, ed. (Baltimore: Johns Hopkins University Press, 1996), pp. 107–41.

Probst, Christopher, "Welcome to the Machine," *American Cinematographer* 80.4 (April 1999): pp. 32–36.

Oiñek, Slavoj, "The Desert of the Real," *In These Times*, October 29, 2001, pp. 25–27.

WEBSITES

Matrix Unfolded. www.suspensionofdisbelief.com/matrix/faq.html. December 14, 2001.

PETER B. LLOYD

GLITCHES

IN THE

MATRIX...

AND

HOW TO

FIX THEM

Why, exactly, do the rebels have to enter the Matrix via the phone system (which after all doesn't physically exist)? And what really happens when Neo takes the red pill (which also doesn't really exist)? And how does the Matrix know what fried chicken tastes like? Technologist and philosopher Peter Lloyd answers these questions and more.

As the essays throughout this book demonstrate, the Wachowski brothers designed *The Matrix* to work at many levels. They carefully thought through the film's philosophical underpinnings, religious symbolism, and scientific speculations. But there are a few riddles in *The Matrix*, aspects of the film that seem nonsensical or defy the laws of science. These apparent glitches include:

- The Bioport—how can a socket in your head control your senses? How can it be inserted without killing you?
- The Red Pill—since the pill is virtual, how can it throw Neo out of the Matrix?
- The Power Plant—can people really be an energy source?
- Entering and Exiting the Matrix—why do the rebels need telephones to come and go?
- The Bugbot—what's the purpose of the bugbot?
- Perceptions in the Matrix—how do the machines know what fried chicken tastes like?
- Neo's Mastery of the Avatar—how can Neo fly?
- Consciousness and the Matrix—are the machines in the Matrix alive and conscious? Or are they only machines, intelligent but mindless?

This essay addresses these questions and shows how these seeming glitches can be resolved.

THE BIOPORT

Can the machines really create a virtual world through a bioport? And how does it work? The bioport is a way of giving the Matrix computers full access to the information channels of the brain. It is located at the back of the neck—probably between the occipital bone at the base of the skull, and the first neck vertebra. Wiring would best enter through the soft cartilage that cushions the skull on the spinal column, and pass up through the natural opening that lets the spinal cord into the skull. This avoids drilling through bone, and maintains the mechanical and biological integrity of the skull's protection. A baby fitted with a bioport can easily survive the operation.

The bioport terminates in a forest of electrodes spanning the volume of the brain. In a newborn, the sheathed mass of wire filaments is pushed into the head through the bioport. On reaching the skull cavity, the sheath would be released, and the filaments spread out like a dandelion, gently permeating the developing cortex. Nested sheaths would release a branching structure of filamentary electrodes. As each sheathed wire approaches the surface of the brain, it releases thousands of smaller electrodes. In the neonate, brain cells have few synaptic connections, so the slender electrodes can penetrate harmlessly.

With its electrodes distributed throughout the brain, the Matrix could deliver its sensory signals in either of two places: at the sensory portals or deep inside the brain's labyrinth. For example, vision could be driven by electrodes on the optic nerves where they enter the brain. Artificial signals would then pass into the visual cortex at the back of the brain, which would handle them as if they had come from the eyes. Correspondingly, outgoing motor nerves would also have electrodes at the boundary of brain and skull. This simple design mirrors the natural state of the brain most closely. It is not, however, the only possibility. Electrodes could alternatively be attached in the depths of the brain, beyond the first stages of the visual cortex. This would greatly simplify the data processing. In normal perception, most of the incoming information isn't processed; information you aren't paying attention to is filtered out. If the Matrix were to deliver information directly to the output axons from the sensory cortex—as opposed to the input to the cortex—then it would save itself the job of filling in all those details.

One scene tells us which method the Matrix uses. When Neo wakes and finds himself in a vat, he pulls out the oxygen and food tubes, drags himself out of the gelatinous fluid, and—perceives the world. The fact that he can see and hear proves that the visual and auditory cortices of his brain are working. This wouldn't be possible if the Matrix had put its sensory data into the deeper centers of his brain. For then his sensory cortex would have been bypassed: it would never have received any stimulation, and would have wasted away. In that case, Neo would wake from his vat and find himself blind and deaf, with no sense of smell or taste, no feeling of touch or heat in his skin, no awareness of whether he was vertical or horizontal, or where his arms or legs were. The Matrix must have input its visual data just where the optic nerve from the eyeball passes into the skull, rather than in the midst of the brain's vision processing. Likewise, Neo's ability to walk and use his arms shows that the motor cortex is also developed and functioning. Indeed, even the cerebellum, which controls balance, must be working. So, the Matrix must be capturing its motor signals from the brain's efferent nerves after they have finished with the last stage of cortical processing, but before the nerves pass out of the skull.

The rebels use the bioport to load new skills into their colleagues' brains—writing directly into permanent memory. The Matrix itself never implants skills in this way; folks in the virtual world learn things in the usual manner by reading books and going to college. So, why did the architects of the Matrix build into the bioport this capability to download skills? It is actually a by-product of how the bioport is installed. They could have attached electrodes to just the sensory and motor nerve fibers. That, though, is difficult: the installer must predict where each nerve fiber will be anchored, which is hard to do reliably, given the plasticity of the neonate brain; and it must navigate through the brain tissue to find these sites. A more robust and adaptable method is to lay a carpet of electrodes throughout the whole brain, and let the software locate the sensory and motor channels by monitoring the data flows on the lines.

That spare capacity remains available for others to exploit, and the rebels use it to download kung-fu expertise into Neo's brain and to implant helicopter piloting skills into Trinity's. If the Matrix ever learned this technique, it could create havoc for the rebels, implanting impulses to serve its own ends.

THE RED PILL

Morpheus offers Neo the choice of his lifetime, in the form of the famous red and blue pills. But what can a virtual pill do to a real brain? We have seen that the Matrix interacts with the brain only in the sensory and motor nerve fibers. It does not affect the inner workings of the brain, where a real psychoactive chemical would have to act. Minor analgesics such as aspirin would work by having their effect outside the brain centers, canceling out pain inputs from the avatar software.

The blue pill is probably a placebo. Morpheus says only, "You take the blue pill and the story ends. You wake in your bed and you believe whatever you want to believe." We never know what, if anything, the blue one would do.

So, how does the active pill, the red one, work? Since virtual aspirin can work as a painkiller, the avatar's software module must be able to accept instructions to cancel out any given sensory input. Evidently, the red pill gives the avatar a blanket command to cancel all such input. It thereby obliterates Neo's perception of the virtual world, which the Matrix has been feeding to him throughout his life. Instead of sitting on a chair in a hotel room, Neo sees and feels for the first time that he is immersed in a fluid. The perception of this filters through into his perceptions of the Matrix's own imagery. Neo touches a mirror, and finds it a viscous fluid that clings to his finger and then seeps along his arm, covering his chest and slithering down his throat. A blend of bodily perceptions and mental imagery is typical of what happens when you wake from a dream; external perceptions are distorted to fit the contents of the dream. Your dream of falling off a cliff might fade into falling out of bed. In the film, the liquefied mirror is seen only by Neo, not the others in the room. His real bodily sensations are, for the first time, sweeping into his brain, which struggles to integrate them into the stable narrative he has lived in up to that moment.

Another route out of the Matrix, besides the red pill, would be meditation. The Buddhist practice of *vipassana*[1] gives adepts penetrating insights into their own mental processes. It rolls back the barrier between conscious awareness and the subconscious. An adept of *vipassana*, living in the Matrix, would discover the interface between the Matrix's electrodes and the brain's wetware. The expert practitioner could override the Matrix's stream of imagery, and see reality. Morpheus mentions that someone did break free from the Matrix. Perhaps meditation was the key. To attain that expertise, however, would take years of effort. Leading other people to the truth would require a school of meditation to train new recruits for years, to pursue what one individual claimed was the truth, but everyone else dismissed as fantasy. No doubt this is what the Oracle is

---

1 In the oldest form of Buddhism, Theravada, the two major forms of meditation are Vipassana (the Pali word for "insight") and its complement Samatha ("tranquility").

Vipassana consists in systematically attending to the individual elements that make up the contents of consciousness. It involves persistently turning away from the ceaselessly arising tide of chatter in the mind. Over time, the chatter subsides, and preconscious activity becomes more readily observed. Laboratory data support claims that long-term practitioners acquire a conscious awareness of brain microprocesses, possibly down to the cellular level. See Shinzeng Young's works.

gently encouraging. But it is not surprising that the red pill was invented as a fast-track route.

Morpheus's team monitors Neo's progress. As he realizes that he is immersed in fluid, Neo panics, and his instinct to escape drowning compels him to drag the tubes out of his mouth. Like waking out of a dream, Neo finds the sensible world rushing in on him, and it is remarkable that his manual coordination has been so well preserved by the Matrix system. He grabs the tubes and yanks them out, using weak hands that had never before grasped anything.

When Neo's exit from the Matrix is detected, a robot inspects him and flushes him out of his pod. Too weak to swim, he must be pulled out of the wastewater pool without delay. How are the rebels to find him? In a power plant vast enough to house the human race, there would be thousands of effluent drains. As Morpheus mentions to Neo, "the pill you took is part of a trace program." Besides cancelling Neo's sensory inputs, the red pill also puts a unique reference signal onto the Matrix network. When the *Nebuchadnezzar*'s computer locates that signal, it can work out Neo's physical location and order the hovercraft to the appropriate chute. In the tense moment before that reference signal is located, the worried Morpheus says, "We're going to need the signal soon," and Trinity exclaims that Neo's heart is fibrillating as the panic threatens to bring on a heart attack. Apoc finds the reference signal just in time, before Neo's brain disengages from the Matrix network and the signal vanishes.

THE POWER PLANT

During the armchair scene, we have what is probably the most criticized element in *The Matrix* story line. Morpheus claims that the human race is imprisoned in a power station, where human bodies are used as a source of bioelectricity. This is engineering nonsense; it violates the fundamental law of energy conservation. The humans would have to be fed, and the laws of physics demand that the energy consumed as food must be greater than the energy generated by the human body. That Morpheus has misunderstood what is going on is underscored by his mention in the same speech of the machines' discovery of a new form of nuclear fusion. Evidently, the fusion is the real source of energy that the machines use. So what are humans doing in the power plant? Controlled fusion is a subtle and complex process, requiring constant monitoring and micromanaging. The human brain, on the other hand, is a superb parallel computer. Most likely, the machines are harnessing the spare brainpower of the human race as a colossal distributed processor for controlling the nuclear fusion reactions. (Sawyer comes to a similar conclusion elsewhere in this volume—Ed.)

ENTERING AND EXITING THE MATRIX

The virtual world of the Matrix is not bound by physical laws as we know them, but for the virtual world to be consistently realistic, the laws of physics must be followed where they can be observed by humans. Access into and out of a virtual world is a problem, because materializing and dematerializing violate the conservation of mass and energy. Furthermore, whatever was previously in the space occupied by the materializing body must be pushed out of the way; and would be pushed with explosive speed if the materialization is instantaneous. Conversely, on dematerialization, the surrounding air would rush in to the vacated space with equal implosive force. There are no such explosions and implosions in *The Matrix,* so how do the rebels do it?

In the Matrix computer, software modules represent the observable objects in the virtual world, and these modules interact by means of predefined messages. One such message issued by a virtual human body, or "avatar," is, "What do I see when I look in the direction V?" A module whose object lies on the line of sight along V will respond with a message specifying the color, luminosity, and texture that the human should see in that direction. If a rebel's avatar is to be visible to other people who are immersed in the Matrix world, the *Nebuchadnezzar*'s computer must pick up those "What-do-I-see" requests and reply with its own "You-see-this" message.

A virtual human body does not send "What-do-I-see?" message to all other modules in the Matrix, or else it would overload the network. It refers to "registers" of modules, which record the virtual objects' shape, size, and position. Simple geometry then tells it which modules to target. For efficiency, each visible volume of space, such as the room of a building, has its own register.

The key step in materializing a body in a given space is for its module to be inserted into that space's register. For dematerializing, it is deleted from the register. Once it is registered, anyone looking in that direction will see that module's virtual body. The Matrix cannot let a software module insert itself arbitrarily into a register, since that could violate the conservation of mass if it led to an object's materializing in an area that has a conscious observer.

Registers for unobserved spaces are not constrained in this way. If nobody is watching a room and its entrances, then a body can safely materialize in it without observably breaking the simulated laws of physics.

This does not mean that the laws of physics break down as soon as all observers leave a room. The table and chair do not start to float around against the law of gravity when nobody is looking. Rather, the Matrix simply does not bother to run the simulation for a room that nobody is looking at. In its register, it retains details of where each object is, but the room is no longer rendered as visual and tactual imagery.

So, when the *Nebuchadnezzar*'s computer wants to materialize a rebel, it must find some unobserved room, and insert the data module for the rebel's body into the register for that room. Subsequently, if someone else enters the room, he will see the rebel just like any other object in the room. And the rebel can walk out of the room into any other part of the Matrix world in the normal manner. This is how rebels materialize in the Matrix without causing explosions or breaching the integrity of the simulation.

When a rebel exits, the module that simulates her body is deleted from the register. This must happen only when the body is not being observed. There is, however, an intermediate state, "imperception," which effectively takes the body out of the virtual world even while the data module is still in the register. This is an emergency procedure that the *Nebuchadnezzar*'s software uses for fast escapes.

Although the Matrix software cannot insert or delete a module while its object is being observed, it does allow any module to change its appearance. The agents use it whenever they enter the world. An agent never materializes or dematerializes, but changes the appearance of another person's avatar to match the personal qualities of the agent.

To make a rebel imperceptible, the *Nebuchadnezzar*'s computer changes the body's visible appearance to be transparent; and the body's mechanical resistance to that of the air. From an observer's perspective, the body has melted into air. From a software perspective, the data module is still on the register but simulating a body indistinguishable from thin air. Later, when the scene is no longer being observed by anybody, the module will be deleted.

We see this happen only once, when Morpheus leaves the subway. Once the *Nebuchadnezzar*'s computer has located his avatar, it sends an instruction to make it invisible. This does not affect the whole avatar at once: the module has to calibrate its appearance to match exactly its surroundings. The first part of the body to receive the instruction is the nervous tissue of the ear, and this at first glows bright white, before settling down to a state of transparency. The rest of the body follows. Its appearance oscillates around whatever is visible in the background, settling down to transparency: where the Morpheus stood, we see the background shimmer momentarily. The solidity of the body then fades: moments after Morpheus's body has become invisible, the telephone handset that had rested in his hand drops, slowly at first, toward the ground. The observed sequence is consistent not with the sudden deletion of the body's module, but rather with its changing its appearance.

HARD LINES

Telephones play a key role in entering and leaving the Matrix. But the rebels do not travel through the telephone lines as energy pulses. There is no device at the end of the telephone for reconstructing a human body from data: all you would get is noise in the earpiece. Furthermore, the bandwidth of a telephone line is too narrow to ship an entire human being. Finally, nothing at all ever really travels along the lines in the Matrix world, as they are only virtual.

Instead of being a conduit for transporting dematerialized rebels, the telephone line is a means of navigation. It pinpoints where a rebel is to enter or leave the Matrix.

To enter the vast Matrix requires specifying where the avatar is to materialize. To get an avatar into the Matrix world, the rebels must use some strictly physical navigation. This is done with the telephone network, which has penetrated every corner of the inhabited world with electronic devices, each of which has a unique, electronically determined label. Without knowing anything of human society and its conventions, the physics modules of the Matrix can determine where any given telephone number terminates.

How are the rebels to give a telephone number to the Matrix? They must dial it, but they cannot simply pick up a handset and make a call to a number inside the Matrix world, for any handset in the *Nebuchadnezzar* is connected to the real world telephone network, not the Matrix's virtual network. Inside the Matrix, a call must be placed subtly, without observably breaching the simulated laws of electromechanics.

To see how this can be done, we need to know something of the infrastructure of the Matrix. Monolithic computer systems are unreliable, so the Matrix is instead an assemblage of independent modules, each having a unique "network address." For a module to communicate with another, it will put a data message on the network with the address of the intended destination. Neither module need know where the other one is inside the electronic hardware of the Matrix computer. They might be inches apart, or a mile away.

This scheme is robust and flexible. There is no central hub, and individual modules can be plugged into, or taken out of, the network without disturbance. Conversely, the rebels can easily hack into it. Once they are linked into the network, their equipment can simply pretend to be another module. It can place data messages onto the system, which will be routed just like authentic messages, and be received and read by the addressed module. So, to initiate a telephone call, the crew will place a data message on the network, addressed to any module that simulates an aerial for receiving calls from cell phones. Some such node will pick up and read the counterfeit data message just as if the message had been sent by a bona fide source. On getting this message, the aerial module will carry out its role in handling a telephone call.

The *Nebuchadnezzar*'s operator maintains contact with rebels who are in the Matrix even while the hovercraft is moving, so they must use radioports onto the network. The rebels might have installed their own rogue radio receiver—mechanically securing it in some dark corner, and plugging its data cable into a spare socket of a router. More likely, the Matrix itself uses radio as part of its network infrastructure, and the rebels broadcast their counterfeit messages on the same frequency.

Materializing or dematerializing, however, needs a network address, which is gotten as follows. When the *Nebuchadnezzar* makes a "phone call" into the Matrix, it places on the network a packet saying "Place this call for (212) 123-4567" or whatever the telephone number is, together with the *Nebuchadnezzar*'s own network address as a return label, such as 9.54.296.42. When the call is picked up, the Matrix will return a data packet, addressed to the *Nebuchadnezzar*, saying "Message for 9.54.296.42: call connected to telephone (212) 123-4567." All the *Nebuchadnezzar*'s computer has to do is listen out for its own address, and it will find attached to it the network address of the telephone equipment.

As soon as the answering machine picks up the incoming call, the *Nebuchadnezzar* will get the network address of that destination.

Essentially the same job must be done when a rebel leaves the Matrix world. In order to disengage the rebel from his or her avatar, the *Nebuchadnezzar*'s computer must again get a fix on the avatar's location within the virtual world. As before, it is not enough to locate the avatar's virtual body in terms that relate to human culture. It is no use to say that Neo is at 56th and Lexington. Rather, it needs a network address that the Matrix's operating system can follow. Of course, the *Nebuchadnezzar* gets it by calling a telephone in the Matrix world, which must be answered for the network address to be passed back to the *Nebuchadnezzar*. Once that has happened, the avatar's module can be deleted from the register for that location.

Why don't the crew navigate their exits with the stylish cell phones that all the rebels carry? Why hunt for a land line (called a "hard line" in the film) under hot pursuit from the agents? The answer is that the cell phones are not part of the Matrix world and do not have network addresses known to the Matrix software. The cell phone is projected into the Matrix world by the *Nebuchadnezzar*'s computer, along with the avatar's body and clothes—and the weapons that Neo and Trinity eventually bring in with them. The software that simulates the cell phones is running inside the *Nebuchadnezzar*'s computer, not the Matrix's computer, so the rebels must find a land line—which are somewhat scarce in an era when everyone has a cell phone.

THE BUGBOT

Before Neo is taken to meet Morpheus, the agents insert a robotic bug into him. Trinity extricates the bugbot before it can do any harm. But what was the bugbot for? Given that it operates inside the human body, the bugbot should be as small as possible. Yet, it is clearly much bigger than a miniature radio beeper needed for tracking Neo's whereabouts. Trinity says that Neo is "dangerous" to them before he is cleaned. We can infer that the bugbot is actually a munition, probably a semtex device that will detonate when it hears Morpheus's voice, killing both Neo and Morpheus and everyone else in the room.

Just before it is implanted, the bugbot takes on the appearance of an animate creature, with claws writhing. Yet, after Trinity has jettisoned it out of the car window, it returns to an inert form. It is another illustration of the agents' limited use of the shapeshifting loophole in the Matrix software, that lets an object transform its properties under programmed commands.

PERCEPTIONS IN THE MATRIX

At dinner on the *Nebuchadnezzar*, Mouse ponders how the Matrix decided how chicken meat should taste, and wonders whether the machines got it wrong because the machines are unable to experience tastes.

A nonconscious machine cannot experience color any more than taste. A computer can store information about colored light, such as a digitized photograph, but it does so without a glimmer of awareness of the conscious experience of color. The digitized picture will evoke conscious colors only when someone looks at it. All other sensations that you can be conscious of will elude the digital computer. The feel of silk, the texture of the crust of a piece of toast, feelings of nausea or giddiness: these are all unavailable to insentient machines. This being so, Mouse could have doubted whether the Matrix would know what anything should taste, smell, look, sound, or feel like.

But the Matrix doesn't need to experience the perceptual qualities to get them right. As we have seen, the Matrix feeds its signals into the incoming nerves where they enter the brain, not into the deeper nerve centers. So when you eat (virtual) fried chicken inside the Matrix, the Matrix will activate nerves from the tongue and nose, and the brain will interpret them as taste sensations. What the Matrix puts in will be a copy of the train of electrical impulses that would actually be produced if you were eating meat. Because of the way that the Matrix has been wired into the brain, it has less freedom than Mouse assumed. Whilst the Matrix cannot know tastes itself, it can nonetheless know which chemosensory cells in a human's nose and mouth yield the requisite smell and taste.

NEO'S MASTERY OF THE AVATAR

For purists of science-fiction plausibility, Neo's superhuman control over his avatar body is a troubling element in the film. The final triumphal scene, where Neo flies like Superman, has especially come under criticism. But is it completely at odds with what we have inferred about the Matrix? And how does Neo transcend his human limits?

The Matrix interacts with the brain, but the brain in turn affects the body. When Neo is hurt in training, he finds blood in his mouth. He asks Morpheus, "If you are killed in the Matrix, you die here?" and gets the cryptic reply: "The body cannot live without the mind." But it cuts both ways; ultimately, Neo's avatar is killed inside the Matrix, causing the vital functions to cease in his real body.

Mental states and beliefs can affect the body in several ways. In the placebo effect, the belief that a pill is a medicine can cure an illness; in hypnosis, imagining a flame on the wrist can induce blisters. In total virtuality, the mind accepts completely what is presented. If the Matrix signals that the avatar's body has died, then the mind will shut down the basic organs of the heart and lungs. Actual death will inevitably ensue, unless fast action is taken to get the heart pumping again.

In the climactic scene, Agent Smith kills Neo's avatar within the Matrix. Neo's brain accepts this fate: it stops his heart and loses conscious awareness. His real brain, however, retains enough oxygenated blood to keep it functioning for approximately three minutes, after which it would begin to suffer irreversible damage and, a few minutes later, brain-death. During this time, the auditory cortex keeps on working and digests what Trinity says, albeit unconsciously. Trinity's message is comprehended by Neo's subconscious mind, and a deep realization that the Matrix world is illusory crystallizes in his mind. At an intellectual level, Neo already believed this, but now he knows it at the visceral level of the mind, the level that interfaces with his physiology. Empowered by the insight that his avatar's death is not his death, Neo regains control of his avatar—not only resurrecting it but attaining superhuman powers: the avatar can stop bullets, and fly into the air.

Neo's new powers contrast with the rigid compliance with simulated physical laws that the Matrix generally adheres to. It reveals that Neo has gained direct access to the software modules that simulate his avatar body. That raises two questions: Why does the avatar software accept commands to transform itself, when normally it strictly follows a physical simulation? And, how can Neo's brain issue such commands, which are obviously outside the scope of the normal muscular signals?

The software that simulates the avatar must have a special port, intended for use only by agents, which accepts commands to change the internal properties of the avatar's body. Agents use this facility to embody themselves in human avatars. Like all software, the avatar will obey such commands wherever they originate, provided that they are correctly formulated. We saw earlier how the *Nebuchadnezzar*'s computer used this transformative power to make Morpheus disappear from the subway station. Now Neo's brain is directly using the same command port.

Commands to transform the body cannot travel on the wires that carry the regular muscular signals from the brain to the avatar module. So, they use some of the many other, seemingly redundant, data lines that terminate throughout the rest of the brain. That those lines are hooked up at all on the Matrix end is a spin-off from the Matrix architect's use of general-purpose interfaces. When a newborn human baby is connected to the software module that runs its avatar, there is no way to predetermine which wires carry which data streams. So, at the Matrix end, each line is free to connect to any data port of the avatar module. Some data ports emit simulated signals from virtual eyes and other sense organs, and they will connect with the brain's sensory cortex; others will accept motor commands to carry out simulated contractions of virtual muscles, and they will link up with the motor cortex. In a feedback process that mirrors how the natural plasticity of the brain is molded to its function, useful connections are strengthened and the useless are weakened. As a baby grows into an infant, it gains feedback through using the simulated senses and muscles of the avatar, and therefore its brain builds up the normal strong connections to the conventional input and output channels. But it lacks the abstract concepts needed to use the special port that accepts transformation commands. So the brain's connection with those lines atrophies. Nevertheless, the hardware for that potential connection remains in place. In Neo's kung fu training, his brain rediscovers the abandoned data lines, and he starts to issue rudimentary transformations, giving his avatar's muscles superhuman strength. Only with the deep insight that he gains from being woken after his avatar's death, does he acquire the mental attitude needed to harness that transformative function fully.

The existence of the transformational back door into the avatar software is a security hole that the architects of the Matrix never imagined would be used by mere humans—but now it threatens the very existence of the Matrix, as Neo exploits the power it gives him.

CONSCIOUSNESS AND THE MATRIX

The last question I will address in this essay is a complex one, and one that continues to be explored and debated in scientific and philosophical circles. Can machines be conscious? In everyday life, the machines are so dumb that we can ignore this question, and so we do not have an established criterion for judging whether the intelligent machines of science fiction are conscious. How similar must a machine be to a human for it to be conscious? Humans have a cluster of properties that always hang together: they have conscious perceptions and emotional feelings, they have opinions and beliefs, intuition and intelligence, they use language, and they are alive and warm-blooded, and have a biological brain. We do not, in everyday life, have to separate out those concepts and decide which ones are necessary and sufficient for sentience. The properties all come as a package. In contrast, the lower animals are like us but do not use language and are not as intelligent as we are. So, it is believed that the higher animals probably have basic conscious perceptions—such as colors and sounds, heat and cold—much as we do, but they lack the superstructure of thought. But what about machines that are intelligent and use language, but are not made of biological tissue? Could they be conscious?

To respond rationally to this emotive challenge, we need to be clear about the ideas that are involved. The commonest and most damaging conflation is that of "intelligence" and "consciousness." Alan Turing, in his celebrated paper that introduced the Turing Test, used the terms interchangeably—but mathematicians are notorious for playing fast and loose with their terms. Philosophers, whose trademark is the careful delineation of concepts, have always insisted on maintaining the distinction. Intelligence is the capacity to solve problems, while consciousness is the capacity for the subjective experience of qualities.

As we shall see, intelligence can be attained without consciousness.[2] A digital computer can be programmed to perform intelligent tasks such as playing chess and understanding language by well-defined deterministic processes, without any need to introduce enigmatic conscious experiences into the software. On the other hand, a conscious being can have subjective experiences—such as seeing the color red, or feeling anger—with needing to use intelligence to solve any problems. An android could be vastly more intelligent than any human and still lack any glimmer of interior mental life. On the other hand, a creature might be profoundly stupid and still have subjective experiences.

Agent Smith is an example of a machine that manifests human-like behavior—which, if you witnessed such words and gestures in a human, you would immediately regard them as showing conscious emotions and volitions. Indeed, it is the immediacy of the interpretation that is deceptive. When you see someone laugh with joy, or scream in pain, you do not knowingly infer the person's mental state from

2 For an alternative perspective, see Kurzweil's essay in this volume. —Ed.

those outward signs. Rather, it is as if you see the emotions directly. Yet, we know from accomplished actors that these signs of emotions can be faked. Therefore, you are indeed making an inference, albeit an automatic one. It is a job of philosophy to scrutinize such automatic inference. When you see another human being emoting, your inference is not based wholly on what you see, but also on background information (such as whether the person is acting on the stage). More fundamentally, you are relying on the reasonable assumption that the person's behavior arises from a biological brain just as yours does. Whenever those premises are undermined, you inevitably revise any inferences you have made from the emoting. If the emoting stops and people around you clap, you realize it was a piece of street theatre, and the person was only acting out those emotions. Or, if the person has a nasty car accident that breaks open his head, revealing electronic circuitry instead of a brain, you realize that it was only an android and you may conclude that it was only simulating emotions.

A key step in the inference is the premise that the emotion plays a role in the causal loop that produces the outward words and gestures. If, instead, we have established that the observed words and gestures are wholly explained in some other way, without involving those emotions—then the inference collapses. The exterior emoting behavior then ceases to count as evidence for an interior emotional experience. If we know that an actor's words and gestures are scripted, then we cease to regard them as evidence for an inward mental state. Likewise, if we know that the words and gestures of an android or avatar are programmed, then they too cease to support any inference of a mental state.

In an android, or in a software simulation of a human such as an agent, words and gestures are produced by millions of lines of programmed software. The software advances from instruction to instruction in a deterministic manner. Some instructions move pieces of information around inside memory, others execute calculations, others send motor signals to actuators in the body. Each line of code references objective memory locations and ports in the physical hardware. It may do so symbolically, and it may do so via sophisticated data structures, for example, using the tag "vision-field" to reference the stabilized and edge-enhanced data from the eye cams. Nevertheless, nowhere in the software suite does the code break out of that objective environment and refer to the enigmatic contents of consciousness. Nor could the programmer ever do so, since she would need an objective, third-person pointer to the conscious experience—which, being a subjective, first-person thing, cannot be labeled with such a pointer.

Everything that the android says and does is fully accounted for by its software. There is no explanatory gap left for machine consciousness to fill. When the android says, "I see colors and feel emotions just as humans do," we know that those words are produced by deterministic lines of software that functions perfectly well without any involvement of consciousness. It is because of this that the android's emoting does not provide an iota of evidence for any interior mental life. All the outward signs are faked, and the programmer knows in comprehensive detail how they are faked.

This point is systematically ignored by the mathematicians and engineers who enthuse about artificial intelligence. You have to go next door, to the philosophy department, to find people who accord due importance to it. Even if, by some unknown means, the android possessed consciousness, it could never tell us about it. As we have seen, everything the android says is determined by the software. Even if, somewhere in the depths of its circuit boards, there was a ghostly glimmer of conscious awareness or volition, it could never influence what the android says and does.

Could it be that the information in the computer just *is* the conscious experience? This argument is popular with information engineers, as it seems to allow them to gloss over the whole mind-body problem. It is flawed because information and conscious experience have different logical structures. Namely, information exists only as an artifact of interpretation; but experience does not stand in need of interpretation in order for you to be aware of it. If I give you a disk holding numerical data (21, 250, 11, 47; 22, 250, 15, 39. etc), those numbers could mean anything. In one program, they are meteorological measurements—temperature, humidity, rainfall. In another, they are medical—pulse rate, blood pressure, body fat. The interpretation has no independent reality; the numbers have no inherent meaning by themselves. In contrast, conscious experience is fundamentally different. If you jam your thumb in a door, your sensation does not need first to be interpreted by you as pain. It immediately presents as pain. Nor can you reinterpret it as some other sensation, such as the scent of a rose. Conscious experiences have real, subjectively witnessed qualities that do not depend for their existence on being interpreted this way or that. They intrinsically involve some quality over and above mere information.

Another popular argument is to appeal to "emergence." Higher-level systems are said to "emerge" from lower-level systems. The simple classic example is that of thermodynamic properties, such as heat and temperature, which emerge from the statistical behavior of ensembles of molecules. Yet the concept of "temperature" just does not exist for an isolated molecule, although billions of those molecules collectively do have a temperature. In like manner, it has been suggested, consciousness emerges from the collective behavior of billions of neurons, which individually could never be conscious on their own. But emergent properties are, in fact, artifacts of how we describe the world, and have no objective existence outside of mathematical theories. An ensemble of molecules may be described in terms of either the trajectories of individual molecules or their aggregate properties, but the latter are invented by human observers for the sake of simplifications. The external reality comprises only the molecules: the statistical properties, such as average kinetic energy, exist only in the mind of the physicist. Likewise, any dynamic features of the aggregate behavior of brain cells exist only in the models of the neuroscientists. The external reality comprises only the brain cells. Yet, as you know, when you jam your thumb in the door, the pain is real and present in the moment; it is not a theoretical construct of a brain scientist.

So there are good reasons for believing that machines are not conscious. But—wouldn't these arguments apply equally to brains? Surely a brain is just a bioelectrochemical machine? It obeys deterministic programs that are encoded in the genetic and neural wiring of the brain. Yet, if our argument that machines are not conscious can also apply equally to brains, then the argument must be flawed—since we know that our own brains are indeed conscious!

The answer is that there are certain processes in brain tissue that involve nondeterministic quantum-mechanical events. And, working through the chaotic dynamics of the brain, those minute phenomena can be amplified into overt behavior. The nondeterminism opens a gateway for consciousness to take effect in the workings of the brain.

As we saw earlier, you can report only the conscious experiences that are in the causal loop that gives rise to the speech acts. If you can report that you are in pain, then the pain sensation must exert a causal influence somewhere in the chain of neural events that governs what you say and write. A step that is physically nondeterministic provides a window of opportunity for consciousness to enter into that causal chain. Since we, as humans, know that we do express our conscious perceptions, we can infer that there must be some such nondeterminism somewhere in the brain. So far, quantum-mechanical events constitute the only known candidate for this. For example, Roger Penrose and Stuart Hammeroff have formulated a detailed theory of how quantum actions in the microtubules of brain cells could play this role. The jury is still out on whether the microtubules really are the locus at which consciousness enters the chain of cause and event.

A conventional, deterministic computer has no such gateway into consciousness. So androids, and virtual avatars, that are driven by computers of that kind, cannot express conscious awareness and their behavior therefore can never be evidence for consciousness. But, if a machine were to be built that used quantum computation in the same way that the brain does, then there is no philosophical reason why that machine could not have the same gateway to consciousness that a living being does. This is not because the quantum module lets the machine carry out computations that a classical computer cannot do. Whatever the quantum computer can do, a classical one can also do, albeit more slowly. Rather, it is the specific implementation of the quantum computer that provides the bridge into conscious processes.

In *The Matrix*, there is no reason to think that the machines are equipped with the kind of quantum computation needed to access consciousness. Quantum computation is not mentioned in the film, and there is circumstantial evidence that the Matrix and its agents are devoid of conscious thought.

Therefore the agents—which are software modules within the Matrix—are intelligent but mindless automata. For the most part, the agents behave unimaginatively, and we might naively think that this corroborates their lack of awareness. Yet, Agent Smith exhibits initiative and seems, in his speech to Morpheus, to evince a conscious dislike of the human world. But is he genuinely conscious, or only mimicking humans? In fact, Smith gives himself away when he says about the human world, "It's the smell, if there is such a thing . . . I can taste your stink and every time I do, I fear that I've somehow been infected by it." Smith's own logical integrity obliges him to doubt the existence of that noncomputable quality that humans talk about: the conscious experience of smell. When Smith says, ". . . the smell, if there is such a thing," he is exhibiting the mark of the automaton. This is corroborated when he then tells Morpheus that he can "taste your stink," revealing that Smith simply does not understand the differentiation of senses in the human mind. For a computer, data are interchangeable, but for a human, tastes, smells, colors, sounds, and feels, are irreducibly different. This fact eludes Agent Smith.

Smith is mimicking human behavior as a tactic to trick Morpheus into cooperation. As the interrogation is getting nowhere, Brown suggests, "Perhaps we are asking the wrong questions." So Smith pretends to talk like a human, to gain Morpheus's empathy. Needless to say, the tactic fails completely.

JAMES L. FORD

BUDDHISM,

MYTHOLOGY,

AND

THE

MATRIX

Is Neo the Buddha? Is there really no spoon? And can it be a coincidence that Keanu Reeves once played Prince Siddhārtha in Little Buddha?

Professor and Buddhist scholar James Ford explores the complex relationship between Buddhism and The Matrix.

Humans are mythologizing and, one might say, "world building" creatures. We fashion epic narratives to express our self-understanding and contribute to a structure of meaning for our lives. Myth in this sense is not a "fairy tale" or forged history—it is rather the deepest expression of our fears, aspirations, and symbolic understanding of life and the world around us. Stories from the Bible, creation accounts from any number of ancient cultures, biographies of nation founders, and even contemporary movies such as *Star Wars* qualify as myth. Part historical fact, part imaginary fiction, or sometimes *complete* imaginary fiction, such accounts inform to various degrees the way we see the world and interpret our experience within the world. But myths are highly fluid and interrelated. The author(s) of a new myth does not generally create a narrative out of a vacuum. He or she will often borrow from the mythological symbols or narrative motifs from the surrounding context and transform their meaning in some new and creative way. For example, we know from scholarly research that the flood narrative found in Genesis borrows considerably from the Babylonian tale of Utnapishtim within the *Epic of Gilgamesh*. But the Biblical authors radically transformed the story by integrating the Hebrew god Yahweh into the narrative. And George Lucas readily admits that he borrowed heavily from the paradigmatic hero journey delineated by the famous mythologist Joseph Campbell. But he also placed the narrative in a futuristic setting and highlighted the potential threat of technology to human compassion and existence.

The Matrix can be seen as a modern example of this myth-making process as well. In an interview with *Time* magazine, the Wachowski brothers stated their mythological intent directly:

> "We're interested in mythology, theology and, to a certain extent, higher-level mathematics. All are ways human beings try to answer bigger questions, as well as The Big Question. If you're going to do epic stories, you should concern yourself with those issues. People might not understand all the allusions in the movie, but they understand the important ideas. We wanted to make people think, engage their minds a bit."[1]

Mixing metaphors from Christianity, Buddhism, Greek mythology, and even cyber technology, *The Matrix* offers a mythological account of the human existential condition. In this essay, I will approach this classic movie from a

Buddhist perspective. How does *The Matrix* reflect a Buddhist "worldview" and analysis of the most fundamental human problems? I am assuming no prior knowledge of Buddhism and will begin with a basic introduction to Buddhism and important historical and doctrinal developments within the tradition that are relevant to my interpretation of *The Matrix*.

LIFE AND CONTEXT OF THE BUDDHA

The founder of Buddhism is known by several different names. Born Siddhartha Gautama, a given family name, he is often referred to as Sakyamuni, literally "Sage of the Sakya clan." Upon achieving enlightenment, he earned the title of Buddha or the "awakened one." As with "Christ" or "Messiah" in relation to the historical figure Jesus, "Buddha" is actually a title rather than a personal name. Siddhartha lived and taught in northern India around the middle of the first millennium B.C.E. The most common dates for his life are 566–486 B.C.E. According to the traditional sources, he renounced the life of a wealthy prince sometime around the age of thirty and embarked on a spiritual quest for a way to overcome suffering and death.

This renouncement of the "world" and his privileged life was not entirely novel for the time. Siddhartha was born into an era of great social tension and transition in northern India. Sacred literature such as the *Upanishads* voiced a challenge to the established priest-centered religion (sometimes known as Brahminism), which emphasized purity, class distinctions, and ritual efficacy. Most important, time was (and is) understood cyclically within Indian religion. Just as seasons and years come and go, so also does the world itself. Conceived in cycles measured by inconceivable blocks of time, a world comes into being, evolves, devolves, and is finally destroyed only to be followed by another world. The process has virtually no beginning and no end. Similarly, sentient beings pass endlessly through various incarnations (e.g., animal, human, god, and so forth).

This general cycle of life after life is known as *samsara*. *Atman*, analogous in many ways to the soul in Western religious terms, is the essence of sentient beings that passes from one life to the next. And one's *karma* determines the status of one's life and rebirth. *Karma*, literally "action," is the moral law of cause and effect based on one's actions. Thus, virtuous actions lead to happiness and favorable rebirth, and nonvirtuous actions lead to suffering. The ultimate goal known as *moksha* (liberation) within this conceptual worldview is to escape from *samsara* and the endless cycle of life and suffering. By Siddhartha's time, perhaps the most effective means of achieving *moksha* was to the renounce the world and pursue the path of a *sannyasin* (wandering ascetic). Through severe denial of the body (i.e., the material self) and demanding meditative and yogic discipline, it was thought that one could realize liberation from *samsara*.

According to tradition, Siddhartha pursued this path of a *sannyasin* for some six years after leaving his luxurious life as a prince, and studied under two prominent gurus. He lived an extremely ascetic life, meditating most hours of the day and consuming a barely sustainable amount of food—the goal being to identify with one's spiritual essence (i.e., *Atman*), not the material body that is but a temporary vessel. In the end, Siddhartha found this path too extreme and abandoned his colleagues to search for another way. Upon regaining his physical strength, he determined to sit beneath a particular tree until he discovered the true nature of reality and the way to overcome suffering. As he broached the threshold of realization, he encountered Mara, the demon god that rules *samsara*. Mara attempted to distract Siddhartha through temptation, fear, and doubt, but in the end Siddhartha prevailed. Upon achieving ultimate enlightenment, the Buddha went on to teach others the content of his realization. In fact, he traveled through northern India for some forty-five years building a Buddhist monastic community (*sangha*) and teaching the monks, nuns, and laypersons that gathered wherever he went.

"DR. BUDDHA" AND THE DHARMA

The content of the Buddha's enlightenment is found in the Four Noble Truths, his most basic teaching. As we will see, these truths constitute a prescriptive analysis of the fundamental human problem and the way to overcome this problem. Or, put another way, the format of the truths is analogous to a doctor's diagnosis of a sick patient. The first truth defines the sickness; the second analyzes the cause of the sickness; the third reveals what it looks like to be cured; and the fourth is the remedy. They are titled "noble" truths because they are self-evident "truths" to someone who is truly enlightened and wise (i.e., "noble").

So what are these Four Noble Truths? They can be listed quite succinctly, but understanding them takes a bit more explication and reflection. They are:

1. The truth of suffering (*dukkha*)
2. The truth of the arising of suffering
3. The truth of the cessation of suffering (*Nirvana*)
4. The truth of the path that leads to the cessation of suffering (eightfold path)

Some say that all of these truths are contained in the first truth of suffering. In other words, if you truly understand the truth of suffering, you will naturally grasp the truths that follow.

"All is suffering" is another way the first truth is often stated. The Pali term that is translated as "suffering" here is *dukkha*. In fact, "suffering" may be a somewhat misleading translation. Consequently, some teachers feel that something like "dissatisfactoriness" better conveys the gist of *dukkha*. The idea here is that there is a universal feeling of dissatisfaction that characterizes all of human experience. It is not difficult to accept that life is indeed filled with suffering of one degree or another. But the Buddha emphasized that this is indeed the fundamental character of life in general. Even in our happiest moments—when we fall in love, have a child, or reach a long-pursued goal— there often is a deep level of angst still present. We know that the moment will not last forever and there may even be an underlying fear that something terrible will undercut our joy. This is, perhaps, much like the feeling of discontent Neo feels, the "splinter in his mind" telling him of the wrongness of the universe around him.

While this might appear to be a rather depressing starting point for a religion, Buddhism would argue that it is "realistic" as opposed to "pessimistic." In fact, I would contend that this deep sense of angst that characterizes the "human condition" is the root of all religion and philosophy. While various religious and philosophical systems may articulate the fundamental human problem in different ways, all endeavor to lead us beyond the difficult and mundane human experience that most fundamentally defines our existence. And while we might expect Buddhists to appear rather dour, angry, or even downright depressed given this starting point, the reality is quite different. Anyone who has seen the Dalai Lama speak immediately senses a buoyant lightness and humor that is anything but sorrowful. Statues of the Buddha himself are often depicted with a slight smile of contentment. So whatever one might say about the starting point of Buddhism in this first noble truth, it does not necessarily lead to a negative or morose view of the world.

The Second Noble Truth reveals the causal process that leads to suffering and, more existentially, the perpetual cycle of transmigration known as *samsara*. First of all, Buddhism asserts that because we are ignorant of the true nature of reality, we perceive and experience the world in a distorted way. "Ignorance" may be misleading here because it is not precisely a lack of knowing that is the problem—it is rather a mis-knowing. In other words, we think we understand to one degree or another the nature of the world around us— but in reality, our perception is quite distorted. For example, one of the "three marks of existence" (truisms about the nature of reality) is that all things are impermanent (*anitya*). Everything is forever changing—nothing stays the same. At a superficial level, we can easily comprehend this dictum. A simple examination of the physical world around us would confirm that indeed nothing remains static. But if one honestly examines the way we live our lives, it is apparent that despite this evident truth of impermanence, we often act as though we are surprised when things do not stay the same. We get angry or upset when something we value disappears, dies, or breaks down. Indeed, we are constantly searching for something of permanence, and when we find something that seems to yield "happiness," we cling to it as if we can keep it from changing. This is where desire comes in. Our encounters with the things of the world lead to positive, negative, and neutral feelings. Where there is something positive, we want more of it; and when it is negative, we do our utmost to avoid it (hatred and aversion are the flip side of desire and attachment). So our desire propels us forward and we become attached, even addicted, to the pleasurable experiences of life. It does not take much to see that if our happiness is dependent on things staying the same, we will forever be discontent. We are like the drug addict, demanding more and more. From this perspective, life is a perpetual experience of loss, loss, loss, . . . because those things we desire and cling to invariably change or disappear altogether.

Another aspect of impermanence is interdependence. Everything arises and exists dependent on any number of other factors. Something as simple as a piece of paper is dependent upon a seedling, a tree, rain, soil, sunlight, a lumberjack, paper mill, etc. And each of those things is dependent on infinitely more things for its own existence. If we move to something as complex as a human, the web of dependence grows ever more complex. Each of us is dependent on our father and mother for birth and sustenance, along with food, shelter, education, protection, etc. In other words, as much as we might like to think that we are independently existing creatures, in reality we are deeply dependent on the web of life surrounding us. In fact, the Buddha asserted via the doctrine of no-self (*anatman*) that it is the illusion that we are somehow distinct, independent "selves" that leads us to act egotistically. And it is this egotistic tendency that perpetuates suffering both for ourselves and others.

If Buddhism stopped here, it would indeed be a rather pessimistic religion (just as *The Matrix* would be a rather pessimistic film if it concluded with all humans trapped within the Matrix). But the third noble truth asserts that there is a way out of this quagmire. There is a way of experiencing reality that is somehow NOT characterized by *dukkha*. This is Nirvana. Nirvana literally means "going out" as in the going out of a flame. The analogy of fire is often evoked in Buddhism. Desire is like a fire that propels us forward constantly demanding new fuel (i.e., attachments), while Nirvana is described as "cool." Nirvana is not a heavenly realm, a perpetual state of bliss, or even nonexistence. The Buddha seemed to imply that Nirvana lies beyond the dualistic distinctions of language. We only need to recall that Sakyamuni realized Nirvana under the Bo tree and proceeded to travel and preach around northern India for some forty years before dying a natural death. From everything we can gather, he interacted with many people, ate, taught, and so forth, so he clearly did not disappear into some transcendent realm. Therefore, Nirvana is not necessarily the cessation of life, *but the cessation of a life characterized by suffering.* Moreover, the Buddha's countenance radiated any number of positive attributes—he is described as peaceful, wise, unattached, selfless, authentic, spontaneous and compassionate. So it is not as though he was a blank slate either. At his death, the Buddha achieved what is known as Pari-Nirvana or "final" Nirvana, defined as a complete escape from rebirth in the realm of *samsara*. Beyond this, it transcends the scope of language. The central point I want to make here is that Buddhism claims that there is a way of experiencing the world that is not characterized by suffering, desire, ignorance, and so forth. This is what it looks like to be cured of the disease of *dukkha*.

So what is the therapy that leads to this cure? The answer is the fourth noble truth—the eightfold path leading to Nirvana. The categories that constitute this path are:

Right Understanding
Right Thought   Wisdom (*prajña*)

Right Speech	
Right Action	Morality (*sila*)
Right Livelihood	
Right Effort	
Right Mindfulness	Mental discipline (*samadhi*)
Right Concentration	

Not a sequential path of training, one develops all of these dimensions simultaneously. As reflected by this chart, Buddhism has generally broken these eight dimensions of practice into what is called the threefold learning. Wisdom is attained through developing right understanding and thought. In other words, by truly comprehending the four noble truths and other Buddhist learnings, we can begin to transform our deluded understanding of reality and conceptions of "self," the world, and so forth. One must also develop proper morality through regulating one's speech, behavior, and work. This means controlling words or actions that may cause suffering for others and avoiding occupations that cause harm to other sentient beings (e.g., butcher, arms dealer, etc.). Finally, since the fundamental problem is one of the mind (i.e., ignorance and delusion), Buddhism asserts that there is a mental discipline necessary to intentionally transform one's consciousness. It is as though our minds are computers that have been programmed incorrectly. Indeed, our "software," the product of many lifetimes of karmic conditioning, must be reprogrammed to conform to the true nature of reality. This is the purpose of meditation within Buddhism. It is not a means of escaping, but a means of transforming one's consciousness so that when one is "in the world," one is able to act, think, and respond wisely and compassionately.

EMERGENCE OF MAHAYANA BUDDHISM

After the death of the Buddha, the tradition carried on and grew significantly around the monastic community. To be sure, there was from the beginning a strong lay movement that centered on popular pilgrimage sites. But the center of Buddhism was the monastic community itself, which represented as it were the ideal Buddhist life. And the ideal of the monastic community was an *arhat*—a fully enlightened disciple of the Buddha who enters Pari-Nirvana upon death. As with many other religious communities, disputes arose over time that resulted in what we might call denominational splits. These divisions resulted from disputes over doctrine and practice, but the various schools that resulted tended not to be very exclusive. By the first century of the Common Era, a new movement emerged that came to be known as Mahayana Buddhism. Followers of Mahayana ("Great Vehicle") distinguished themselves from the more traditional schools, which they labeled Hïnayana ("Small Vehicle"). Scholars prefer the term Nikaya for early Buddhism because it does not carry the obvious pejorative connotation of Hïnayana. By the very title of their movement, Mahayanists claimed that this new vehicle was more universalistic than the old tradition that carried a relative few to the other shore of Nirvana. A number of fundamental characteristics distinguished Mahayana from the earlier tradition, most noteworthy is the ideal of the bodhisattva. In contrast to the *arhat* ideal of Nikaya Buddhism, Mahayana favored the bodhisattva—one who is on the path to Buddhahood. According to Mahayana rhetoric at least, the bodhisattva is motivated not by a desire to achieve Nirvana for him or herself, but to achieve enlightenment for the benefit of all beings. Thus, a bodhisattva intentionally comes back to the world of *samsara* in order to alleviate suffering and help lead others on the same path. A bodhisattva, frequently defined as one who "turns back" from Nirvana, is more accurately pursuing a different goal (i.e., full buddahood) altogether. Some Mahayana texts even claim that Nirvana does not exist and was simply a conceptual tool used by the Buddha to motivate people onto the path.

At any rate, a bodhisattva is motivated by a compassion for all suffering beings and a pursuit of wisdom that facilitates wise action. As a bird requires two wings, a bodhisattva relies on the mutual development of wisdom and compassion. Various delineations of the bodhisattva path emerged, the most popular being a ten-stage progression over many lifetimes in which the bodhisattva perfects the necessary virtues (e.g., generosity, patience, perseverance, etc.) to realize Buddhahood. As one progresses along this path, one gains extraordinary, even miraculous powers. As a result, there developed within the Mahayana tradition a growing assembly of what may be called "celestial bodhisattvas"—advanced bodhisattvas who may reside in heavenly realms from whence they can descend to teach and assist suffering beings. Maitreya in particular is noteworthy because he appears very much like a messianic figure within the Buddhist tradition. At various times and places, there have been significant movements centered around the expected "descent" of Maitreya as the next Buddha.

Before moving onto the significant parallels between Buddhism and *The Matrix*, allow me to introduce one prominent philosophical school of Mahayana Buddhism that is particularly noteworthy for reasons that will become obvious. It should be evident by now that Buddhism is in many ways a philosophy of the mind. The fundamental problem is not "of the world," as it clearly is for those that perceive the world as a battleground between good and evil forces. Rather, the problem is in the (deluded) way we perceive the world. Thus, the solution is rooted in a transformation of one's consciousness and the way one processes reality. Buddhism does emphasize certain moral imperatives to minimize worldly suffering. But even here, conscious *intention* is the most important ingredient. Unlike Jainism, for example, Buddhism contends that there are no negative karmic consequences if we *unintentionally* kill an animal. What is most important is one's conscious intent, not simply the actions that result. Aside from avoiding hurting others, good moral behavior is emphasized because of the interdependent relationship between one's actions and one's mind. Practicing generosity helps one become more mindful of being generous, and vice versa.

This Buddhist analysis of "consciousness" reached its climax in the fourth-century Mahayana school known as Yogacara. Yogacara, also known as the "Consciousness Only" school (Vijñanavada), asserts that the objective world we perceive to be real is ultimately a product of our minds.[2] It is as though one's mind is a movie projector and the world that one experiences is the "projection" of one's consciousness. Because we perceive the "objects" of consciousness to be independently existing, we ceaselessly pursue them or avoid them, depending on feelings of desire or hatred. Yogacara does not assert that the objective world does not exist, though many observers have drawn this conclusion.[3] Rather, this is more accurately an *epistemological* insight. The point is that every "object" is significantly altered by our conscious perception; we know it secondhand as idea and we cannot know it before it is so transformed.

---

2 For a coherent overview of Yogacara thought, see Williams, pp. 77–95.

3 For representative examples of this debate with respect to Yogacara Buddhism, see Keenan, pp. 169 and 209; and Paul Griffiths, p. 83.

Everything that one experiences is filtered through one's consciousness, which invariably distorts the experience in some way. Yogacara claims that once we realize that the objects of consciousness are, in this sense, illusory, then desire, attachment, and suffering cease. At this point the underlying flow of consciousness is transformed into the wisdom of a Buddha.

In order to attain this realization about the nature of consciousness, Yogacara emphasized various meditative and visualization practices—hence, the name of the school ("practitioners of yoga"). Meditation techniques were developed to deconstruct, in a sense, one's conditioned way of seeing the world and help one awaken to the ultimately interdependent and non-dualistic nature of reality. The manner in which one is able to create and control images in the mind through various visualization practices served to reinforce the notion that everyday conscious perceptions, like dreams, are no less "created." The practitioner comes to realize the illusory nature of the self and the external constituents of reality. Ultimately, one endeavors to overcome the subject-object dualism that informs our deluded view that we (and all "objects") are somehow distinct and independently existing entities. The content of this realization of non-duality is beyond verbal description. This realization is the ultimate goal of a Yogacara practitioner.

BUDDHISM AND *THE MATRIX*

Every religion offers an analysis of the human condition. Most also have foundation myths that convey the basic existential problem of human existence. Confucian accounts of the idealized Chou dynasty, for example, reflect that tradition's understanding of the fundamental problem—social disharmony due to the human tendency to neglect ritual and social propriety. Sacred Hindu texts such as the *Bhagavadgïtua* and the *Upanishads* present the human condition as one of perpetual bondage in the endless cycle of *samsara*, life after life. For Christianity and Judaism, the fundamental problem is humanity's alienation from God due to our sinful nature and egoistic tendency to try to be like God. This of course is symbolized in the Genesis creation narrative of Adam and Eve in the Garden of Eden. A core of Christian belief is that God offered his own son, the *messiah*, as a means to overcome that alienation.

While *The Matrix* echoes the messianic motifs of the Christian narrative, the "human problem" is clearly not alienation from God since God is nowhere present in the story—or at least not a personal creator God.[4] Conrad Ostwalt sees this omission of the divine and the rejection of the supernatural as agent for the apocalypse as symptomatic of "the contemporary apocalyptic imagination."[5] God will not bring about the apocalypse—something else will. But *The Matrix* need not be understood only as a "contemporary" adaptation of the Judeo-Christian apocalyptic view; there are other ancient mythological perspectives that also omit the "divine" entirely. It is here, I think, that Buddhism offers an illuminating mythological parallel.

The Buddhist parallels in *The Matrix* are numerous. Clearly, the fundamental problem is one of the mind. The Matrix itself is analogous to *samsåra*, the illusory world that is not the reality it appears to be. Morpheus tells Neo that the "Matrix is everywhere, it's all around us, here even in this very room. You can see it out your window or on your

---

4 For an alternative perspective, see Paul Fontana's essay "Finding God in *The Matrix*" in this volume. —Ed.

5 Ostwalt

television. You feel it when you go to work, or go to church or pay your taxes. It is the world that has been pulled over your eyes to blind you from the truth." In other words, the fundamental problem is ignorance of the true nature of reality. Morpheus later adds that it is our conditioned "attachment" to this delusional reality that prevents most beyond a certain age from breaking away from it. There is the suggestion of reincarnation as when the oracle informs Neo that he is not The One, but adds, "Maybe next life." There is another suggestion of reincarnation in Morpheus's claim that the man who first transcended the Matrix would return as "The One."

There is also a dimension of karma evident in the film in the sense that humans are basically in a condition of their own making. As Morpheus notes, humans have always been dependent on tools for existence. The artificial intelligence that runs the Matrix and controls humanity is of humanity's own making. Moreover, it was humanity that destroyed the world in an effort to defeat the AI by depriving it of the sunlight needed for energy. The point is that the AI did not appear on its own nor is it some "evil force" that has existed from the beginning of the time. It is the (karmic) result of past actions.

Another important parallel between *The Matrix* and Buddhism relates to the realm of discipline and practice. Recall that an important dimension of the eightfold path of Buddhism is meditation and mental concentration. One must learn to discipline and control the mind that so fundamentally distorts reality and imputes permanence and selfhood onto things that are ultimately empty. Meditation is a means of "reprogramming" the mind, as it were, so that our perception of reality conforms to the way the world really is. The process of Neo's own training is a wonderful analogy of this decidedly "mental" transformation process.

His mind is literally reprogrammed so that, like a bodhisattva, he is able to enter the Matrix (i.e., *samsara*) with increasing powers of perception and control. In other words, the very process of Neo's training is a techno-cyber version of meditation. The filmmakers also adopt the motif of martial arts training, which has historically close ties with Buddhist monastic training in China and Japan. I might also note that the vital moment for one embarking on the bodhisattva path is the arousal of the aspiration for enlightenment known as *bodhicitta*. A crucial episode for a monk within Mahayana Buddhism is the declaration of his intent to pursue enlightenment for the benefit of all beings. Through a formal ritual of declaring vows, one intentionally commits to the path. It strikes me that Neo's decision to take the red pill is a kind of ritualistic expression of his own intent before embarking on the adventure "down the rabbit hole." Along these same lines, the lifestyle of the rebels is strikingly monastic in flavor. Their food, clothing, and living quarters are quite austere. Indeed, Cypher revolts in part because he would rather live the deluded life of desire than endure the frugal and disciplined "monastic" life of the rebels.

While we do not find explicit discussions of impermanence, interdependence, or emptiness in the dialogue of *The Matrix*, there is the clear message that the world humans experience is a complete distortion. It is literally a computer program input into our minds to keep us entertained. In other words, it is "empty" of any substantive "reality." We are not the "selves" we perceive ourselves to be. We are in fact "slaves," as Morpheus says to Neo: " . . . like everyone else, you were born into bondage . . . kept inside a prison that you cannot smell, taste, or touch. A prison for your mind." It is here that the parallels with Yogacara philosophy seem quite apropos. As noted above, Yogacara emphasizes that our *only* access to reality is through our conscious minds. We must first realize that the "projected" image of the world that we experience is not the "reality" we perceive it to be. It is distorted by our individual and collective karma that conditions us to impute a degree of permanence and independence upon things of the world that is not there. In the same way, the Matrix is quite clearly a delusional reality. "What is real?" Morpheus asks Neo. "How do you define real? If you're talking about what you feel, taste, smell, or see, then real is simply electrical signals interpreted by your brain. This is the world that you know. The world as it was at the end of the twentieth century. It exists now only as part of a neural-interactive simulation that we call the Matrix. You have been living in a dreamworld, Neo." What is needed is an extraordinary being who can penetrate the maze of this "cinematic prison" and reveal the nature of our plight to us. This is precisely what bodhisattvas and Buddhas do . . . and so with Neo. It remains to be seen exactly how Neo will proceed from here.

According to the Mahayana tradition, as one progresses along the path to Buddhahood, one procures powers to manipulate the perceived "objective" world. Buddhas and advanced bodhisattvas can transform and manipulate objects at will. They can also manifest themselves at different places, even at the same time. Recall the young "Potentials" in the living room of the Oracle's apartment. Some appear to be practicing meditation while others manipulate wooden blocks, spoons, and so forth. We might consider these Potentials the equivalent to young bodhisattvas learning to transform elements of the "objective" world through powers of consciousness. A Buddha actually possesses the power to create his/her own cosmic realm.[6] However, Sakyamuni Buddha did not transform the world in such a radical way. People continued to suffer, live illusory existences, and die. But he did offer a new path and way of overcoming our distorted perception of the world. Thus, there remains a strong sense of free will and responsibility. In the same way, it does not appear as though Neo is going to radically transform the world or destroy the Matrix created by AI, despite the fact that this is what Morpheus is expecting.[7] Indeed, it is not clear what he is going to do with the Matrix. But it is apparent that he, like the prior One, is going to reveal the truth to those willing to listen. At the conclusion of the film, Neo offers what might be described as a rather compassionate warning to AI:

> "I know you're out there. I can feel you now. I know that you're afraid. You're afraid of us. You're afraid of change. I don't know the future. I didn't come here to tell you how this is going to end. I came here to tell you how it's going to begin. I'm going to hang up this phone and then I'm going to show these people what you don't want them to see. I'm going to show them a world without you, a world without rules and controls, without borders or boundaries, a world where anything is possible. Where we go from here is a choice I will leave to you."

6 The most famous example here is Amitabha (Japan: Amida), the central Buddha of the Pure Land tradition of Buddhism in East Asia. Amitabha, while a bodhisattva, vowed to create his own Pure Land upon achieving Buddhahood. All who invoke the name of Amitabha with a sincere heart can be reborn in that majestic realm where enlightenment is more easily attained.

7 At one point, Morpheus explains to Neo the origin of the rebels and the prophesy of the Oracle concerning the coming One: "When the Matrix was first built, there was a man born inside who had the ability to change whatever he wanted, to remake the Matrix as he saw fit. It was he who freed the first of us, taught us the truth: 'As long as the Matrix exists the human race will never be free.' After he died the Oracle prophesized his return and that his coming would hail the destruction of the Matrix, end the war, bring freedom to our people."

We might imagine the Buddha having the same conversation with Mara, the demon-god that lords over *samsara*. He did not destroy Mara. Mara, symbolizing the power that keeps us in *samsara*, lives on. We can imagine, however, that Mara proceeds with a sense of fear knowing that Sakyamuni has escaped and may indeed show others the way out of *samsara*.

Recall that in the Yogacara vision of enlightenment, it is not as though the substratum of flowing consciousness disappears or is destroyed. Rather it is transformed and a Buddha sees it for the interdependent web that it is without the afflictive emotions of desire and hatred that lead to attachment and suffering. And by so doing, he is able to move through the interdependent web of *samsara* spontaneously, without fear, doubt, or temptation. He is not constrained by the conventional laws of cause and effect (i.e., *karma*) that govern *samsara*. Now recall the moment when Neo is resurrected (i.e., reborn). He is able to glide through the Matrix, turning bullets into suspended debris and exploding "Mara" (i.e., Agent Smith) into white light. No longer constrained by fear, doubt, or ignorance, Neo, like a Buddha, has transcended all dualities, even the ultimate duality of life and death.

THE MATRIX AS MYTH

As with any myth, *The Matrix* is metaphorical and begs for some kind of interpretation. Myths are ultimately symbolic and operate on many different levels. For example, humans have created all kinds of "systems" (i.e., constructed ways of conceptualizing and understanding the world). There are political systems (e.g., democratic, socialist, communist, dictatorial, monarchical, etc.). Similarly, there are various social, economic, and religious "systems" adopted by various societies that structure the way people brought up in these systems see and even experience the world. Moreover, these "systems," once established, tend to have a life of their own and even act back on humans in ways that their creators probably did not anticipate. In short, the Matrix and *samsara* can be seen as metaphors for the "systems" that impose themselves upon us. And Neo and the Buddha are analogous to those unique "saviors" that reveal to us the sometimes perverted and destructive nature of such "systems."

So we could also understand the Matrix to be a metaphor for the various "systems" that sometimes compel us to act in ways that are not in our best collective or even individual interest. For example, some might say that our dependence on and attachment to technology is out of control. Of course, there are innumerable benefits from technology. But one perhaps negative result is that it sometimes undermines or impedes genuine human interaction. Others might argue that industrialization and capitalism, two interrelated "systems," can be destructive to the environment or undermine genuine human compassion, respectively. For example, capitalism, when not balanced with other ethical imperatives, can lead to an inequitable distribution of suffering or an imbalance between the haves and have-nots. Without always being fully aware of it, we are conditioned socially and otherwise, by growing up within such "systems," so that we can no longer see their constructed nature. We are "blind," as Morpheus might say, to the degree to which the "system" controls us. In short, with respect to the Matrix, one need not understand the issues of delusion, attachment, control, and so forth, only in reference to one "ultimate reality." And this is also the case for the Buddhist analysis of the human condition;

samsara also can be seen as a metaphor for any of the various dimensions of our perceived reality.

From this more mundane perspective, *The Matrix* challenges our conditioned way of seeing the world. How are WE "programmed," it seems to ask? What aspect of OUR reality is artificially constructed and enslaving us within a conceptual prison? Is technology liberating or imprisoning us? Is materialistic capitalism leading to true happiness or unrequited addiction? Do our cherished religious views bring us together or divide us? These are fruitful questions for stimulating one's own interpretation of this modern myth and its relevance to *our* social reality. In addition to the mesmerizing action scenes, it may well be that this implicit skepticism toward "institutional" control explains the popularity of this film among young adults.

Beyond the noted parallels to the Buddhist and Christian worldviews, it is also important to note how this "myth" diverges from some of the core values of these traditions. For example, in many respects *The Matrix* is a glorification of violence and patriarchal dominance. The one token female is, on the surface, notably androgynous or even masculine. And the graphic violence merited an "R" rating for the film. One might argue that the killings are not actual but analogous to killing the demons of one's mind or destroying the symbolic manifestations of hatred, greed, and delusion (i.e., Sakyamuni's encounter with Mara beneath the Bo tree on the eve of his enlightenment). The fact is, however, that each person killed within the Matrix is the death of a "real" person within the human battery chambers. I would contend that the mesmerizing process of destruction, amplified by the technology of VFX or "bullet time" photography, transcends metaphorical license and clearly cultivates a more literal form of violence. The moral dimension of the Buddhist eightfold path or the moral imperatives of Christianity are basically absent from the film narrative. It is here, as with all mythology, that we must pay due attention to the context of this myth and especially its commercial aims. The glorification of violence has clear commercial appeal to one of the primary target audiences of Hollywood producers—young teenage boys. So while on an abstract level, *The Matrix* indeed evokes many "religious" parallels to Christianity, Buddhism, and other mythological traditions, it also integrates arguably contradictory values of violence and male dominance for commercial (or other) ends. One might say that it glorifies some of the "social matrices" it purports to challenge.

This evident tension between the "religious" dimension of this myth, on the one hand, and the "Hollywood" and cultural elements of the film, on the other, speaks directly to the contextual nature of the mythologizing process. Myths are not the product of an individual author but a collective representation developed over time. Myths are always produced in "institutional" contexts. Thus, they are the by-product of a dialectical process that often yields internally conflictive elements.

With all that said, the parallels between *The Matrix* and Buddhism make it a useful tool for comprehending some of the most insightful teachings of the latter. The Matrix is a metaphor for many of the culturally programmed "realities" that our consciousness tells us are ultimately real. They constitute "the world that has been pulled over your eyes to blind you from the truth."

From a Buddhist perspective, we often fail to see the interdependent web that links each and every sentient being. We impute a false degree of permanence onto things of the world—objects, our claims of truth, our conceptual systems, even the independent status of our "selves"—that leads to egotism, desire, attachment, and suffering. We must first open our eyes and wake up to the "matrix" that may indeed be imprisoning each of us. Given the chance, which pill would you take . . . blue or red? Every moment, the choice is yours.

SOURCES

BOOKS

Williams, Paul. *Mahayana Buddhism: The Doctrinal Foundations* (London: Routledge, 1989).

Keenan, John. *The Meaning of Christ: A Mahayana Theology* (Maryknoll, New York: Orbis Books, 1989).

Griffiths, Paul. *On Being Mindless: Buddhist Meditation and the Mind-Body Problem* (La Salle, Illinois: Open Court, 1986).

ARTICLES

Ostwalt, Conrad. "Armageddon at the Millennial Dawn." In *The Journal of Religion and Film*, vol. 4, no. 1, (April 2000). Available at *www.unomaha.edu/~wwwjrf/armagedd.htm*.

Corliss, Richard, "Popular Metaphysics." *Time*, vol. 153, no. 15, April 19, 1999.

PETER J. BOETTKE

HUMAN

FREEDOM

AND

THE

RED PILL

The red pill or the blue pill? Responsibility or comfort? Reality or illusion? Every day we make our choices and the choices define who we are. Economist Peter Boettke argues that societies also have choices, and would do well to avoid the temptations of the blue pill . . .

NEO: "You mean this isn't real?"

MORPHEUS: "What is real? How do you define real? If you are talking about what you can feel, taste, smell, or see, then real is simply electrical signals interpreted by your brain."

MORPHEUS: "I didn't say it would be easy Neo, I just said it would be the truth."

NEO: "I can't go back, can I?"

MORPHEUS: "No. But if you could, would you really want to?"

CYPHER: "I know what you're thinking 'cause right now I'm thinking the same thing. Actually, to tell you the truth, I've been thinking the same thing ever since I got here. Why, oh why, didn't I take the blue pill!?"

We each have our fantasies. From travel agencies to prostitution and virtual-reality games, major industries have arisen to cater to our fantasy life. We all need to escape from reality every once in a while. Consumer demand for narcotics, alcohol, and even sports is fueled by a desire to escape everyday life. Like millions of other fans, I watched Michael Jordan's basketball career in utter amazement. From his winning shot in the 1982 NCAA finals as a college freshman to his last second shot to win the 1998 NBA title against the Utah Jazz, I could only imagine the thrill he experienced in achieving such a high level of athletic excellence.[1] Would I willingly plug myself into a machine that would enable me to "experience" that joy? Would I do so even if in "reality" I was only a body in a tank, plugged into a computer system that provided that "be like Mike" moment? I have dreamed of such a moment since I was a boy, and now I could experience it. So why not accept that bargain? And, if I say yes, am I simultaneously affirming the choice that Cypher makes in *The Matrix*?

Of course I (and millions of others) would plug in, if it entailed a momentary departure from reality. I could be like Mike for an afternoon or evening, and then return to my life. But this is *not* the choice we are confronted with in *The Matrix*. Instead we are confronted with an all-or-nothing choice. Either we *live* our life, or we *experience* life.[2] Once the deal is put this way, the obviousness of plugging in

---

1 Jordan still amazes basketball fans now, playing for the Wizards after returning to the game in 2001 at the age of 38.

2 I have been told of experiments with rats where they were confronted with the following choices—they could either learn to press a lever and receive food, or they could press another lever that would send an electronic stimulus that simulated sexual satisfaction. The rats would continually press on the second lever and starve to death. Human beings need not be rats. Even as staunch a utilitarian as John Stuart Mill argued that there was more to human betterment than experienced pleasure when he wrote: "It is better to be a human dissatisfied than a pig satisfied; better to be Socrates dissatisfied than a fool satisfied." (Mill, p. 10)

disappears. Depending on certain conditions, we could still see the logic of plugging in—e.g., a person diagnosed with a fatal disease, who has no immediate family, may prefer to plug in rather than suffer through the final stages of life alone. But again, this is not the choice we are confronted with in *The Matrix*. At best we get a one-time either/or decision, such as Cypher's. I either live my life as I have constructed it, or I experience a life constructed for me. At worst, you get no choice at all because you remain ignorant of your real existence as fuel for the AI's power plant.

The Matrix puts this choice before us in stark visual terms. The real world is tough and ugly, while the Matrix provides us with the experience of normal human life in 1999. If Neo chooses the blue pill, he doesn't have to experience eating goop inside the real world. He can continue to enjoy eating noodles at the local Chinese restaurant, safe from the knowledge that he's being fed intravenously. His reality as a "battery" is certainly worse than reality as a revolutionary fighter, but inside the matrix life as Mr. Anderson is one of material comfort compared to the harsh conditions on-board the hovercraft. Why should he choose the reality of fighting rather than the experience of living as a computer programmer?[3]

In this essay, I argue that one of the important lessons we should learn from contemplating the decision to take either the red or blue pill is the connection between individual freedom and responsibility, the link between living a free and responsible life and living a *meaningful* life. Living a meaningful life requires us to have the freedom to construct our life *and* be responsible for the decisions we

---

3 Neo's restless mind already has detected the unreality of the Matrix before he is freed by Morpheus. There is a "splinter" in his mind that he seeks to understand. The overwhelming number of humans in the Matrix are not the least bit uneasy. To convey the unreality of the Matrix, the Wachowski Brothers added a green tint to all scenes inside the Matrix and a blue tint to all scenes outside the Matrix to depict reality.

make in constructing that life. Any step away from that burden of responsibility is a step toward opting for the blue pill; it atrophies our humanity to that extent. This argument can be extended from individual choice to the realm of public choice with respect to political, legal, and economic institutions. Choosing between institutions is analogous to choosing between the red and blue pill; opting for "blue pill" institutions can have the same negative consequences on our humanity as when we choose the blue pill in our private lives. To take the red pill is to choose to take responsibility for our lives, both on the personal and larger social levels.

THE RELEVANCE OF *THE MATRIX* TO POLITICAL ECONOMY

Theoretical knowledge, especially in the disciplines of moral philosophy and political economy, advances through the use of thought experiments and imaginary constructions. *The Matrix* draws our attention to the thought experiment of Plato's cave. In Plato's simile of the cave, we are asked to consider the situation of prisoners chained since birth and unable to see anything but the images their controllers project against the wall as shadows from a tended fire. The prisoners do not know they are in fact prisoners; they are blind to their ignorance. When this ignorance is revealed, there is not immediate enlightenment, but instead outrage and disbelief.[4] A prisoner freed from the cave faces a tough transition, but once he adjusts to reality he can flourish. Liberation from ignorance is a precondition for nourishing our humanity. As Charles Griswold has put it: "Clearly,

---

4 Consider Neo's original reaction upon learning the truth from Morpheus. In the next scene, Morpheus apologizes, because he states that after a certain age the mind is unable to accept the truth and thus they don't attempt to rescue those individuals.

one must discover for oneself that one has been living in illusion, that one is not free but a slave of a system, that there exists the good and true by nature. Coming to the truth is a transformation of soul that is as much a discovery of self—that one has a soul, and that soul has a certain nature—as a discovery of what is real."[5] Only through this transformation can we attribute meaningfulness to our lives. That meaningfulness, however, is assigned through our being free and responsible individuals—people who must make choices in the face of nature and truth.

Robert Nozick also covered this ground in his justly celebrated *Anarchy, State and Utopia* with his example of the experience machine. Nozick's thought experiment is directly related to the Matrix because it entails being plugged into the machine and having neuropsychologists stimulate your brain to give you any experience you desire. You would really be just a body floating in a tank with electrodes attached to your brain, but you would experience all of life's desires. Nozick asks, "Should you plug into this machine for life, preprogramming your life's experiences?"[6] Nozick argues that once we think hard about the situation, we should *not* plug in for three reasons: (1) what matters for us is to *do* certain things, not just experience those things; (2) what matters is we want to *be* a certain type of person, we want to be courageous, kind, intelligent, witty, or loving— not a blob floating in a tank; and (3) what ultimately matters is that our imagination of what we want to achieve in our life is *unbounded*, whereas the experience machine will limit

5 Griswold, p. 8

6 Nozick, *Anarchy, State and Utopia*, p. 42. Note the either/or nature of Nozick's question, if the question was instead put as one entailing a choice on the margin Nozick modifies his answer. We do not need to engage reality 100 percent of the time (Nozick, *The Examined Life*, p. 121). The problem is not plugging into the experience machine per se, the problem would be not returning to reality from the experience machine. Not learning to make free choices and burden the responsibility for the choices made. Not constructing a life, but merely experiencing a life.

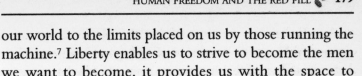

our world to the limits placed on us by those running the machine.[7] Liberty enables us to strive to become the men we want to become, it provides us with the space to incorporate the unknown and the unpredictable into our lives and modify our life plans; it instills in us a sense of responsibility as well as adventure. In a discussion of Nozick's experience machine, David Schmidtz asks us to recollect our visits to the zoo with small children. Aren't we often amazed at the bored reaction of small children to seeing the tigers and zebras in their confined space? These same children will squeal with excitement at watching a rambunctious squirrel foraging for stray food on the sidewalk or chasing another squirrel up a tree. "The kids know: The squirrel is real in a way zoo animals are not. Somehow, there is more meaning, more reality, in the wild—in experiences that have not been scripted, especially by someone else."[8] Gerald Erion and Barry Smith state bluntly that "Neither the experience machine nor the Matrix allows for genuine, meaningful action; instead they merely give the *appearance* of meaningful action."[9] Inside the Matrix, our contact with reality is denied in any meaningful sense and thus our lives are devoid of meaning.

---

7 When Morpheus fights with Neo in the training simulator he attempts to free his mind from the illusions of the Matrix, to learn that the Matrix is bounded by rules governed by their programmers, but as a human he can bend and break those rules. Neo asks whether this means he will be able to dodge bullets, and Morpheus replies that when he comes to fully understand who he is he will not have to. The human mind can step beyond the bounds that the rules of a program require. A criticism of hard Artificial Intelligence made by Roger Penrose runs along similar lines when he deploys Godel's theorem to challenge the idea that a mind can fully know itself. John Searle makes a different but equally compelling argument against hard AI when he points out the difference between syntactic clarity and semantic meaning. Human thought is grounded in semantic meaning, not just syntactic clarity. For a discussion of the relevance of the philosophy of mind to questions of political economy see Boettke and Subrick, "From Philosophy of the Mind to Philosophy of the Market."

8 Schmidtz p. 211

9 Erion, Smith p.26

And herein lies the relevance of the Matrix for political economy. Not only would we not plug in because of what it means to live a life, but once we think about what it means to construct a life we realize that we actually need certain social institutions. These are necessary for us to construct a meaningful life as well. Our ability to make *free* choices, to *do* certain things, to *become* the type of people we want to become and to *imagine* goals we hope to achieve is a function of the political and legal institutional context in which we find ourselves (which gives us the freedom to make the most of natural talents and material circumstances). While individuals may make responsible choices under any conceivable set of institutions, our ability to make morally meaningful choices and live a flourishing human life is not invariant with regard to the institutions. Our choice of institutions is analogous to our choice of taking either the red or blue pill. "Red pill" institutions that promote our freedom to choose are a *necessary* condition for human flourishing, whereas the "blue pill" institutions that attempt to script our lives tend to atrophy our humanity.[10]

---

10 Socialism and communism, for example, did not just lead to poor economic performance but atrophied the human moral sense. Political informants, party loyalists, and perpetrators of purges were often ordinary people who were lead to commit heinous acts because of the institutional arrangement. Sovietologists talk of the "dual reality" of life within the Soviet Union and the necessity for individuals to "live the lie"; even ordinary language was perverted to convey the fact that people had to live one way to survive and speak another way to conform to the official ideology. The original aspiration of communism was one of advanced material production, economic security, and social harmony between the classes, yet the reality was one of poverty and arbitrary power. Political leaders of the post-Lenin period made Cypher's choice and chose the illusion of power and relative affluence over the ugly reality of a failed ideology. Communism did not fail because humanity failed to live up to its ideal, but because its ideals failed to live up to humanity. On the history, collapse, and transition from communism in the former Soviet Union see Boettke, *The Political Economy of Soviet Socialism*, *Why Perestroika Failed*, and *Calculation and Coordination*.

SOME EMPIRICAL OBSERVATIONS ON FREEDOM AND FLOURISHING

This discussion of red- and blue-pill institutions is not as abstract as it may first appear. It is, in fact, very concrete when we understand the connection between institutions, human freedom, and economic growth. Institutions are required for us to live a free and responsible life. These very institutions also enable individuals to realize improvements in the productive capacity of mankind. Institutions and material means work together to lift individuals out of ignorance and squalor.

For much of history, human beings have lived in wretched poverty. The vast majority of individuals lived a life that was so filled with misery that they didn't even know the extent of their misery—like the prisoners in Plato's cave. The struggle for survival was hard, children either died before maturing or sacrificed their childhood to work; women who lived to adulthood often died in childbirth, and even as civilization advanced they continued to be denied access to education and opportunity; men were illiterate, bore the burden of difficult labor, and frequently died young. Life expectancy was short, and prospects for improvement of one's lot in life was negligible.

Mankind was able to overcome this miserable state because of the adoption of institutions of freedom— recognition of private-property rights, the establishment of a rule of law, and the opening of the economy to trading opportunities from afar.[11] The sad reality is that while mankind has found the way beyond its miserable existence, much of mankind still lives under wretched conditions in the underdeveloped world.[12]

---

11 The basic book on this subject in my opinion is Rosenberg and Birdzell.

12 See Easterly for a discussion of the human tragedy of underdevelopment.

It is not my purpose here to provide a detailed institutional explanation of why some nations are rich and other nations are poor, but instead simply to argue that an instrumentalist view of the institutions of economic freedom link tightly to the institutions necessary for human freedom. Put another way, *the material preconditions for human flourishing are produced by the same set of institutions that are necessary for us to effectively choose freely.* Without those institutions we will not only be denied the material means to move beyond the mere struggle for survival, but also *denied the social space for us to make meaningful choices—to construct our lives.*[13]

The relationship between economic freedom and economic growth is positive. Security of property and the freedom of contract, free pricing, low levels of regulation and taxation, stable currency and open international trade are positively correlated with economic growth throughout the world. Countries that adopt institutions that differ from this recipe perform decidedly worse. Moreover, the relationship between economic growth and human capabilities is also positively correlated. Life expectancy rises, nutritional content of the average diet improves, great strides are made in sanitation, and educational access for women and minorities increases.[14] Ignorance and squalor are overcome through modernization and economic development.

To connect this discussion to our earlier discussion of illusion and reality, we must recognize that without the modernization move, individuals remain chained inside

---

13 For an examination of the relationship between development and human freedom see Sen. His position deviates significantly from the one in this paper, but the topic is similar.

14 See Boettke, *Calculation and Coordination* for a discussion of these issues. Also see Boettke and Subrick, "The Rule of Law and Human Capabilities," for an examination of the relationship between the rule of law, economic growth, and human capabilities.

Plato's cave, watching images on the wall. Development breaks those chains, and development is only brought about by the adoption of certain key institutions. These institutions, in fact, are the mechanism by which our prisoners escape the cave and achieve enlightenment. As mentioned above, this transformation is not easy and often brings in its wake outrage and disbelief. Recent protests of globalization aside, however, we must realize that the greatest hope for lifting the world's poor from misery is the spread of *real* capitalism.[15]

THE FREEDOM TO RIGHT AND WRONG

Our choices are never as stark as the one Morpheus offers to Neo—blue pill or red pill. We often trade off the reality of the "red pill" and the responsibility to live a free life for the illusion of security the "blue pill" of socialism and the modern welfare state supposedly provides. I don't want to argue here about the efficiency of socialism, but instead focus attention on the impact on our ability to live meaningful lives once we adopt the institutions of socialism or even the mixed economy of the welfare state.[16] My argument is simple. Whenever we move away from notions of individual responsibility we lose something of ourselves. It is not just the incentive effect, once we are able to socialize the costs of our decisions that result in perverse consequences. The welfare state's "help" is tantamount to feeding the poor a blue pill.

---

15 See Norberg for a nice summary of the evidence on this claim. By real capitalism I mean an unhampered market economy and not the defense of corporations. Capitalism is not a defense of the corporate order, but an institutional regime that enables individuals to pursue their projects and realize the mutual benefits from exchange through voluntary cooperation.

16 For a documentary history of the economic assessment of socialism see Boettke, ed., *Socialism and the Market Economy*.

In order to make a moral choice we must also have the ability to make wrong choices. To do the right thing, in other words, we must have the freedom to do the wrong thing. If we don't have that freedom, then in what sense did we really *choose* the right thing? Our moral sensibility emerges through our experience with free choices.

We can argue that Cypher's choice was a poor one because he had the freedom to choose, in a way that we wouldn't argue that the police in the opening scene of the movie were choosing poorly because they attempted to arrest Trinity. In one instance a free choice was being made, in the other no choice at all was being made—the police were simply playing a pre-scripted role inside the Matrix.

In addition to learning to do the right thing, our experience of living with our choices teaches us prudence and other virtues associated with *thoughtful decision-making*.[17] The freedom to choose is directly tied to our accepting responsibility for our choices. If we are not responsible for our choices, our moral sense and our prudent self are truncated to our detriment as free individuals. F. A. Hayek stressed how the expansion of the corporate welfare state influenced individual psychology and threatened to transform individuals from being able to live free and responsible lives into entities within a "social" machine. Protection from the consequences of our choices results in a retardation of our humanity. In short, institutions that protect us from our choices distort our incentives and our fundamental humanity. "It is important to realize," Hayek argued, "that we are not educating people for a free society if we train technicians who expect to be 'used,' who are incapable of finding their proper niche themselves, and who regard it as somebody else's responsibility to ensure the appropriate use of their ability or skill."[18] To be truly

17 See Searle for a discussion of rationality and action.

18 Hayek p.81–82

"human" means to choose freely and bear responsibility for those choices. We may try to avoid the responsibility but we cannot if we hope to be the masters of our own lives. "It is doubtless because the opportunity to build one's own life also means an unceasing task, a discipline that man must impose upon himself if he is to achieve his aims, that many people are afraid of liberty."[19]

Moral esteem is worthless without freedom. In *The Matrix*, Cypher is the lowliest character. He is despicable. Is it because he turns his back on his friends and betrays their trust? We value trust in others precisely because there are always others who are untrustworthy. But Cypher's violation of the trust is a particularly egregious one. He makes his choice in full knowledge that he will achieve a better *experience,* not a better *life.* In his proposed deal with the "agents," he will not remember anything, and he will be programmed as a successful and powerful actor, but he will in reality be nothing more than a battery in the powerhouse. At the moment of his decision, he knows the full magnitude of his choice. Perhaps a life lived as a battery is a fitting future for someone who would make that deal. Cypher is choosing to not live a human life but to experience a life scripted by someone else. He is, in short, sacrificing his humanity. Neo, on the other hand, must choose between saving Morpheus and risking himself (as the Oracle foretold), and in making that choice he learns that he indeed is "The One," and his humanity is affirmed. As Erion and Smith state: "Cypher's decision is, in fact, *immoral.* In contrast, Neo's decision to face 'the desert of the real' allows him to undertake genuine action and have genuine experiences that give his life meaning, and thus a moral value."[20]

---

19 Hayek p.72
20 Erion, Smith p.27

Just as Neo must go through electronic stimulation to build up the muscles that have atrophied over the years of his life in the power plant, individuals who live under a situation under circumstances where the costs and benefits of their decisions are not internalized will experience an atrophying of their humanity. When we attempt to exchange our freedom for security we may in fact get neither. Ultimately, our humanity is lost.

CONCLUSION

Trinity corners Neo and whispers in his ear, "It is the question that drives us." And she is certainly correct. Nature has not endowed mankind with sharp teeth and claws, or thick and tough skin. Instead, we are at the mercy of nature. In brute struggle for survival with nature and other animals, we are one of the weaker species. But we are endowed with the facility to reason. This ability allows us to communicate with others, to cooperate with them, and to innovate in our dealings with nature (the uses of tools) and others (the relationships we form). It is our capacity to question and learn through both abstract deduction and experience that empowers us.

The Matrix is a wonderful artistic depiction of the basic human dilemma caused by the burden of free choice. If we take the "blue pill" and run from the burden, we don't live a meaningful life. We may experience a life, but not live it. If, on the other hand, we take the "red pill," we travel deep inside the rabbit hole and must cope with a reality of tough moral choices, decisions that sometimes go wrong, and relationships that lead to pain. But we also know the joys of adventure and achievement. Living a flourishing human life is only possible once we take Morpheus's challenge. Once we do, the question truly is not whether we can go back or not, but whether we would *want* to go back even if we could.

Morpheus's challenge is not limited to our private life. At a foundational level, our public choice of institutions is analogous to the individual choice between the red and blue pill. If we take the blue pill and do not adopt institutions that require us to make free choices and accept responsibility for those choices at an individual level, then our ability to live meaningful lives will be truncated and our moral sense atrophied. On the other hand, the establishment of guarantees of individual freedom in political, legal, and economic realms brings with it prosperity and an enhancement of our capabilities to live a flourishing human life.

SOURCES

BOOKS

Boettke, Peter, *The Political Economy of Soviet Socialism: The Formative Years, 1918–28* (Boston: Kluwer Academic Publishers, 1990).

———, *Why Perestroika Failed: The Politics and Economics of Socialist Transformation* (London: Routledge, 1993).

———, *Calculation and Coordination: Essays on Socialism and Transitional Political Economy* (London: Routledge, 2001).

———, ed., *Socialism and the Market Economy: The Socialist Calculation Debate Revisited*, 9 volumes (London: Routledge, 2000).

Easterly, William, *The Elusive Quest for Growth* (Cambridge, Massachusetts: MIT Press, 2002).

Hayek, Friedrich A., *The Constitution of Liberty* (Chicago: University of Chicago Press, 1960).

Mill, John Stuart, *Utilitarianism* (Indianapolis, Indiana: Hackett, 1979).

Norberg, Johan, *In Defense of Global Capitalism* (Stockholm: Timbro, 2001).

Nozick, Robert, *Anarchy, State and Utopia* (New York: Basic Books, 1974).

Nozick, Robert, *The Examined Life* (New York: Simon and Schuster, 1989).

Rosenberg, Nathan and Birdzell, L. E., *How the West Grew Rich* (New York: Basic Books, 1986).

Schmidtz, David, "The Meanings of Life," in David Schmidtz, ed., *Robert Nozick* (New York: Cambridge University Press, 2002).

Searle, John, *Rationality in Action* (Cambridge, Massachusetts: MIT Press, 2002).

Sen, Amartya, *Development as Freedom* (New York: Random House, 1999).

ARTICLES

Boettke, Peter, and John Robert Subrick, "From Philosophy of the Mind to Philosophy of the Market," *Journal of Economic Methodology*, vol. 9, no. 1, 2002.

——, "The Rule of Law and Human Capabilities," *Supreme Court Economic Review*, 10, 2003.

Erion, Gerald J., and Barry Smith, "Skepticism, Morality and *The Matrix*," in William Irwin, ed., *The Matrix and Philosophy* (Chicago: Open Court, 2002).

Griswold, Charles, "Happiness and Cypher's Choice: Is Ignorance Bliss?" in *The Matrix and Philosophy* (Open Court Publishing, 2002.

PAUL FONTANA

FINDING

GOD

IN

THE

MATRIX

Among the most enthusiastic fans of The Matrix *are devout Christians, who see numerous parallels between* The Matrix *and the story of Christ. Paul Fontana explores these fascinating parallels and reveals the critical role God plays in* The Matrix.

"Here are the bare bones of a tale that will be popular with the young everywhere: A man travels a lot, is often alone. He seeks spiritual comfort and avoids boring work. He is more intelligent than his parents and most of the people he meets. He encounters many queerly lovely hints that spiritual comfort really can be found."
— *Kurt Vonnegut,*
"Why They Read Hesse."[1]

In late August 1999 I went with some friends to see *The Matrix* at a cinema in New York's East Village. We had all seen the film a number of times, but we share the

1 Vonnegut, p. 107

philosophy that a movie worth watching once is worth watching over and over. When we entered the theater ten minutes before showtime, I was amazed to find that there was not a seat in the house. *The Matrix* had been open for over four months already and yet it was standing room only. After the film began to play it was apparent that nearly everyone there had seen the movie countless times because the audience cheered and yelled with all the zeal that consumes cult-film fans.

In its opening weekend alone *The Matrix* made over fifty million dollars; it sold more copies on DVD in the United States and Great Britain than any film that preceded it. Surprised by the popular reception of *The Matrix,* film critic Steven Armstrong writes that "even the best action and sci-fi movies come and go, and most cult films bomb at the box office before finding a loyal audience on video, but *The Matrix* has broken all the rules."[2]

Critical reception of *The Matrix* was mixed and its notable success with popular audiences occurred more in spite of its reviews than because of them. Janet Maslin of the *New York Times* echoed the comments of many of the film's critics when she said that "*The Matrix* should be commended for its special effects but it lacks depth in other crucial areas."[3] The Academy of Motion Picture Arts & Sciences made its own statement when it gave *The Matrix* Oscars for its special effects, sound, and editing, but did not even nominate it in any category that pertained to the substance of the film.

One reason young audiences received *The Matrix* so well is its placement in a popular genre of movies such as *The Graduate, Ferris Bueller's Day Off, Trainspotting, Fight Club*, and *American Beauty* (among many others), which advocate free

---

2 Armstrong

3 Maslin

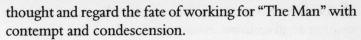

thought and regard the fate of working for "The Man" with contempt and condescension.

Yet, beyond the surface message of "free your mind" there is a theme that runs much deeper. Anyone with a religious background can notice some of the more obvious Biblical parallels in *The Matrix*. However, as one analyzes the overarching themes in the movie it becomes apparent that *The Matrix* resounds with the elements of Jewish and Christian apocalyptic thought. The theology of *The Matrix* is informed by the concerns of apocalyptic expectation characteristic of this period, specifically hope for messianic deliverance, restoration and establishment of the Kingdom of God. This film is surprisingly true to Biblical theology—despite its unorthodox appearance. And, despite its seemingly secular plot, God isn't absent from *The Matrix*. As we shall see, the Wachowskis have subtly but unmistakably made God a critical element of the film.

The Matrix's character allegory provides the most evidence of Christian themes, and the natural place to begin is with Neo. Early in the film Morpheus announces to Neo that he is "The One," the person who can manipulate the Matrix and liberate humanity. In ancient Israelite tradition there was an expectation that a great military leader—probably from the Davidic line—would arise and restore Israel to its former glory while subjugating all of Israel's enemies.[4] This person was referred to as the messiah ("anointed one" in Hebrew) because anointing was a sign of kingliness. All the canonical Gospels report that when Jesus arrived in Jerusalem the people hailed him as a king; they hoped he was the one who would finally free Israel from foreign rule and restore it to its proper relationship with God. Evangelists

---

4 Cf. Isaiah 9, 11, 42, 61

like Paul went to great lengths to explain that Jesus' mission was not at all military. However, the claim that Jesus was the Messiah was confusing because no one in ancient Israel expected a suffering spiritual king—Jesus did nothing to further the cause of a sovereign Israel. In many ways Neo is closer to the military messiah that Israel expected than to the soteriological[5] role that Jesus fulfilled.

In the second scene of the movie we meet this would-be Christ figure. Thomas Anderson works as a software programmer and moonlights as "Neo," a notorious computer hacker. Our first equation of Neo with Jesus happens at first sight; the audience sees him asleep at his computer with music blaring in his headphones.[6] An anonymous message on the computer wakes Neo: "Wake up, Neo . . . The Matrix has you . . . knock, knock. . . ." This message is followed immediately by a loud knocking at his door. As he is greeted by Choi (someone looking for illegal computer software) we have our first messianic foreshadowing. As Choi thanks Neo, he emphatically states: "Hallelujah! You're my savior, man. My own personal Jesus Christ!" There is even an indication of the Markan[7] messianic secret; Neo warns Choi not to tell anyone about the transaction and Choi responds, "Yeah, I know. This never happened. You don't exist." This scene craftily hints at Neo's messianic significance.

In what is no doubt a subtle Biblical pun, Neo's introductory scene is followed by his call narrative. Though this is not a Jesus reference per se, many important figures

---

5 Soteriology is the doctrine of salvation made possible by Christ's sacrifice. —Ed.

6 The fact that it is "Massive Attack" playing in his headphones foreshadows Neo's role later in the film.

7 In the Gospel of Mark, Jesus is reticent to accept the title of Messiah. For example, when Peter confesses his belief that Jesus is Christ, the Messiah, Jesus instructs him to reveal this information to no one. Most Biblical scholars believe that Jesus' reluctance to be identified as Messiah has much to do with him avoiding the label of military messiah that dominated the popular imagination of Jewish messianic expectation.

in the Bible are "called" by God—sometimes with an annunciation by an angel, others by God directly—and given instructions. (For example, Abraham is called and told to go out into the land of Canaan.)

In the archetypal format of a call narrative, as illustrated in the calling of Abraham[8] in the Hebrew Scriptures and the Virgin Mary in the New Testament,[9] God states the name of the person being called and that person responds, "Here I am, Lord." In the version of this type-scene played out in *The Matrix,* the angel is replaced by a Federal Express agent who says "Thomas Anderson?" Neo replies, "That's me." When he opens the package he finds a cellular phone. He immediately receives his "call" from Morpheus wherein he is given instructions.

As the film progresses, the audience receives conflicting data as to whether or not Neo is "The One." To confirm Neo's "Oneness," Morpheus (whose faith in Neo is unwavering) brings Neo to see the Oracle. The Oracle's message to Neo is mixed: she implies (but never says) that he is *not* The One. She further adds the bad news that Morpheus, who is convinced that he has found The One, will offer his life to save Neo, and that Neo must decide if he will let Morpheus die or will give his own life in exchange. This becomes theologically significant in the film's last scenes.

However, before the grand, climactic confirmation that Neo is The One, there is an overt allusion to the miracle of the raising of Lazarus.[10] When Morpheus is taken captive, Neo realizes that the Oracle's prophesy is coming true, and goes to rescue him in what turns out to be the most dramatic and exciting action sequence in the film. During this scene,

8 Genesis 12:1, 22:1

9 Luke 1:38

10 John 11

Morpheus is held in a long, narrow room much like the cave in which Lazarus was buried. Neo swoops down in a helicopter to rescue a nearly comatose Morpheus. Neo's command "Morpheus, get up! Get up!" echoes Jesus' command, "Lazarus, come out!"[11] In both these instances it is the power that emanates from the agents of salvation (Neo and Jesus) that raises the men in the tombs who each come out with their hands and feet bound.[12] From a theological standpoint, both these instances mark a turning point in the careers of Jesus and Neo. In the Gospel of John the raising of Lazarus is seen as the climax and turning point of Jesus' ministry because it is during this last and most dramatic of Jesus' miracles that he attracts a large enough crowd to become a public threat.[13] Correspondingly, in *The Matrix* this dramatic and seemingly impossible rescue—which is nothing short of miraculous—banishes any last doubts that Trinity and Tank had about Neo being The One. Also, it is here that the agents who had previously set their sights only on Morpheus turned their attention to Neo.

The scenes that follow contain many of the elements of the passion narratives.[14] Neo boldly and violently enters the government building with the dramatic flair of Christ cleansing of the Temple—though Neo's actions are admittedly more violent. This comparison is less far-fetched than it might appear, because the Temple and this government building are centers of the governing authorities that Jesus and Neo oppose. Of course, in Jesus' eyes the Temple is inherently good but has become corrupt, whereas the government building is the home of a purely evil power with no redeeming qualities.

---

11 Ibid., 11:43

12 Ibid., 11:44

13 Ibid., 11:48,53; cf. 12:21

14 The passion narratives are the anecdotes about Jesus' life and work that are found in the Gospels.

In another parallel with the passion narratives, Neo, like Jesus, is killed, resurrected and ascends bodily into the sky. In the scene following Morpheus's rescue, Neo is left to face Agent Smith alone. After a showdown in a subway station, Neo flees to a nearby motel to room 303,[15] where there is a viable exit. Upon entering the room, Neo is shot by Agent Smith and he falls and dies. The prevalent screen placement of "303" should alert the sensitivities of any New Testament—savvy audience member who is aware of the numerical significance of the number three in the Gospels. Since it would not be possible within the plot of the film to have Neo dead for three days, this symbolic visual cue is all the film needs to provide to alert the audience members to the significance of this momentary death.[16] Yet, like in the Gospels, this death is not the end of the story, because moments later Neo comes back to life. In all the Gospels, it is a woman or a group of women who find the empty tomb and are the first to see Jesus (and/or a heavenly figure). *The Matrix* does not miss this opportunity to draw a further parallel between these two stories. In a dramatic Pieta fashion, Trinity holds the lifeless Neo and is the first to see him as he comes back to life.

While we are looking further at the resurrection parallel, it is significant to note the differences between the pre- and postresurrection Neo. Though all four canonical Gospels tell of the resurrection, its true centrality within Christianity theology can be traced to Paul. In First Corinthians 15, which is one of the most theologically significant passages of the New Testament, Paul explains the centrality of the resurrection—both Jesus' and the full resurrection of

15 In the first scene Trinity was also in room 303 of an abandoned motel. Here we have the envelope sequence: the film ends where it began.

16 Like the Gospels, the makers of The Matrix make it clear that Neo really is dead (literally flat-lined). If he just rallies after getting shot that would not be as miraculous, just as it would not have been significant if Jesus or Lazarus just "swooned' and were then resuscitated.

believers at the end of days—to Christian belief.[17] The significance of this passage for our discussion is Paul's idea of what the resurrected body will be like. He uses the enigmatic phrase "*soma pneumatikon*,"[18] which is translated in the New Revised Standard Version as "spiritual body." Scholars have spilled much ink in arguing what exactly Paul envisioned a *soma pneumatikon* to be. However, we need not concern ourselves with the details of this debate here but merely need to compare Paul's description of the *soma pneumatikon* to the characteristics of the risen Neo. Comparing the fleshly body to the resurrected body, Paul writes: "What is sown is perishable, what is raised is imperishable. It is sown in dishonor, raised in glory. It is sown in weakness, raised in power."[19]

When we view the risen Neo in light of Paul's description of the *soma pneumatikon*, we find remarkable similarities. The postresurrection Neo is able to do things that were unimaginable in his former life, such as stopping bullets with a command, jumping inside an agent's body and exploding it, and ascending into the sky at will. We know that the risen Neo is "imperishable," because there is nothing that the agents can do to hurt him. After they try shooting him, Agent Smith lunges at Neo, but Neo effortlessly fights him off with one hand behind his back. This postresurrection Neo even has an unmistakable radiance about him, though not like the brilliant white reported of the risen Jesus.[20]

Just as the disciples only understand Jesus' predictions about the Temple after Easter morning,[21] Neo's resurrection make sense of the things he was told earlier by Morpheus

---

17 I Corinthians 15:12–19

18 Ibid., 15:44

19 Ibid., 15:42b–43

20 Matthew 28:3, Mark 16:5, Luke 24:4, Acts 26:13

21 John 2:22

and the Oracle. For example, Neo asks, "Are you saying I can dodge bullets?" and Morpheus responds: "I'm saying, when you're ready, you won't have to." This exchange foreshadows Neo's postresurrection changed nature.[22] We know that Neo is only "ready" after his resurrection, because just moments earlier he tried dodging bullets and was hit by one. But after his resurrection he is indeed ready, and just as Morpheus predicted, untouchable by bullets. All postresurrection appearances of Neo clearly indicate that his body is raised in "power, glory, and imperishability." The things Neo does after his resurrection are only possible for a *soma pneumatikon*, because even Neo's powerful fleshly (i.e., virtual) body is still nothing compared to his postresurrection body.

When we combine the above-quoted prophesy of Morpheus with the prediction given by the Oracle that Neo's full potential will only be realized in his "next life" (that is, after his resurrection), we get a clear picture that the death and resurrection of Neo *had* to happen in order for the war to eventually be won. In other words, unless Neo was killed and resurrected, the war could not be won, because Neo only reaches his state of full actualization after the resurrection. The inevitability and necessity of the Passion/Easter events is a theme well known in the Gospels. They also tell us that Jesus freely gave himself up to be killed so that all may partake in the Kingdom of God. We see this sacrificial element in *The Matrix* passion story; as Neo goes to save Morpheus, he does so despite the forewarning of the Oracle that he will have to sacrifice his own life. Further, because it is the codes to Zion that the agents want (so that they can obliterate human civilization), Neo's self-sacrifice saves humankind.

---

22 The Oracle's prediction that Neo's "got the gift" but is waiting for his next life is also illuminated and proven true after he is resurrected.

Another resurrection similarity is that neither the disciples nor Morpheus were expecting the messiah to die or be resurrected, because there was no explicit prediction of this given by the scriptures or the Oracle. Though the messianic texts of the canonical Hebrew Scriptures are varied, vague, and few, none even hint that the messiah will be executed and/or resurrected. The fact that in all four Gospels the disciples are frightened and confused by Jesus' death and then subsequently surprised by his postresurrection appearances strongly suggests that none of Jesus' disciples were expecting the resurrection. We see the same shock and utter confusion in Morpheus when Neo is killed—"It can't be!"—which indicates that in all the prophecies he received from the Oracle he was never told of the coming death and resurrection of The One.

The final similarity to note between the Gospels and *The Matrix* is their respective endings. The last shot of *The Matrix* (Neo flying up into the sky) directly follows the narrative of Mark, Luke, and Acts, which all tell of the ascension of the risen Jesus.

One notable dissimilarity which needs to be mentioned is that though the actions of Neo's life mirror those of Jesus, the eschatological[23] significance of Neo—as the one whose return will end the battle and usher in a new age of peace— is much more closely aligned with that of the risen Christ expected in the second coming. Some people might object to the idea of a supposed Jesus figure shooting people with guns. However, violent destruction of God's enemies was a live option for establishing the Kingdom of God and the

---

23 Eschatology is a belief or doctrine that concerns itself primarily with an apocalyptic end of the world. Jesus' eschatological significance is easily located; he promised to return to rapture the faithful, signaling the beginning of Armageddon and the end of the world. Judas' betrayal is evidence that he did not believe Jesus could make good on this promise. —Ed.

fact that Jesus did not do this led to confusion among his followers.[24]

Though Morpheus wears a number of allegorical hats throughout the film, his most prevalent role is John the Baptist, especially John as he appears in the Fourth Gospel. The role of John the Baptist in the Fourth Gospel is to be a witness to Jesus, a witness to the light.[25] John downplays his own importance, and makes it clear that his only duty is to make way for the coming of Jesus. These following verses summarize John's mission:

> "Among you stands one whom you do not know, the one who is coming after me; I am not worthy to untie the thong of his sandal. . . ."[26]

> The next day he saw Jesus coming toward him and declared "Here is the lamb of God who takes away the sins of the world! This is of whom I said 'after me comes a man who ranks ahead of me because he was before me.'"[27]

Morpheus and John the Baptist both take on the role of announcer of the coming savior; they both display unwavering certainty that Neo/Jesus is The One. Morpheus's faith certainty does not waver throughout the film even when Neo doubts that he is The One. Morpheus also expresses a particular reverence to Neo similar to that which John the Baptist showed Jesus.

---

24 In *The Climax of the Covenant* N. T. Wright points out that the Qumran War Scroll speaks of military tactics and establishing the kingdom of God in the same sentence (p. 306).

25 John 1:7

26 Ibid., 1:26–27

27 Ibid., 1:29–30

Though this parallel works well for certain aspects of Morpheus's role, Morpheus also assumes a more complex and extensive relationship with Neo (guru, leader, substitutionary sacrifice) than John had with Jesus. While John quickly disappears from the plot of the Gospels and is killed in obscurity off scene, Morpheus remains in the center of the drama and lives to the end.

It's fairly easy to pinpoint the connections between Morpheus and Neo and specific characters found in the Bible. Trinity, however, can be a bit more vexing. While her name certainly resonates with Christian mythos, the word "trinity" does not actually appear in the Bible. Rather, it's the name that Christians have given that which they understand to be the Godhead. One really can't argue that Trinity exhibits characteristics displayed by Christ, God, and the Holy Ghost. But the word "trinity" came about after Christ sent the comforter (the Holy Ghost) after his ascension. Christians had to find a way to explain how God, Christ, and the Holy Spirit could all be "God" and yet maintain their basic monotheistic doctrine. The Holy Ghost, or Holy Spirit, is the more comforting and spiritual entity of the trinity—these are certainly characteristics that can be attributed to Trinity. But this connection is tenuous at best. Could Trinity have more in common with Mary Magdalene?

There is a knee-jerk reaction to equating Trinity with Mary Magdalene, because they are both prominent women in a world of men. While there is something to this allegorization, it is also problematic. Though Mary Magdalene's historicity is not doubted due to her appearance in Matthew, Mark, and John (and perhaps in Luke), we actually know very little of her relationship with Jesus and her role in early Christianity. What the Gospels do tell us is that she was with Jesus for the time of his public ministry and that it was she who found the empty tomb and was the first to see Jesus. John further reports that it was Mary (no last name) who anoints Jesus with her hair before he is killed.[28]

Trinity mirrors this elusive role—she is with Neo when he is killed and she is the first to see him when he is resurrected.[29] Further, her embracing of Neo as he comes out of the Matrix echoes the Gospel of John wherein Mary Magdalene runs to embrace the risen Jesus. Trinity also appears to anoint Neo when she tears her clothes to wipe his head. The use of her clothes is similar to the personal giving of Mary Magdalene, who uses her hair.

One notable dissimilarity is that even though the Gospel stories of Mary Magdalene have been carefully examined, there is no indication that her relationship with Jesus was sexual. Though some would (and certainly do) argue differently, there simply is no textual evidence found in the New Testament to substantiate the claims of a sexual relationship between them. Therefore the kiss Trinity gives Neo (which hints at a future relationship) tends to further obscure rather than strengthen her allegorical equation to Mary Magdalene.

Trinity's character seems to be a mixed bag of subtle Biblical references; it's very unlike the clear match between Cypher and Judas, the betrayer.

———

The Oxford English Dictionary reports a number of meanings for the word "cypher" (or cipher): "1. A method of secret writing . . . 2. A secret message . . . 4. An obsolete name for zero . . . " The "secret" applies both to Cypher and Judas:

---

28 John 12:1–6

29 One could make the case that it was somehow through Trinity's power that Neo comes back to life. In this case she would have to be allegorized as God–an assertion which is further strengthened by her name which is overtly theistic.

Cypher's clandestine rendezvous with Agent Smith mirrors Judas's secret meeting with the high priests where he makes arrangements to betray Jesus.[30] Also, Cypher, like Judas, is a "zero," because "it would have been better if he had not been born."[31, 32]

Both Cypher and Judas are paid for their actions. In the Gospel of Matthew Judas receives thirty silver pieces to turn sides. In a bit of ironic humor, Cypher gets a nice dinner and the opportunity to be reincarnated (or, more precisely, rein*virtuated*) as an actor. The fact that both are paid for their actions highlights their common greed, selfishness, and myopia.

Moreover, neither believes for a moment that the person he is betraying has any ontological,[33] eschatological, or soteriological significance. Unlike the other disciples, Judas is never recorded referring to Jesus as "Lord."[34] Even at the Last Supper, when Jesus predicts his betrayal and all the disciples say "Surely not I, Lord," Judas proclaims: "Surely, it is not I, Rabbi."[35] Right from the outset of *The Matrix* Cypher makes it clear that he does not have any faith in Neo. When Trinity tells him that Morpheus believes Neo is The One, Cypher replies, "We're gonna kill him. Do you understand that!?" When meeting in private with Neo,

---

30 Mark 14:10, Matthew 26:14, Luke 22:4

31 Mark 14:20b

32 Though it could be argued that without Cypher's betrayal, the sequence of events that led to Neo's death and resurrection would never have been set into motion. Likewise, without Judas's kiss Christ would ostensibly not have been crucified and then risen to save the souls of humanity. Thus, weren't Cypher and Judas born to fulfill a certain role in a divine plan?

33 Ontology is the metaphysical discourse on the nature of being—for Christ to have ontological significance would mean that he answers the questions raised when considering the nature of existence. In Christian doctrine, Christ himself is the answer. —Ed.

34 "The Matrix as Messiah Movie" (awesomehouse.com/matrix)

35 Matthew 26:25

Cypher mocks the whole idea of "The One," saying: "So you're here to 'save the world!' Jesus, what a mind job! What do you say to something like that!?" Neither Judas nor Cypher believed that the object of their betrayal was the savior of the world or, presumably, they would not have gone through with their actions.

The particular elements of Judas played out in Cypher rely on both Johannine and synoptic material.[36] In the story of the Last Supper, the Beloved Disciple asks Jesus who his betrayer will be. Jesus responds, "It is the one to whom I give this piece of bread when I have dipped it in the dish."[37] After Jesus makes this identification, Judas immediately leaves to meet with the authorities, "and it was night".[38] Cypher and Neo's version of the Last Supper (where they sip moonshine) alludes to this identification of the betrayer; immediately following this scene, Cypher meets with Agent Smith. Further, Neo drinks this liquor even though it tastes like gasoline, thus echoing Jesus' prophetic statement "Am I not to drink from the cup my father has given me?."[39]

Allusions to the synoptic accounts of Judas can be seen in Matthew, Mark, and Luke's report that Judas identified Jesus to the authorities by embracing him with a kiss. The nervous smile that Cypher flashes at Neo (on which the camera lingers) just as he alerts the agents as to their whereabouts with his cell phone is reminiscent of the betrayal with a kiss.

The only qualification about equating Cypher with Judas is that Morpheus, not Neo, is the person for whom the agents are specifically looking. This is not, however, fatal

---

36 The first three Gospels are referred to as the synoptic Gospels, because they share such similar content. John, the fourth Gospel, differs drastically from the first three.

37 John 13:26

38 John 13:30

39 John 18:11

to the allegory because in turning over Morpheus, Cypher is betraying the whole crew and all of humanity.

———

The rest of Morpheus's crew—Tank, Dozer, Apoc, Switch, and Mouse—approximately fit into the role of the disciples. Of course, there are not twelve, so we cannot take this analogy too far. However, there are two other noteworthy similarities. First, it is worth mentioning that among Jesus' disciples, each of the Gospels reports a pair (or pairs) of brothers. The fact that there are brothers within the small crew of Morpheus does not seem coincidental.

Second, just as the twelve disciples and the general public were confused about Jesus' nature, Morpheus's crew share mixed opinions about Neo. The two extremes in *The Matrix* are polarized by Trinity, who believes from the beginning that Neo is The One, and Cypher, whose last line is "No, I don't believe it!" Everyone else falls somewhere in between. In the synoptic Gospels, Jesus asks his disciples, "who do you say that I am?" Peter answers, "the Messiah . . ."[40] Jesus rewards Peter's faith by declaring that on this "rock" (which is a word play on Peter[41]) he will build his church. Shortly after Peter's declaration, each of the synoptics also report an event wherein Jesus is transfigured before Peter, James, and John, who then have the decisive pre-Easter "aha!" moment of the Gospels.[42] The name "Tank" suggests the same sort of power and stability that Peter has, and indeed there are some parallels between these two. Most noteworthy is *The Matrix* version of transfiguration wherein

---

40 Mark 8:28, Matthew 16:16, Luke 9:20, cf. John 1:41

41 Peter is from the Greek Petros, meaning "rock." Peter's name was actually Simon, but Christ renamed him Peter because of its etymology.

42 None of the disciples expected Jesus' resurrection, as evidenced by their intense sorrow following the crucifixion. The big 'aha!' moment arrived when Jesus appeared to them—they realized that he was truly the Son of God.

Neo amazes Tank as he miraculously rescues Morpheus and Trinity from the agents' building; Tank's joy and certainty is expressed in the phrase "I knew it. He's The One." The fact that Neo pulled off this rescue is Tank's (and the audience's) decisive "aha!" moment that Neo indeed is The One, as Morpheus predicted.

———

The final characters of this allegorical scheme are the agents. The closest Biblical parallel is to Satan (or the devil, or the Antichrist), but this is not at all a perfect fit. The Apocrypha and the New Testament contain conflicting and varied understandings of Satan, so it is difficult to locate a starting point in this allegorization. In the synoptic Gospels, Satan plays the role of the tempter who attempts to foil Jesus' earthly mission before it begins by offering him worldly power in exchange for his worship. Neo is offered a similar "deal" by Agent Smith, but he too refuses to cooperate with the powers of evil.[43]

The synoptic Gospels also tell us of numerous instances of demonic possession, which are mirrored by the agent's ability to possess the bodies of anyone hardwired to the system. However these two meanings and uses of "possession" are wholly dissimilar beyond the surface.

One interesting parallel with the three agents is that in the Book of Revelation there is an "unholy trinity" made up of dragon/Satan, the First Beast, and the Second Beast,[44] who are defeated by the risen Christ just as the risen Neo defeats the agents. However, this too is approximate.

The true difficulty with equating the agents with Satan is that the agents are not really the enemy in *The Matrix* in the same way that Satan is the enemy of God in Biblical

43 "The Matrix as Messiah Movie"
44 Revelation 12–13

theology.[45] The true enemy in this film is not a being at all but rather a larger, self-conscious computer system. The death of Agent Smith in no way signifies that the war is over, but something more akin to a turning of the corner: now humanity finally has a chance. This is unlike the Book of Revelation, where the death of Satan is the final hurdle before the creation of the New Heaven and the New Earth.

I believe that in this particular case it will be prudent to resist our allegorical urge to cast the three agents as specific Biblical characters, and instead view them as generally representing agents of evil, who must be defeated on the way to the realization of human freedom.

———

The *Nebuchadnezzar* and the city of Zion are also Biblical allusions of great import; though we've only heard a bit of Zion in the first film, it's sure to play a bigger role in the coming sequels.

The name "Nebuchadnezzar" first appears in the Bible in the Second Book of Kings. As king of the Babylonian Empire, it was Nebuchadnezzar who led the armies that sacked Jerusalem and exiled the two remaining tribes of Jacob, which inhabited the southern Kingdom of Judah. Nebuchadnezzar's name appears often in the three major prophets and most of the minor prophets. The Babylonian Empire (and therefore its leader, in turn) was frequently used as catch phrase and pseudonym for present evil authorities, just as we might nowadays call any adversary a "Nazi."[46]

---

45 I use the phrase "Biblical theology" to get around the fact that there is no single Biblical consensus on who Satan is or what is the extent of his power/freedom. The idea that there are equally powerful forces of Good and Evil competing for sovereignty in the universe is a dualistic, Eastern notion unknown to the Bible.

46 In Revelation, though the evil empire is called Babylon, it is widely agreed that the author intended Rome. Likewise, Daniel wrote about the Temple desecration of Antiochos IV Epiphanes, though he refers to this king as "Nebuchadnezzar." For a modern parallel, *M*A*S*H* was set in the Korean War, though it was a critique of the Vietnam War.

Why would the filmmakers name this ship after an agent of destruction, when Morpheus's mission is one of freedom? Clearly Morpheus and his crew exist on the side of goodness; the artificial intelligence that enslaves the planet is evil and needs to be defeated. The use of this name in reference to goodness is problematic. The solution I propose is something of a subtle point in Biblical theology that runs counter to common wisdom. The answer lies not in the Book of Kings but in the prophets, especially Jeremiah.

In ancient Israelite cosmology there was no post-enlightenment understanding of a natural world governed by natural forces. The deistic notion that God exists on a transcendent plane removed from the day-to-day affairs of the human realm was unknown. Instead, the Israelite's God was an ever-present reality, active in history and human affairs. In the mindset of Ancient Israel, nothing happens that God does not allow. In the words of Biblical scholar Dominic Crossan, "whatever happens to Jews in the contemporary world empire is interpreted in terms of God's punitive and slavific designs."[47] According to this worldview, then, the destruction of the Temple and the exile had to be explained within the parameters of justice. We find it to be the case in all of the major prophets that the exile and the Temple's destruction were just retribution for the people's (especially the kings') wickedness in worshiping false gods. Thus, if the exile occurred as part of God's plan, and was handed out as punishment by God, then Nebuchadnezzar was an agent of God's justice, like a bailiff in a courtroom. That is, Nebuchadnezzar did what God *wanted* Him to do. Speaking for God, Jeremiah tells the people: "if any nation or kingdom will not serve this king, Nebuchadnezzar of Babylon, and put its neck under the yoke of the king of

47 Crossan, p. 31

Babylon then I will punish them with the sword, with famine, and with pestilence, says the LORD, until I have completed its destruction by his hand."[48, 49]

In keeping with this theological framework, Nebuchadnezzar is an agent of God's wrath, just as "Death" is sent by God to punish the wicked in Revelation 6. God's blessing on King Nebuchadnezzar is the only theologically acceptable way to understand his victory over Judah, according to ancient Israelite theology.

Thus Morpheus's ship, the *Nebuchadnezzar,* has the dual connotation of having God's blessing ("we're on a mission from God") as well as an agent of mass destruction sent to wreak havoc on the corrupt establishment.

The word "Zion" has rich and varied meanings in the Bible. Perhaps the most consistent understanding of it appears in Psalm 76:2 as the dwelling place of the LORD. Like Israel itself, Zion is both a place and a people; while Zion refers to the mountain that is home to the Temple, it is also often used to signify the whole people of Israel.[50] Yet, it is essential to understand that in both these terms the meaning is somewhat transcendent. Because of God's presence, Zion is a *cosmic* mountain as well as a *holy* people. Mount Zion was seen as existing in sacred space, apart from the confines of ordinary time. Thus even during the Exile, while the physical Temple lay in ruins, the cosmic Zion remained alive in the holy people during their time in Babylon.

––––––

48 Jeremiah 27:8

49 First-century Jewish historian Josephus also understood the destruction of the Second Temple in 70 c.e. as a sign that God has switched his Most Favored Nation Status to Rome (Jewish War).

50 Isaiah 51:16; cf. Levenson, p.137

Three important aspects of Biblical Zion traditions correspond directly to *The Matrix*. First, Zion is the promised land. According to the Book of Exodus, God was saddened to see His people enslaved under Pharaoh, so He promised them deliverance. Yahweh appoints Moses the leader of His people and assures them of passage to a land that flows with milk and honey.[51] This new land is Zion. In *The Matrix*, Tank echoes Yahweh's overarching promise to Israel in his line "If you live long enough you might even get to see it [Zion]." In both these cases Zion is held out as a promise of the way things can and will be in the future. But more than Zion, the geographic place, there was an understanding of a heavenly Zion, which remains in cosmic sync with its mundane twin. For this reason, a longing for Zion among ancient Israelites was a desire for union with God, whose presence was immanent in Zion.

Second is the utter importance of Zion. Though this is not strictly Biblical, there was rabbinic understanding that Zion was the blueprint from which the world was created. In the Talmud and Midrash, Zion is equated with the Garden of Eden, a paradise, the first of God's creation, the ultimate firewall that prevents the flood of chaos from overtaking the world. We see a similar understanding of the ultimate importance of Zion in *The Matrix*. Here, instead of being the first of God's creation, it is the last remaining human city. Since Zion is all humans have left, they will do anything to defend it; without Zion all is lost and the war is over. Tank is even willing to sacrifice his commander if it means that he can save this last human dwelling: "Zion is more important than you, me, even Morpheus."

After the fall of Jerusalem in 587 B.C.E., "Zion became a poignant symbol of national disgrace, of the contradiction between the great royal city of promise and memory and

51 Exodus 3:8

the pitiful ruins of the present era."[52] The third parallel between the Zion of the Bible and that of *The Matrix* is that the new Zion, wherein God's people will be restored to their intended glory, will be brought about by the messiah.

———

If we are to make the claim that *The Matrix* is a religious movie, we must ask, "So, where is God?" One might notice that no character in the movie can be properly allegorized as God. To explain this seeming omission, it is now time to move beyond allegory and begin to view *The Matrix* through the lens of first-century apocalyptic thought.

The observation that there is no mention of or reference to God in *The Matrix* leaves us with two options. First, we can conclude that there is no understanding of God in *The Matrix*. If we accept this claim then we effectively undermine the carefully constructed allegorical model to which we have devoted the previous pages, because if there is no God, then the idea of a messiah is meaningless. However, the second route of interpretation that we can take is that God is played by God. That is, the God figure in *The Matrix* is somewhat akin to the Judeo-Christian notion of an intangible God, who, though transcendent, is active in the affairs of human history and the economy of salvation.

Since this theistic read of *The Matrix* is not immediately apparent, such claim requires further explanation. Against the argument that an understanding of God exists in *The Matrix* is the fact that this film contains precisely as many references to God as the *Song of Songs*: none. Except for Morpheus's single, passing remark about "going to church" as one of the vacuous things that one can do within the Matrix, and the garden-variety blasphemy that peppers the film's dialogue, this film is free from theistic references of

---

52 Levenson, p.1102

any kind. Yet the key to finding God in *The Matrix* is not to look for God directly, but rather to observe God's presence in the general flow of the film.

To explain this point I must borrow a metaphor from astronomy: by definition, it is impossible to see a black hole. However, scientists have detected about a dozen black holes in space by charting the movements of the stellar bodies that orbit these black holes. The same can be done with God in *The Matrix*. Though we cannot readily see God *within The Matrix,* we can triangulate God's whereabouts by carefully observing the film's plot. The answer to the question "Where is God in *The Matrix?*" lies in certain theological issues that plagued the religious thinkers of the first century C.E.

———

The answer to this question does tend to change throughout the film. In the beginning of the film and during the two hundred years prior, God has been absent. But by the end of the narrative, God has returned.

The first of these realities, that God is absent, was a feeling held by the exiles of the sixth century B.C.E. N. T. Wright explains that for these people, "the present age was a time when the creator God seemed to have been hiding His face." The feeling of abandonment by God is quite common for people undergoing suffering.[53] This sentiment was uttered by Job's wife, who encouraged her husband to curse God and die[54] and was also held by the author of Psalm 22 who wrote the line (later made famous by Jesus' reiteration of it) "My God, my God, why have You forsaken me?"[55]

---

53 Isaiah 54:8
54 Job 2:9
55 Psalm 22:1

The feeling that "God is not with us or else this could not have happened" was surely felt by the people in the year 2199 of *The Matrix* just as it was felt by the exiles and others who have undergone intense suffering. It is a likely scenario that if humanity had to undergo two hundred years of exile and slavery, people would reach a unanimous conclusion that God was dead. If the word "God" had not totally fallen away from language as a meaningless concept, its mention would probably be an aggravating reminder of how naive the humans of old were about the fate of the world. For Morpheus's crew living in the year 2199, God was a belief of people long ago, and these people must have been wrong because this God, if there ever were such a being, has been absent for two centuries. Yet during the last moments of the film, in a subtle way, God reappears. In fact, God breaks into the action of the film a second and third time, in case the audience members missed this first appearance. The script provides us with all the clues we need to figure these out.

As the action of the film progresses, it becomes clear that Neo is the last hope of humanity. Other would-be messiahs have been tested and failed. The crew is getting impatient, and Cypher is ready to throw in the towel for the whole human race. Yet right when doubt reaches its high-water mark as Cypher is about to wipe out what is left of the human race by turning over Zion, God returns to the drama. In a twist of irony, when Cypher quips that it would "take a miracle" to stop him, Tank suddenly gets up and stops Cypher. (Enter God, stage left.) Later, as Neo is about to go back into the Matrix to rescue Morpheus, Tank asks, "so what do you need, besides a miracle?" Sure enough, this miracle is granted and Morpheus comes back alive. Finally, as it seems that all is lost in the final seconds of the movie, before activating the EMP as sentinels are about to destroy everyone aboard the *Nebuchadnezzar,* Neo comes back to life and the day is saved. All three of these events are true miracles, unexplainable without God's renewed favor.

The motif of a hero abandoning his people and then suddenly reappearing at the last moment to save the day is a cinematic convention which, in a very subtle way, has been employed here regarding the presence of God.

Though the people in *The Matrix* seem to be atheistic in that they betray no knowledge or belief in God, the film itself is deeply theistic in that it tells of the exiles returning to Zion. Or, to be more precise, Zion returning to its intended place on earth. Without God acting in the wings, it is impossible to explain Neo's resurrection and the other miraculous events of the film. Where did "The One" come from if not God? How could the Oracle have known what was coming without being in touch with a divine plan for salvation? God may have "hidden His face" for the two centuries preceding the commencement of the plot of *The Matrix*, but as of the finding of Neo, God returns and the restoration begins. Zion, which is currently buried underground, will soon be resurrected and restored to new life due to the intervention of The One, who has been sent by God. The remaining few human survivors in *The Matrix* are like the valley of dry bones in Ezekiel 37, the last remnants of what once was. It is with these building blocks that God will make humanity anew, free of the oppression of the Matrix.

The long-awaited restoration is at hand.

———

The Wachowski brothers by no means intended *The Matrix* as a subtle evangelical attempt to inject religious ideas into the popular psyche. To claim that *The Matrix* is a "Christian movie" would be to ignore the fact that it's replete with myriad other ancient religious and philosophical ideas, most of which are decidedly not Christian. One could easily have written an essay that views *The Matrix* through the lens of Gnosticism, Berkeley's metaphysics, Buddhism, Pythagorean numerology, Neoplatonism, and, no doubt, countless other ideological viewpoints.

It is interesting to note that during an online chat, the Wachowski brothers were asked: "are all the religious symbolism [sic] and doctrine thought throughout the movie intentional or not?" to which they responded, "most of it was intentional."[56] However, I will not make too much of this point because I believe that it ultimately does not matter if the religious motifs that have been discussed in the previous pages were added "intentionally" or not. I agree with the postmodern literary critics who posit that artists are influenced by "floating signifiers," which are ideas (such as the theme of exile and restoration) that permeate culture and are waiting to be digested and reused in a new way. It is highly possible that the Wachowski brothers felt that the (secular) motifs of restoration and new creation are themes that would resonate well with their target audience. They turned out to have been right.

A final question to consider: why did the Wachowski brothers choose to tell this particular story? That is, why combine the disparate vehicles of a quasi-religious story with high-speed ultraviolence? Would it not have been easier to simply choose one or the other? The likely answer is that the Wachowski brothers know their audience. Few young people today are interested in watching a Charlton Heston epic about the Bible. They included the excessive violence in the film for the same reason that farmers have to annually increase the strength of pesticides: young people have been so anesthetized by violence and irreverence that

---

56 Text of this conversation is available at awesomehouse.com/matrix.

the only way to speak to the young moviegoing public today is to up those standards by using cooler effects to make things sexier and faster or else nobody cares. For this reason, the blistering pace of the action scenes is something one *has* to include to reach a wide audience; innocuous films do not command much publicity. Yet, it is not the action or effects that sustain the enduring popularity of this movie. The action scenes in *Terminator 2* are just as exciting—and *T2* even has the apocalyptic motif of a man from the destroyed future coming back to warn us to turn back from our drive to make artificial intelligence. Yet after the film left theaters it failed to command nearly the dedicated cult following *The Matrix* has. The instant cult status of *The Matrix,* is, I believe, due to the subtext of exile, restoration and the fulfillment of eschatological hope, which, in a roundabout way, speaks to its audience.

What is essential to realize about the concept of restoration is that the point is not to make things as they were, but to make them as they are meant to be. The hope of getting things back as they were is reactionary—like Jay Gatsby's dream of reliving his past. The eschatological hope for restoration is for *radical newness*, a complete reversal of the evil present—this is the scenario that Isaiah and Revelation predict. Moreover, this is the hope of the exiles.

This applies to *The Matrix* because its target audience, the 18–35-year-old moviegoing middle class, are the members of Generation Exile. The idea that there is another way that things can be resonates well with us. Every vacuous hour of MTV, every superficial fashion magazine, every dot.com telling us to "click here!" further alienates us from any scrap of an idea that might lend some sort of transcendent or enduring meaning to our allotted eighty years. We have tried dyeing our hair, piercing our bodies, and moving to California, but nothing seems to endure. We long for something meaningful, whole, and new.

Though the Book of Revelation was written to Christian communities facing persecution from Roman authorities, its message of patient endurance—hold on, for the end is near and soon we will all be vindicated—is still widely popular with contemporary audiences who live under the yoke of oppression.[57] Similarly, the "Battle Hymn of the Republic," which is shot through with Biblical apocalyptic imagery, was sung by soldiers as they marched into battle in the Civil War because the promise that their war will someday be over was an empowering and revitalizing message.

In contemporary American society, as the stakes are lower, so too are the hopes for radical newness. However, for people imprisoned in office cubicles everywhere, the satire of *Dilbert* is embraced as a statement of their Sisyphus-like existence. It is popular because it explains the existential anxiety that can build up while one is doing meaningless work for a large corporation.

Young people watching *The Matrix* might notice that the cubicles they occupy at work bear a remarkable similarity to the pods in the power plant of *The Matrix*. They might think that the stale coffee they are served is the equivalent of the liquefied dead, which is intravenously fed to sustain the billions of human slaves who power the Matrix with their bioelectricity. Likewise, dress-down Fridays, two weeks of paid vacation, and stock options are there for the same reason that the Matrix itself was created: "What is the Matrix? Control. The Matrix is a computer-generated dream world built to keep us under control."

---

57 Boff, p. 17

It is not a coincidence that Thomas Anderson's boss at the Meta Cortechs Corporation has the same haircut as Agent Smith, and that the squeak made by the window washers is the same sound that Neo's hand makes against the glass as he is sucked out of his pod. The agents who enforce the tyranny of the Matrix are not entirely different from Mr. Rhineheart, who bawls Neo out and keeps him penned up in that little cubicle in his gray-on-gray office. The idea that there is another possibility, that by "freeing our minds" we can become spiritually enlightened and escape this prison, is a very attractive prospect to us, modern-day exiles. As Kurt Vonnegut points out, these are the bare bones of a story that will continue to resonate with young people everywhere.

SOURCES

BOOKS

Anchor Bible Dictionary, The, David Noel Freedman, ed. (New York: Doubleday, 1990).

Badham, Paul, *Christian Beliefs About Life After Death* (London: Macmillan Press, 1976).

Barrett, C. K., *A Commentary on the First Epistle to the Corinthians* (London: Adam and Charles Black, 1968).

Boff, Leonard, *Systematic Theology* (Orbis Books, 1987).

Borg, Marcus, *Meeting Jesus Again for the First Time* (San Francisco: HarperSanFrancisco, 1994).

Brown, Raymond, *The Gospel According to John* (New York: The Anchor Bible, Doubleday, 1976).

Crossan, Dominic, *Jesus: a Revolutionary Biography* (San Francisco: HarperSanFrancisco, 1994).

Fee, Gordon D., *The First Epistle to the Corinthians* (Grand Rapids, Michigan: Eerdmans Publishing Co., 1987).

Hays, Richard B., *First Corinthians* (Louisville, Kentucky: John Knox Press, 1997).

Koester, Helmut, *History and Literature of Early Christianity* (Berlin: Walter de Gruyter, 1995).

———, *History, Culture and Religion of the Hellenistic Age* (Berlin: Walter de Gruyter, 1995).

Levenson, Jon D. "Zion Traditions," in *Anchor Bible Dictionary*.

Longenecker, Richard N., ed., *Life in the Face of Death* (Grand Rapids, Michigan: Eerdmans Publishing Co., 1998).

Orr, William F. and James Arthur Walter, *The Anchor Bible, First Corinthians* (New York: Doubleday, 1976).

Perkins, Pheme, *Resurrection: New Testament Witness and Contemporary Reflection* (New York: Doubleday, 1984).

Rahner, Karl, *Foundations of the Christian Faith* (New York: Crossroads, 1972).

Schilling, S. Paul, *God and Human Anguish* (Nashville: Abingdon Press, 1977).

Sobrino, Jon and Ignacio Ellacuría, eds., *Systematic Theology* (New York: Orbis Books, 1993).

Torrance, Thomas F., *Space, Time and Resurrection* (Grand Rapids, Michigan: Eerdmans Publishing Co., 1976).

Vonnegut, Kurt, *Wampeters, Foma and Granfalloons* (New York: Dell, 1989).

Wright, N. T., *The New Testament and the People of God* (Minneapolis: Fortress Press, 1992).

———, *The Climax of the Covenant* (Minneapolis: Fortress Press, 1992).

ARTICLES

Armstrong, Stephen, "The Gospel According to Keanu," *London Sunday Times,* Feb. 13, 2000

Bowman, James, "Moody Blues," *American Spectator,* June 1999.

De Jonge, Marinus, "Messiah," in *Anchor Bible Dictionary*.

Devito, Robert A., "The Demarcation of Divine and Human Realms in Genesis 2–11," *Catholic Biblical Quarterly*, 1992.

Ebert, Robert, "The Matrix," *Chicago Sun-Times,* March 31, 1991.

Lim, Dennis, "Grand Illusions," *The Village Voice,* March 30, 1999.

Mare, W. Harold, "Zion," in *Anchor Bible Dictionary*.

Maslin, Janet, "The Reality Is All Virtual and Desperately Complicated," *New York Times*, March 31, 1999.

Nickelsburg, George, "Eschatology (OT)," in *Anchor Bible Dictionary*.

Osborne, Grant R., "Theodicy in the Apocalypse," *Trinity*, 1993.

Perkins, Pheme, "Gnosticism," in *Anchor Bible Dictionary*.

Schweitzer, R. Eduard, "Body," in *Anchor Bible Dictionary*.

Segal, Alan F., "Paul's Thinking Resurrection in Its Jewish Context," *New Testament Studies*, vol. 44, 1998.

WEBSITES

Elliot, Michael, "The Matrix," *www.christiancritic.com/movies/matrix.htm*

Horsley, Jake, "Gnosticism Reborn," *A Cinema of Savagery: Volume II, Millennial Blues, www.wynd.org/matrix.htm*

Murphy, Jason, "The Matrix," *www.christiananswers.net/spotlight/reviews/I-The Matrix.html*

"The Matrix as Messiah Movie," *awesomehouse.com/matrix*

RAY KURZWEIL

THE
HUMAN
MACHINE
MERGER:

ARE WE

HEADED FOR

THE MATRIX?

Most viewers of The Matrix *consider the more fanciful elements—intelligent computers, downloading information into the human brain, virtual reality indistinguishable from real life—to be fun as science fiction, but quite remote from real life. Most viewers would be wrong. As renowned computer scientist and entrepreneur Ray Kurzweil explains, these elements are very feasible and are quite likely to be a reality within our lifetimes.*

The Matrix is set in a world two hundred years in the future, a world offering a seemingly miraculous array of technological marvels—sentient (if malevolent) programs, the ability to directly download capabilities into the human brain, and the creation of virtual realities indistinguishable from the real world. For most viewers these developments may appear to be pure science fiction, interesting to consider, but of little relevance to the world outside the movie theatre. But this view is shortsighted. In my view, these developments will become a reality within the next three to four decades.

I've become a student of technology trends as an outgrowth of my career as an inventor. If you work on creating technologies, you need to anticipate where technology will be at points in the future so that your project will be feasible and useful when it's completed, not just when you started. Over the course of a few decades of anticipating technology, I've become a student of technology trends and have developed mathematical models of how technologies in different areas are developing.

This has given me the ability to invent things that use the materials of the future, not just limiting my ideas to the resources we have today. Alan Kay has noted, "To anticipate the future we need to invent it." So we can invent with future capabilities if we have some idea of what they will be.

Perhaps the most important insight that I've gained, which people are quick to agree with but very slow to really internalize and appreciate all of its implications, is the accelerating pace of technical change itself.

One Nobel laureate recently said to me: "There's no way we're going to see self-replicating nanotechnological entities for at least a hundred years." And yes, that's actually a reasonable estimate of how much work it will take. It'll take a hundred years of progress, at today's rate of progress, to get self-replicating nanotechnological entities. But the rate of progress is not going to remain at today's rate; according to my models, it's doubling every decade. We will make a hundred years of progress at today's rate of progress in twenty-five years. The next ten years will be like twenty, and the following ten years will be like forty. The twenty-first century will therefore be like twenty thousand years of progress—at today's rate. The twentieth century, as revolutionary as it was, did not have a hundred years of progress at today's rate; since we accelerated up to today's rate, it really was about twenty years of progress. The twenty-first century will be about a thousand times greater, in terms of change and paradigm shift, than the twentieth century.

A lot of these trends stem from thinking about the implications of Moore's Law. Moore's Law refers to integrated circuits and famously states that the computing power available for a given price will double every twelve to twenty-four months. Moore's Law has become a synonym for the exponential growth of computing.

I've been thinking about Moore's Law and its context for at least twenty years. What is the real nature of this exponential trend? Where does it come from? Is it an example of something deeper and more profound? As I will show, the exponential growth of computing goes substantially beyond Moore's Law. Indeed, exponential growth goes beyond just computation, and applies to every area of information-based technology, technology that will ultimately reshape our world.

Observers have pointed out that Moore's Law is going to come to an end. According to Intel and other industry experts, we'll run out of space on an integrated circuit within fifteen years, because the key features will only be a few atoms in width. So will that be the end of the exponential growth of computing?

That's a very important question as we ponder the nature of the twenty-first century. To address this question, I put forty-nine famous computers on an exponential graph. Down, at the lower left-hand corner is the data processing machinery that was used in the 1890 American census (calculating equipment using punch cards). In 1940, Alan Turing developed a computer based on telephone relays that cracked the German enigma code and gave Winston Churchill a transcription of nearly all the Nazi messages. Churchill needed to use these transcriptions with great discretion, because he realized that using them could tip off the Germans prematurely. If, for example, he had warned Coventry authorities that their city was going to be bombed, the Germans would have seen the preparations and realize that their code had been cracked. However, in the Battle of Britain, the English flyers seemed to magically know where the German flyers were at all times.

In 1952, CBS used a more sophisticated computer based on vacuum tubes to predict the election of a U.S. president, President Eisenhower. In the upper right-hand corner is the computer sitting on your desk right now.

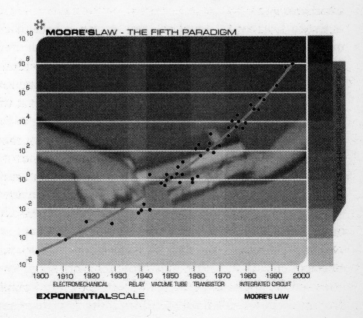

One insight we can see on this chart is that Moore's Law was not the first but the fifth paradigm to provide exponential growth of computing power. Each vertical line represents the movement into a different paradigm: electro-mechanical, relay-based, vacuum tubes, transistors, integrated circuits. Every time a paradigm ran out of steam, another paradigm came along and picked up where that paradigm left off.

People are very quick to criticize exponential trends, saying that ultimately they'll run out of resources, like rabbits in Australia. But every time one particular paradigm reached its limits, another, completely different method would continue the exponential growth. They were making vacuum tubes smaller and smaller but finally got to a point where they couldn't make them any smaller and maintain the vacuum. Then transistors came along, which are not just small vacuum tubes. They're a completely different paradigm.

Every horizontal level on this graph represents a multiplication of computing power by a factor of a hundred. A straight line in an exponential graph means exponential growth. What we see here is that the rate of exponential growth is itself growing exponentially. We doubled the computing power every three years at the beginning of the century, every two years in the middle, and we're now doubling it every year.

It's obvious what the sixth paradigm will be: computing in three dimensions. After all, we live in a three-dimensional world and our brain is organized in three dimensions. The brain uses a very inefficient type of circuitry. Neurons are very large "devices," and they're extremely slow. They use electrochemical signaling that provides only about two hundred calculations per second, but the brain gets its prodigious power from parallel computing resulting from being organized in three dimensions. Three-dimensional computing technologies are beginning to emerge. There's an experimental technology at MIT's Media Lab that has three hundred layers of circuitry. In recent years, there have been substantial strides in developing three-dimensional circuits that operate at the molecular level.

Nanotubes, which are my favorite, are hexagonal arrays of carbon atoms that can be organized to form any type of electronic circuit. You can create the equivalent of transistors and other electrical devices. They're physically very strong, with fifty times the strength of steel. The thermal issues appear to be manageable. A one-inch cube of nanotube circuitry would be a million times more powerful than the computing capacity of the human brain.

Over the last several years, there has been a sea change in the level of confidence in building three-dimensional circuits and achieving at least the hardware capacity to emulate human intelligence. This has raised a more salient issue, namely that "Moore's Law may be true for hardware but it's not true for software." From my own four decades of experience with software development, I believe that is not the case. Software productivity is increasing very rapidly. As an example from one of my own companies, in fifteen years we went from a $5,000 speech-recognition system that recognized a thousand words poorly, without continuous speech, to a $50 product with a hundred-thousand-word vocabulary that's far more accurate. That's typical for software products. With all of the efforts in new software development tools, software productivity has also been growing exponentially, albeit with a smaller exponent than we see in hardware.

Many other technologies are improving exponentially. When the genome project was started about fifteen years ago, skeptics pointed out that at the rate at which we can scan the genome, it will take ten thousand years to finish the project. The mainstream view was that there would be improvements, but there was no way that the project could be completed in fifteen years. But the price-performance and throughput of DNA sequencing doubled every year, and the project was completed in less than fifteen years. In twelve years we went from a cost of $10 to sequence a DNA base pair to a tenth of a cent.

Even longevity has been improving exponentially. In the eighteenth century, every year we added a few days to human life expectancy. In the nineteenth century, every year, we added a few weeks. We're now adding about 120 days every year, to human life expectancy. And with the revolutions now in an early stage in genomics, therapeutic cloning, rational drug design, and the other biotechnology transformations, many observers including myself anticipate that within ten years we'll be adding more than a year, every year. So, if you can hang in there for another ten years, we'll get ahead of the power curve and be able to live long enough to see the remarkable century ahead.

Miniaturization is another very important exponential trend. We're making things smaller at a rate of 5.6 per linear dimension per decade. Bill Joy, in the essay following this one, has, as one of his recommendations, to essentially forgo nanotechnology. But nanotechnology is not a single unified field, only worked on by nanotechnologists. Nanotechnology is simply the inevitable end result of the pervasive trend toward making things smaller, which we've been doing for many decades.

Below is a chart of computing's exponential growth, projected into the twenty-first century. Right now, your typical $1000 PC is somewhere between an insect and a mouse brain. The human brain has about 100 billion neurons, with about 1,000 connections from one neuron to another. These connections operate very slowly, on the order of 200 calculations per second, but 100 billion neurons times 1,000 connects creates 100 trillion-fold parallelism. Multiplying that by 200 calculations per second yields 20 million billion calculations per second, or, in computing terminology, 20 billion MIPS. We'll have 20 billion MIPS for $1000 by the year 2020.

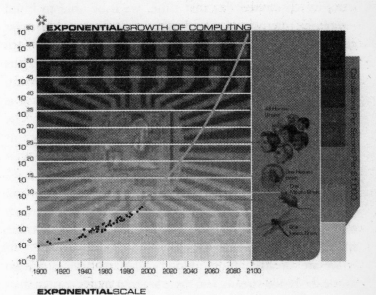

Now, that won't automatically give us human levels of intelligence, because the organization, the software, the content and the embedded knowledge are equally important. Below I will address the scenario in which I envision achieving the software of human intelligence, but I believe it is clear that we will have the requisite computing power. By 2050, $1000 of computing will equal one billion human brains. That might be off by a year or two, but the twenty-first century won't be wanting for computational resources.

Now, let's consider the virtual-reality framework envisioned by *The Matrix*—a virtual reality which is indistinguishable from true reality. This will be feasible, but I do quibble with one point. The thick cable entering Neo's brainstem made for a powerful visual, but it's unnecessary; all of these connections can be wireless.

Let's go out to 2029 and put together some of the trends that I've discussed. By that time, we'll be able to build nanobots, microscopic-sized robots that can go inside your capillaries and travel through your brain and scan the brain from inside. We can almost build these kinds of circuits today. We can't make them quite small enough, but we can make them fairly small. The Department of Defense is developing tiny robotic devices called "Smart Dust." The current generation is one millimeter—that's too big for this scenario—but these tiny devices can be dropped from a plane, and find positions with great precision. You can have many thousands of these on a wireless local area network. They can then take visual images, communicate with each other, coordinate, send messages back, act as nearly invisible spies, and accomplish a variety of military objectives.

We are already building blood-cell-sized devices that go inside the blood stream, and there are four major conferences on the topic of "bioMEMS" (biological Micro Electronic Mechanical Systems). The nanobots I am envisioning for 2029 will not necessarily require their own navigation. They could move involuntarily through the bloodstream and, as they travel by different neural features, communicate with them the same way that we now communicate with different cells within a cell phone system.

Brain-scanning resolution, speeds, and costs are all exploding exponentially. With every new generation of brain scanning we can see with finer and finer resolution. There's a technology today that allows us to view many of the salient details of the human brain. Of course, there's still no full agreement on what those details are, but we can see brain features with very high resolution, provided the scanning tip is right next to the features. We can scan a brain today and see the brain's activity with very fine detail; you just have to move the scanning tip all throughout the brain so that it's in close proximity to every neural feature.

Now, how are we going to do that without making a mess of things? The answer is to send the scanners inside the brain. By design, our capillaries travel by every interneuronal connection, every neuron and every neural feature. We can send billions of these scanning robots, all on a wireless local area network, and they would all scan the brain from inside and create a very high-resolution map of everything that's going on.

What are we going to do with the massive database of neural information that develops? One thing we will do is reverse-engineer the brain, that is understand the basic principles of how it works. This is an endeavor we have already started. We already have high-resolution scans of certain areas of the brain. The brain is not one organ; it's comprised of several hundred specialized regions, each organized differently. We have scanned certain areas of the auditory and visual cortex, and have used this information to design more intelligent software. Carver Mead at Caltech, for example, has developed powerful, digitally controlled analog chips that are based on these biologically inspired models from the reverse engineering of portions of the visual and auditory systems. His visual sensing chips are used in high-end digital cameras.

We have demonstrated that we are able to understand these algorithms, but they're different from the algorithms that we typically run on our computers. They're not sequential and they're not logical; they're chaotic, highly parallel, and self-organizing. They have a holographic nature in that there's no chief-executive-officer neuron. You can eliminate any of the neurons, cut any of the wires, and it makes little difference—the information and the processes are distributed throughout a complex region.

Based on these insights, we have developed a number of biologically inspired models today. This is the field I work in, using techniques such as evolutionary "genetic algorithms" and "neural nets," which use biologically inspired models. Today's neural nets are mathematically simplified, but as we get a more powerful understanding of the principles of operation of different brain regions, we will be in a position to develop much more powerful, biologically inspired models. Ultimately we can create and recreate these processes, retaining their inherently massively parallel, digitally controlled analog, chaotic, and self-organizing properties. We will be able to recreate the types of processes that occur in the hundreds of different brain regions, and create entities—they actually won't be in silicon, they'll probably be using something like nanotubes—that have the complexity, richness, and depth of human intelligence.

Our machines today are still a million times simpler than the human brain, which is one key reason that they still don't have the endearing qualities of people. They don't yet have our ability to get the joke, to be funny, to understand people, to respond appropriately to emotion, or to have spiritual experiences. These are not side effects of human intelligence, or distractions; they are the cutting edge of human intelligence. It will require a technology of the complexity of the human brain to create entities that have those kinds of attractive and convincing features.

Getting back to virtual reality, let's consider a scenario involving a direct connection between the human brain and these nanobot-based implants. There are a number of different technologies that have already been demonstrated for communicating in both directions between the wet, analog world of neurons and the digital world of electronics. One such technology, called a neurotransistor, provides this two-way communication. If a neuron fires, this neuron transistor detects that electromagnetic pulse, so that's communication from the neuron to the electronics. It can also cause the neuron to fire or prevent it from firing.

For full-immersion virtual reality, we will send billions of these nanobots to take up positions by every nerve fiber coming from all of our senses. If you want to be in real reality, they sit there and do nothing. If you want to be in virtual reality, they suppress the signals coming from our real senses and replace them with the signals that you would have been receiving if you were in the virtual environment.

In this scenario, we will have virtual reality from within and it will be able to recreate all of our senses. These will be shared environments, so you can go there with one person or many people. Going to a website will mean entering a virtual-reality environment encompassing all of our senses, and not just the five senses, but also emotions, sexual pleasure, humor. There are actually neurological correlates of all of these sensations and emotions, which I discuss in my book *The Age of the Spiritual Machines*.

For example, surgeons conducting open-brain surgery on a young woman (while awake) found that stimulating a particular spot in the girl's brain would cause her to laugh. The surgeons thought that they were just stimulating an involuntary laugh reflex. But they discovered that they were stimulating the perception of humor: whenever they stimulated this spot, she found everything hilarious. "You guys are just so funny standing there," was a typical remark.

Using these nanobot-based implants, you will be able to enhance or modify your emotional responses to different experiences. That can be part of the overlay of these virtual-reality environments. You will also be able to have different bodies for different experiences. Just as people today project their images from webcams in their apartment, people will beam their whole flow of sensory and even emotional experiences out on the web, so you can, à la the plot concept of the movie *Being John Malkovich*, experience the lives of other people.

Ultimately, these nanobots will expand human intelligence and our abilities and facilities in many different ways. Because they're communicating with each other wirelessly, they can create new neural connections. These can expand our memory, cognitive faculties, and pattern-recognition abilities. We will expand human intelligence by expanding its current paradigm of massive interneuronal connections as well as through intimate connection to nonbiological forms of intelligence.

We will also be able to download knowledge, something that machines can do today that we are unable to do. For example, we spent several years training one research computer to understand human speech using the biologically inspired models—neural nets, Markov models, genetic algorithms, self-organizing patterns—that are based on our crude current understanding of self-organizing systems in the biological world. A major part of the engineering project was collecting thousands of hours of speech from different speakers in different dialects and then exposing this to the system and having it try to recognize the speech. It made mistakes, and then we had it adjust automatically, and self-organize to better reflect what it had learned.

Over many months of this kind of training, it made substantial improvements in its ability to recognize speech. Today, if you want your personal computer to recognize human speech, you don't have to spend years training it the same painstaking way, as we need to do with every human child. You can just load the evolved models, it's called "loading the software." So machines can share their knowledge.

We don't have quick downloading ports on our brains. But as we build nonbiological analogs of our neurons, interconnections, and neurotransmitter levels where our skills and memories are stored, we won't leave out the equivalent of downloading ports. We'll be able to download capabilities as easily as Trinity downloads the program that allows her to fly the B-222 helicopter.

When you talk to somebody in the year 2040, you will be talking to someone who may happen to be of biological origin but whose mental processes are a hybrid of biological and electronic thinking processes, working intimately together. Instead of being restricted, as we are today, to a mere hundred trillion connections in our brain, we'll be able to expand substantially beyond this level. Our biological thinking is flat; the human race has an estimated 10^{26} calculations per second, and that biologically determined figure is not going to grow. But nonbiological intelligence is growing exponentially. The crossover point, according to my calculations, is in the 2030s; some people call this the Singularity.

As we get to 2050, the bulk of our thinking—which in my opinion is still an expression of human civilization—will be nonbiological. I don't believe that *The Matrix* scenario of malevolent artificial intelligences in mortal conflict with humans is inevitable. The nonbiological portion of our thinking will still be human thinking, because it's going to be derived from human thinking. It's will be created by humans, or created by machines that are created by humans, or created by machines that are based on reverse engineering of the human brain or downloads of human thinking, or one of many other intimate connections between human and machine thinking that we can't even contemplate today.

A common reaction to this is that this is a dystopian vision, because I am "placing humanity with the machines." But that's because most people have a prejudice against machines. Most observers don't truly understand what machines are ultimately capable of, because all the machines that they've ever "met" are very limited, compared to people. But that won't be true of machines circa 2030 and 2040. When machines are derived from human intelligence and are a million times more capable, we'll have a different respect for machines, and there won't be a clear distinction between human and machine intelligence. We will effectively merge with our technology.

We are already well down this road. If all the machines in the world stopped today, our civilization would grind to a halt. That wasn't true as recently as thirty years ago. In 2040, human and machine intelligence will be deeply and intimately melded. We will become capable of far more profound experiences of many diverse kinds. We'll be able to "recreate the world" according to our imaginations and enter environments as amazing as that of *The Matrix*, but, hopefully, a world more open to creative human expression and experience.

SOURCES

BOOKS

Kurzweil, Ray, *The Age of Spiritual Machines: When Computers Exceed Intelligence* (Penguin USA, 2000).

BILL JOY

WHY

THE

FUTURE

DOESN'T

NEED

US

In the previous essay, Kurzweil paints an optimistic perspective on the potential of technology for transforming the world as we know it. In this essay, Bill Joy, Chief Scientist for Sun and one of the leaders of the Internet revolution, takes a darker view. While sharing Kurzweil's view of the trajectory we are on, Joy finds much more cause for concern. The horrors of The Matrix *are only one of a range on potential nightmares . . .*

Our most powerful 21st-century technologies—robotics, genetic engineering, and nanotech—are threatening to make humans an endangered species.

From the moment I became involved in the creation of new technologies, their ethical dimensions have concerned me, but it was only in the autumn of 1998 that I became anxiously aware of how great are the dangers facing us in the 21st century. I can date the onset of my unease to the day I met Ray Kurzweil, the deservedly famous inventor of the first reading machine for the blind and many other amazing things.

Ray and I were both speakers at George Gilder's Telecosm conference, and I encountered him by chance in the bar of the hotel after both our sessions were over. I was sitting with John Searle, a Berkeley philosopher who studies consciousness. While we were talking, Ray approached and a conversation began, the subject of which haunts me to this day.

I had missed Ray's talk and the subsequent panel that Ray and John had been on, and they now picked right up where they'd left off, with Ray saying that the rate of improvement of technology was going to accelerate and that we were going to become robots or fuse with robots or something like that, and John countering that this couldn't happen, because the robots couldn't be conscious.

While I had heard such talk before, I had always felt sentient robots were in the realm of science fiction. But now, from someone I respected, I was hearing a strong argument that they were a near-term possibility. I was taken aback, especially given Ray's proven ability to imagine and create the future. I already knew that new technologies like genetic engineering and nanotechnology were giving us the power to remake the world, but a realistic and imminent scenario for intelligent robots surprised me.

It's easy to get jaded about such breakthroughs. We hear in the news almost every day of some kind of technological or scientific advance. Yet this was no ordinary prediction. In the hotel bar, Ray gave me a partial preprint of his then-forthcoming book *The Age of Spiritual Machines,* which outlined a utopia he foresaw—one in which humans gained near immortality by becoming one with robotic technology. On reading it, my sense of unease only intensified; I felt sure he had to be understating the dangers, understating the probability of a bad outcome along this path.

I found myself most troubled by a passage detailing a *dys*topian scenario:

THE NEW LUDDITE CHALLENGE

First let us postulate that the computer scientists succeed in developing intelligent machines that can do all things better than human beings can do them. In that case presumably all work will be done by vast, highly organized systems of machines and no human effort will be necessary. Either of two cases might occur. The machines might be permitted to make all of their own decisions without human oversight, or else human control over the machines might be retained.

If the machines are permitted to make all their own decisions, we can't make any conjectures as to the results, because it is impossible to guess how such machines might behave. We only point out that the fate of the human race would be at the mercy of the machines. It might be argued that the human race would never be foolish enough to hand over all the power to the machines. But we are suggesting neither that the human race would voluntarily turn power over to the machines nor that the machines would willfully seize power. What we do suggest is that the human race might easily permit itself to drift into a position of such dependence on the machines that it would have no practical choice but to accept all of the machines' decisions. As society and the problems that face it become more and more complex and machines become more and more intelligent, people will let machines make more of their decisions for them, simply because machine-made decisions will bring better results than man-made ones. Eventually a stage may be reached at which the decisions necessary to keep the system running will be so complex that human beings will be incapable of making them intelligently. At that stage the machines will be in effective control. People won't be able to just turn the machines off, because they will be so dependent on them that turning them off would amount to suicide.

On the other hand it is possible that human control over the machines may be retained. In that case the average man may have control over certain private machines of his own, such as his car or his personal computer, but control over large systems of machines will be in the hands of a tiny elite—just as it is today, but with two differences. Due to improved techniques the elite will have greater control over the masses; and because human work will no longer be necessary the masses will be superfluous, a useless burden on the system. If the elite is ruthless they may simply decide to exterminate the mass of humanity. If they are humane they may use propaganda or other psychological or biological techniques to reduce the birth rate until the mass of humanity becomes extinct, leaving the world to the elite. Or, if the elite consists of soft-hearted liberals, they may decide to play the role of good shepherds to the rest of the human race. They will see to it that everyone's physical needs are satisfied, that all children are raised under psychologically hygienic conditions, that everyone has a wholesome hobby to keep him busy, and that anyone who may become dissatisfied undergoes "treatment" to cure his "problem." Of course, life will be so purposeless that people will have to be biologically or psychologically engineered either to remove their need for the power process or make them "sublimate" their drive for power into some harmless hobby. These engineered human beings may be happy in such a society, but they will most certainly not be free. They will have been reduced to the status of domestic animals.[1]

In the book, you don't discover until you turn the page that the author of this passage is Theodore Kaczynski—the Unabomber. I am no apologist for Kaczynski. His bombs killed three people during a 17-year terror campaign and wounded many others. One of his bombs gravely injured my friend David Gelernter, one of the most brilliant and visionary computer scientists of our time. Like many of my colleagues, I felt that I could easily have been the Unabomber's next target.

Kaczynski's actions were murderous and, in my view, criminally insane. He is clearly a Luddite, but simply saying this does not dismiss his argument; as difficult as it is for me to acknowledge, I saw some merit in the reasoning in this single passage. I felt compelled to confront it.

Kaczynski's dystopian vision describes unintended consequences, a well-known problem with the design and use of technology, and one that is clearly related to Murphy's law—"Anything that can go wrong, will." (Actually, this is Finagle's law, which in itself shows that Finagle was right.) Our overuse of antibiotics has led to what may be the biggest such problem so far: the emergence of antibiotic-resistant and much more dangerous bacteria. Similar things happened when attempts to eliminate malarial mosquitoes using DDT caused them to acquire DDT resistance; malarial parasites likewise acquired multi-drug-resistant genes.[2]

---

1 The passage Kurzweil quotes is from Kaczynski's Unabomber Manifesto, which was published jointly, under duress, by *The New York Times* and *The Washington Post* to attempt to bring his campaign of terror to an end. I agree with David Gelernter, who said about their decision:

"It was a tough call for the newspapers. To say yes would be giving in to terrorism, and for all they knew he was lying anyway. On the other hand, to say yes might stop the killing. There was also a chance that someone would read the tract and get a hunch about the author; and that is exactly what happened. The suspect's brother read it, and it rang a bell.

"I would have told them not to publish. I'm glad they didn't ask me. I guess." (Gelernter, p.120)

2 Garrett, pp. 47-52, 414, 419, 452

The cause of many such surprises seems clear: The systems involved are complex, involving interaction among and feedback between many parts. Any changes to such a system will cascade in ways that are difficult to predict; this is especially true when human actions are involved.

I started showing friends the Kaczynski quote from *The Age of Spiritual Machines;* I would hand them Kurzweil's book, let them read the quote, and then watch their reaction as they discovered who had written it. At around the same time, I found Hans Moravec's book *Robot: Mere Machine to Transcendent Mind.* Moravec is one of the leaders in robotics research, and was a founder of the world's largest robotics research program, at Carnegie Mellon University. *Robot* gave me more material to try out on my friends—material surprisingly supportive of Kaczynski's argument. For example:

THE SHORT RUN (EARLY 2000S)

Biological species almost never survive encounters with superior competitors. Ten million years ago, South and North America were separated by a sunken Panama isthmus. South America, like Australia today, was populated by marsupial mammals, including pouched equivalents of rats, deers, and tigers. When the isthmus connecting North and South America rose, it took only a few thousand years for the northern placental species, with slightly more effective metabolisms and reproductive and nervous systems, to displace and eliminate almost all the southern marsupials.

In a completely free marketplace, superior robots would surely affect humans as North American placentals affected South American marsupials (and as humans have affected countless species). Robotic industries would compete vigorously among themselves for matter, energy, and space, incidentally driving their price beyond human reach. Unable to afford the necessities of life, biological humans would be squeezed out of existence.

There is probably some breathing room, because we do not live in a completely free marketplace. Government coerces nonmarket behavior, especially by collecting taxes. Judiciously applied, governmental coercion could support human populations in high style on the fruits of robot labor, perhaps for a long while.

A textbook dystopia—and Moravec is just getting wound up. He goes on to discuss how our main job in the 21st century will be "ensuring continued cooperation from the robot industries" by passing laws decreeing that they be "nice,"[3] and to describe how seriously dangerous a human can be "once transformed into an unbounded superintelligent robot." Moravec's view is that the robots will eventually succeed us—that humans clearly face extinction.

I decided it was time to talk to my friend Danny Hillis. Danny became famous as the cofounder of Thinking Machines Corporation, which built a very powerful parallel supercomputer. Despite my current job title of Chief Scientist at Sun Microsystems, I am more a computer architect than a scientist, and I respect Danny's knowledge of the information and physical sciences more than that of any other single person I know. Danny is also a highly regarded futurist who thinks long-term—four years ago he started the Long Now Foundation, which is building a clock

3 Isaac Asimov described what became the most famous view of ethical rules for robot behavior in his book *I, Robot* in 1950, in his Three Laws of Robotics: 1. A robot may not injure a human being, or, through inaction, allow a human being to come to harm. 2. A robot must obey the orders given it by human beings, except where such orders would conflict with the First Law. 3. A robot must protect its own existence, as long as such protection does not conflict with the First or Second Law.

designed to last 10,000 years, in an attempt to draw attention to the pitifully short attention span of our society."[4]

So I flew to Los Angeles for the express purpose of having dinner with Danny and his wife, Pati. I went through my now-familiar routine, trotting out the ideas and passages that I found so disturbing. Danny's answer—directed specifically at Kurzweil's scenario of humans merging with robots—came swiftly, and quite surprised me. He said, simply, that the changes would come gradually, and that we would get used to them.

But I guess I wasn't totally surprised. I had seen a quote from Danny in Kurzweil's book in which he said, "I'm as fond of my body as anyone, but if I can be 200 with a body of silicon, I'll take it." It seemed that he was at peace with this process and its attendant risks, while I was not.

While talking and thinking about Kurzweil, Kaczynski, and Moravec, I suddenly remembered a novel I had read almost 20 years ago—*The White Plague*, by Frank Herbert—in which a molecular biologist is driven insane by the senseless murder of his family. To seek revenge he constructs and disseminates a new and highly contagious plague that kills widely but selectively. (We're lucky Kaczynski was a mathematician, not a molecular biologist.) I was also reminded of the Borg of *Star Trek*, a hive of partly biological, partly robotic creatures with a strong destructive streak. Borg-like disasters are a staple of science fiction, so why hadn't I been more concerned about such robotic dystopias earlier? Why weren't other people more concerned about these nightmarish scenarios?

Part of the answer certainly lies in our attitude toward the new—in our bias toward instant familiarity and unquestioning acceptance. Accustomed to living with almost routine scientific breakthroughs, we have yet to

4 Hillis, p. 78.

come to terms with the fact that the most compelling 21st-century technologies—robotics, genetic engineering, and nanotechnology—pose a different threat than the technologies that have come before. Specifically, robots, engineered organisms, and nanobots share a dangerous amplifying factor: They can self-replicate. A bomb is blown up only once—but one bot can become many, and quickly get out of control.

Much of my work over the past 25 years has been on computer networking, where the sending and receiving of messages creates the opportunity for out-of-control replication. But while replication in a computer or a computer network can be a nuisance, at worst it disables a machine or takes down a network or network service. Uncontrolled self-replication in these newer technologies runs a much greater risk: a risk of substantial damage in the physical world.

Each of these technologies also offers untold promise: The vision of near immortality that Kurzweil sees in his robot dreams drives us forward; genetic engineering may soon provide treatments, if not outright cures, for most diseases; and nanotechnology and nanomedicine can address yet more ills. Together they could significantly extend our average life span and improve the quality of our lives. Yet, with each of these technologies, a sequence of small, individually sensible advances leads to an accumulation of great power and, concomitantly, great danger.

What was different in the 20th century? Certainly, the technologies underlying the weapons of mass destruction (WMD)—nuclear, biological, and chemical (NBC)—were powerful, and the weapons an enormous threat. But building nuclear weapons required, at least for a time, access to both rare—indeed, effectively unavailable—raw materials and highly protected information; biological and chemical weapons programs also tended to require large-scale activities.

The 21st-century technologies — genetics, nanotechnology, and robotics (GNR) — are so powerful that they can spawn whole new classes of accidents and abuses. Most dangerously, for the first time, these accidents and abuses are widely within the reach of individuals or small groups. They will not require large facilities or rare raw materials. Knowledge alone will enable the use of them.

Thus we have the possibility not just of weapons of mass destruction but of knowledge-enabled mass destruction (KMD), this destructiveness hugely amplified by the power of self-replication.

I think it is no exaggeration to say we are on the cusp of the further perfection of extreme evil, an evil whose possibility spreads well beyond that which weapons of mass destruction bequeathed to the nation-states, on to a surprising and terrible empowerment of extreme individuals.

Nothing about the way I got involved with computers suggested to me that I was going to be facing these kinds of issues.

My life has been driven by a deep need to ask questions and find answers. When I was 3, I was already reading, so my father took me to the elementary school, where I sat on the principal's lap and read him a story. I started school early, later skipped a grade, and escaped into books—I was incredibly motivated to learn. I asked lots of questions, often driving adults to distraction.

As a teenager I was very interested in science and technology. I wanted to be a ham radio operator but didn't have the money to buy the equipment. Ham radio was the Internet of its time: very addictive, and quite solitary. Money issues aside, my mother put her foot down—I was not to be a ham; I was antisocial enough already.

I may not have had many close friends, but I was awash in ideas. By high school, I had discovered the great science fiction writers. I remember especially Heinlein's *Have Spacesuit—Will Travel* and Asimov's *I, Robot,* with its Three Laws of Robotics. I was enchanted by the descriptions of space travel, and wanted to have a telescope to look at the stars; since I had no money to buy or make one, I checked books on telescope-making out of the library and read about making them instead. I soared in my imagination.

Thursday nights my parents went bowling, and we kids stayed home alone. It was the night of Gene Roddenberry's original *Star Trek*, and the program made a big impression on me. I came to accept its notion that humans had a future in space, Western-style, with big heroes and adventures. Roddenberry's vision of the centuries to come was one with strong moral values, embodied in codes like the Prime Directive: to not interfere in the development of less technologically advanced civilizations. This had an incredible appeal to me; ethical humans, not robots, dominated this future, and I took Roddenberry's dream as part of my own.

I excelled in mathematics in high school, and when I went to the University of Michigan as an undergraduate engineering student I took the advanced curriculum of the mathematics majors. Solving math problems was an exciting challenge, but when I discovered computers I found something much more interesting: a machine into which you could put a program that attempted to solve a problem, after which the machine quickly checked the solution. The computer had a clear notion of correct and incorrect, true and false. Were my ideas correct? The machine could tell me. This was very seductive.

I was lucky enough to get a job programming early supercomputers and discovered the amazing power of large machines to numerically simulate advanced designs. When I went to graduate school at UC Berkeley in the mid-1970s, I started staying up late, often all night, inventing new worlds inside the machines. Solving problems. Writing the code that argued so strongly to be written.

In *The Agony and the Ecstasy*, Irving Stone's biographical novel of Michelangelo, Stone described vividly how Michelangelo released the statues from the stone, "breaking the marble spell," carving from the images in his mind.[5] In my most ecstatic moments, the software in the computer emerged in the same way. Once I had imagined it in my mind I felt that it was already there in the machine, waiting to be released. Staying up all night seemed a small price to pay to free it—to give the ideas concrete form.

After a few years at Berkeley I started to send out some of the software I had written—an instructional Pascal system, UNIX utilities, and a text editor called vi (which is still, to my surprise, widely used more than 20 years later)—to others who had similar small PDP-11 and VAX minicomputers. These adventures in software eventually turned into the Berkeley version of the UNIX operating

---

5 Michelangelo wrote a sonnet that begins:

> *Non ha l' ottimo artista alcun concetto*
> *Ch' un marmo solo in sè non circonscriva*
> *Col suo soverchio; e solo a quello arriva*
> *La man che ubbidisce all' intelleto.*

Stone translates this as:

> *The best of artists hath no thought to show*
>
> *which the rough stone in its superfluous shell*
> *doth not include; to break the marble spell*
> *is all the hand that serves the brain can do.*

Stone describes the process: "He was not working from his drawings or clay models; they had all been put away. He was carving from the images in his mind. His eyes and hands knew where every line, curve, mass must emerge, and at what depth in the heart of the stone to create the low relief." (Stone, p. 144)

system, which became a personal "success disaster"—so many people wanted it that I never finished my PhD. Instead I got a job working for Darpa putting Berkeley UNIX on the Internet and fixing it to be reliable and to run large research applications well. This was all great fun and very rewarding. And, frankly, I saw no robots here, or anywhere near.

Still, by the early 1980s, I was drowning. The UNIX releases were very successful, and my little project of one soon had money and some staff, but the problem at Berkeley was always office space rather than money—there wasn't room for the help the project needed, so when the other founders of Sun Microsystems showed up I jumped at the chance to join them. At Sun, the long hours continued into the early days of workstations and personal computers, and I have enjoyed participating in the creation of advanced microprocessor technologies and Internet technologies such as Java and Jini.

From all this, I trust it is clear that I am not a Luddite. I have always, rather, had a strong belief in the value of the scientific search for truth and in the ability of great engineering to bring material progress. The Industrial Revolution has immeasurably improved everyone's life over the last couple hundred years, and I always expected my career to involve the building of worthwhile solutions to real problems, one problem at a time.

I have not been disappointed. My work has had more impact than I had ever hoped for and has been more widely used than I could have reasonably expected. I have spent the last 20 years still trying to figure out how to make computers as reliable as I want them to be (they are not nearly there yet) and how to make them simple to use (a goal that has met with even less relative success). Despite some progress, the problems that remain seem even more daunting.

But while I was aware of the moral dilemmas surrounding technology's consequences in fields like weapons research, I did not expect that I would confront such issues in my own field, or at least not so soon.

Perhaps it is always hard to see the bigger impact while you are in the vortex of a change. Failing to understand the consequences of our inventions while we are in the rapture of discovery and innovation seems to be a common fault of scientists and technologists; we have long been driven by the overarching desire to know that is the nature of science's quest, not stopping to notice that the progress to newer and more powerful technologies can take on a life of its own.

I have long realized that the big advances in information technology come not from the work of computer scientists, computer architects, or electrical engineers, but from that of physical scientists. The physicists Stephen Wolfram and Brosl Hasslacher introduced me, in the early 1980s, to chaos theory and nonlinear systems. In the 1990s, I learned about complex systems from conversations with Danny Hillis, the biologist Stuart Kauffman, the Nobel-laureate physicist Murray Gell-Mann, and others. Most recently, Hasslacher and the electrical engineer and device physicist Mark Reed have been giving me insight into the incredible possibilities of molecular electronics.

In my own work, as codesigner of three microprocessor architectures—SPARC, picoJava, and MAJC—and as the designer of several implementations thereof, I've been afforded a deep and firsthand acquaintance with Moore's Law. For decades, Moore's Law has correctly predicted the exponential rate of improvement of semiconductor technology. Until last year I believed that the rate of advances predicted by Moore's Law might continue only until roughly 2010, when some physical limits would begin to be reached. It was not obvious to me that a new technology would arrive in time to keep performance advancing smoothly.

But because of the recent rapid and radical progress in molecular electronics—where individual atoms and molecules replace lithographically drawn transistors—and related nanoscale technologies, we should be able to meet or exceed the Moore's Law rate of progress for another 30 years. By 2030, we are likely to be able to build machines, in quantity, a million times as powerful as the personal computers of today—sufficient to implement the dreams of Kurzweil and Moravec.

As this enormous computing power is combined with the manipulative advances of the physical sciences and the new, deep understandings in genetics, enormous transformative power is being unleashed. These combinations open up the opportunity to completely redesign the world, for better or worse: the replicating and evolving processes that have been confined to the natural world are about to become realms of human endeavor.

In designing software and microprocessors, I have never had the feeling that I was designing an intelligent machine. The software and hardware is so fragile and the capabilities of the machine to "think" so clearly absent that, even as a possibility, this has always seemed very far in the future.

But now, with the prospect of human-level computing power in about 30 years, a new idea suggests itself: that I may be working to create tools which will enable the construction of the technology that may replace our species. How do I feel about this? Very uncomfortable. Having struggled my entire career to build reliable software systems, it seems to me more than likely that this future will not work out as well as some people may imagine. My personal experience suggests we tend to overestimate our design abilities.

Given the incredible power of these new technologies, shouldn't we be asking how we can best coexist with them? And if our own extinction is a likely, or even possible, outcome of our technological development, shouldn't we proceed with great caution?

The dream of robotics is, first, that intelligent machines can do our work for us, allowing us lives of leisure, restoring us to Eden. Yet in his history of such ideas, *Darwin Among the Machines*, George Dyson warns: "In the game of life and evolution there are three players at the table: human beings, nature, and machines. I am firmly on the side of nature. But nature, I suspect, is on the side of the machines." As we have seen, Moravec agrees, believing we may well not survive the encounter with the superior robot species.

How soon could such an intelligent robot be built? The coming advances in computing power seem to make it possible by 2030. And once an intelligent robot exists, it is only a small step to a robot species—to an intelligent robot that can make evolved copies of itself.

A second dream of robotics is that we will gradually replace ourselves with our robotic technology, achieving near immortality by downloading our consciousnesses; it is this process that Danny Hillis thinks we will gradually get used to and that Ray Kurzweil elegantly details in *The Age of Spiritual Machines.*[6]

But if we are downloaded into our technology, what are the chances that we will thereafter be ourselves or even human? It seems to me far more likely that a robotic existence would not be like a human one in any sense that

---

6 (We are beginning to see intimations of this in the implantation of computer devices into the human body, as illustrated on the cover of *Wired* 8.02 February)

we understand, that the robots would in no sense be our children, that on this path our humanity may well be lost.

Genetic engineering promises to revolutionize agriculture by increasing crop yields while reducing the use of pesticides; to create tens of thousands of novel species of bacteria, plants, viruses, and animals; to replace reproduction, or supplement it, with cloning; to create cures for many diseases, increasing our life span and our quality of life; and much, much more. We now know with certainty that these profound changes in the biological sciences are imminent and will challenge all our notions of what life is.

Technologies such as human cloning have in particular raised our awareness of the profound ethical and moral issues we face. If, for example, we were to reengineer ourselves into several separate and unequal species using the power of genetic engineering, then we would threaten the notion of equality that is the very cornerstone of our democracy.

Given the incredible power of genetic engineering, it's no surprise that there are significant safety issues in its use. My friend Amory Lovins recently co-wrote, along with Hunter Lovins, an editorial that provides an ecological view of some of these dangers. Among their concerns: that "the new botany aligns the development of plants with their economic, not evolutionary, success."[7] Amory's long career has been focused on energy and resource efficiency by taking a whole-system view of human-made systems; such a whole-system view often finds simple, smart solutions to otherwise seemingly difficult problems, and is usefully applied here as well.

After reading the Lovins' editorial, I saw an op-ed by Gregg Easterbrook in *The New York Times* about genetically

7 Lovins, p. 247

engineered crops, under the headline: "Food for the Future: Someday, rice will have built-in vitamin A. Unless the Luddites win."

Are Amory and Hunter Lovins Luddites? Certainly not. I believe we all would agree that golden rice, with its built-in vitamin A, is probably a good thing, if developed with proper care and respect for the likely dangers in moving genes across species boundaries.

Awareness of the dangers inherent in genetic engineering is beginning to grow, as reflected in the Lovins' editorial. The general public is aware of, and uneasy about, genetically modified foods, and seems to be rejecting the notion that such foods should be permitted to be unlabeled.

But genetic engineering technology is already very far along. As the Lovins note, the USDA has already approved about 50 genetically engineered crops for unlimited release; more than half of the world's soybeans and a third of its corn now contain genes spliced in from other forms of life.

While there are many important issues here, my own major concern with genetic engineering is narrower: that it gives the power—whether militarily, accidentally, or in a deliberate terrorist act—to create a White Plague.

The many wonders of nanotechnology were first imagined by the Nobel-laureate physicist Richard Feynman in a speech he gave in 1959, subsequently published under the title "There's Plenty of Room at the Bottom." The book that made a big impression on me, in the mid-'80s, was Eric Drexler's *Engines of Creation,* in which he described beautifully how manipulation of matter at the atomic level could create a utopian future of abundance, where just about everything could be made cheaply, and almost any imaginable disease or physical problem could be solved using nanotechnology and artificial intelligences.

A subsequent book, *Unbounding the Future:The Nanotechnology Revolution*, which Drexler cowrote, imagines some of the changes that might take place in a world where we had molecular-level "assemblers." Assemblers could make possible incredibly low-cost solar power, cures for cancer and the common cold by augmentation of the human immune system, essentially complete cleanup of the environment, incredibly inexpensive pocket supercomputers — in fact, any product would be manufacturable by assemblers at a cost no greater than that of wood— spaceflight more accessible than transoceanic travel today, and restoration of extinct species.

I remember feeling good about nanotechnology after reading *Engines of Creation*. As a technologist, it gave me a sense of calm—that is, nanotechnology showed us that incredible progress was possible, and indeed perhaps inevitable. If nanotechnology was our future, then I didn't feel pressed to solve so many problems in the present. I would get to Drexler's utopian future in due time; I might as well enjoy life more in the here and now. It didn't make sense, given his vision, to stay up all night, all the time.

Drexler's vision also led to a lot of good fun. I would occasionally get to describe the wonders of nanotechnology to others who had not heard of it. After teasing them with all the things Drexler described I would give a homework assignment of my own: "Use nanotechnology to create a vampire; for extra credit create an antidote."

With these wonders came clear dangers, of which I was acutely aware. As I said at a nanotechnology conference in 1989, "We can't simply do our science and not worry about these ethical issues."[8] But my subsequent conversations with

---

8 First Foresight Conference on Nanotechnology in October 1989, a talk titled "The Future of Computation." Published in Crandall, B. C. and James Lewis, editors. *Nanotechnology: Research and Perspectives*. MIT Press, 1992: 269. See also www.foresight.org/Conferences/MNT01/Nano1.html.

physicists convinced me that nanotechnology might not even work—or, at least, it wouldn't work anytime soon. Shortly thereafter I moved to Colorado, to a skunk works I had set up, and the focus of my work shifted to software for the Internet, specifically on ideas that became Java and Jini.

Then, last summer, Brosl Hasslacher told me that nanoscale molecular electronics was now practical. This was *new* news, at least to me, and I think to many people—and it radically changed my opinion about nanotechnology. It sent me back to *Engines of Creation*. Rereading Drexler's work after more than 10 years, I was dismayed to realize how little I had remembered of its lengthy section called "Dangers and Hopes," including a discussion of how nanotechnologies can become "engines of destruction." Indeed, in my rereading of this cautionary material today, I am struck by how naive some of Drexler's safeguard proposals seem, and how much greater I judge the dangers to be now than even he seemed to then. (Having anticipated and described many technical and political problems with nanotechnology, Drexler started the Foresight Institute in the late 1980s "to help prepare society for anticipated advanced technologies" — most important, nanotechnology.)

The enabling breakthrough to assemblers seems quite likely within the next 20 years. Molecular electronics—the new subfield of nanotechnology where individual molecules are circuit elements—should mature quickly and become enormously lucrative within this decade, causing a large incremental investment in all nanotechnologies.

Unfortunately, as with nuclear technology, it is far easier to create destructive uses for nanotechnology than constructive ones. Nanotechnology has clear military and terrorist uses, and you need not be suicidal to release a massively destructive nanotechnological device—such devices can be built to be selectively destructive, affecting,

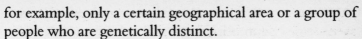

for example, only a certain geographical area or a group of people who are genetically distinct.

An immediate consequence of the Faustian bargain in obtaining the great power of nanotechnology is that we run a grave risk—the risk that we might destroy the biosphere on which all life depends.

As Drexler explained:

> "Plants" with "leaves" no more efficient than today's solar cells could out-compete real plants, crowding the biosphere with an inedible foliage. Tough omnivorous "bacteria" could out-compete real bacteria: They could spread like blowing pollen, replicate swiftly, and reduce the biosphere to dust in a matter of days. Dangerous replicators could easily be too tough, small, and rapidly spreading to stop—at least if we make no preparation. We have trouble enough controlling viruses and fruit flies.
>
> Among the cognoscenti of nanotechnology, this threat has become known as the "gray goo problem." Though masses of uncontrolled replicators need not be gray or gooey, the term "gray goo" emphasizes that replicators able to obliterate life might be less inspiring than a single species of crabgrass. They might be superior in an evolutionary sense, but this need not make them valuable.
>
> The gray goo threat makes one thing perfectly clear: We cannot afford certain kinds of accidents with replicating assemblers.

Gray goo would surely be a depressing ending to our human adventure on Earth, far worse than mere fire or ice, and one that could stem from a simple laboratory accident.[9] Oops.

---

9 In his 1963 novel *Cat's Cradle*, Kurt Vonnegut imagined a gray-goo-like accident where a form of ice called ice-nine, which becomes solid at a much higher temperature, freezes the oceans.

It is most of all the power of destructive self-replication in genetics, nanotechnology, and robotics (GNR) that should give us pause. Self-replication is the modus operandi of genetic engineering, which uses the machinery of the cell to replicate its designs, and the prime danger underlying gray goo in nanotechnology. Stories of run-amok robots like the Borg, replicating or mutating to escape from the ethical constraints imposed on them by their creators, are well established in our science fiction books and movies. It is even possible that self-replication may be more fundamental than we thought, and hence harder—or even impossible—to control. A recent article by Stuart Kauffman in *Nature* titled "Self-Replication: Even Peptides Do It" discusses the discovery that a 32-amino-acid peptide can "autocatalyse its own synthesis." We don't know how widespread this ability is, but Kauffman notes that it may hint at "a route to self-reproducing molecular systems on a basis far wider than Watson-Crick base-pairing."[10]

In truth, we have had in hand for years clear warnings of the dangers inherent in widespread knowledge of GNR technologies—of the possibility of knowledge alone enabling mass destruction. But these warnings haven't been widely publicized; the public discussions have been clearly inadequate. There is no profit in publicizing the dangers.

The nuclear, biological, and chemical (NBC) technologies used in 20th-century weapons of mass destruction were and are largely military, developed in government laboratories. In sharp contrast, the 21st-century GNR technologies have clear commercial uses and are being developed almost exclusively by corporate enterprises. In this age of triumphant commercialism, technology—with science as its handmaiden—is delivering a series of almost magical inventions that are the most phenomenally lucrative

10 Kauffman, p.496

ever seen. We are aggressively pursuing the promises of these new technologies within the now-unchallenged system of global capitalism and its manifold financial incentives and competitive pressures.

> This is the first moment in the history of our planet when any species, by its own voluntary actions, has become a danger to itself—as well as to vast numbers of others.

> It might be a familiar progression, transpiring on many worlds—a planet, newly formed, placidly revolves around its star; life slowly forms; a kaleidoscopic procession of creatures evolves; intelligence emerges which, at least up to a point, confers enormous survival value; and then technology is invented. It dawns on them that there are such things as laws of Nature, that these laws can be revealed by experiment, and that knowledge of these laws can be made both to save and to take lives, both on unprecedented scales. Science, they recognize, grants immense powers. In a flash, they create world-altering contrivances. Some planetary civilizations see their way through, place limits on what may and what must not be done, and safely pass through the time of perils. Others, not so lucky or so prudent, perish.

That is Carl Sagan, writing in 1994, in *Pale Blue Dot,* a book describing his vision of the human future in space. I am only now realizing how deep his insight was, and how sorely I miss, and will miss, his voice. For all its eloquence, Sagan's contribution was not least that of simple common sense—an attribute that, along with humility, many of the leading advocates of the 21st-century technologies seem to lack.

I remember from my childhood that my grandmother was strongly against the overuse of antibiotics. She had worked since before the first World War as a nurse and had a commonsense attitude that taking antibiotics, unless they were absolutely necessary, was bad for you.

It is not that she was an enemy of progress. She saw much progress in an almost 70-year nursing career; my grandfather, a diabetic, benefited greatly from the improved treatments that became available in his lifetime. But she, like many levelheaded people, would probably think it greatly arrogant for us, now, to be designing a robotic "replacement species," when we obviously have so much trouble making relatively simple things work, and so much trouble managing—or even understanding—ourselves.

I realize now that she had an awareness of the nature of the order of life, and of the necessity of living with and respecting that order. With this respect comes a necessary humility that we, with our early-21st-century chutzpah, lack at our peril. The commonsense view, grounded in this respect, is often right, in advance of the scientific evidence. The clear fragility and inefficiencies of the human-made systems we have built should give us all pause; the fragility of the systems I have worked on certainly humbles me.

We should have learned a lesson from the making of the first atomic bomb and the resulting arms race. We didn't do well then, and the parallels to our current situation are troubling.

The effort to build the first atomic bomb was led by the brilliant physicist J. Robert Oppenheimer. Oppenheimer was not naturally interested in politics but became painfully aware of what he perceived as the grave threat to Western civilization from the Third Reich, a threat surely grave because of the possibility that Hitler might obtain nuclear weapons. Energized by this concern, he brought his strong intellect, passion for physics, and charismatic leadership skills to Los Alamos and led a rapid and successful effort by an incredible collection of great minds to quickly invent the bomb.

What is striking is how this effort continued so naturally after the initial impetus was removed. In a meeting shortly after V-E Day with some physicists who felt that perhaps the effort should stop, Oppenheimer argued to continue. His stated reason seems a bit strange: not because of the fear of large casualties from an invasion of Japan, but because the United Nations, which was soon to be formed, should have foreknowledge of atomic weapons. A more likely reason the project continued is the momentum that had built up—the first atomic test, Trinity, was nearly at hand.

We know that in preparing this first atomic test the physicists proceeded despite a large number of possible dangers. They were initially worried, based on a calculation by Edward Teller, that an atomic explosion might set fire to the atmosphere. A revised calculation reduced the danger of destroying the world to a three-in-a-million chance. (Teller says he was later able to dismiss the prospect of atmospheric ignition entirely.) Oppenheimer, though, was sufficiently concerned about the result of Trinity that he arranged for a possible evacuation of the southwest part of the state of New Mexico. And, of course, there was the clear danger of starting a nuclear arms race.

Within a month of that first, successful test, two atomic bombs destroyed Hiroshima and Nagasaki. Some scientists had suggested that the bomb simply be demonstrated, rather than dropped on Japanese cities—saying that this would greatly improve the chances for arms control after the war—but to no avail. With the tragedy of Pearl Harbor still fresh in Americans' minds, it would have been very difficult for President Truman to order a demonstration of the weapons rather than use them as he did—the desire to quickly end the war and save the lives that would have been lost in any invasion of Japan was very strong. Yet the overriding truth was probably very simple: As the physicist Freeman Dyson later said, "The reason that it was dropped was just that nobody had the courage or the foresight to say no."

It's important to realize how shocked the physicists were in the aftermath of the bombing of Hiroshima, on August 6, 1945. They describe a series of waves of emotion: first, a sense of fulfillment that the bomb worked, then horror at all the people that had been killed, and then a convincing feeling that on no account should another bomb be dropped. Yet of course another bomb was dropped, on Nagasaki, only three days after the bombing of Hiroshima.

In November 1945, three months after the atomic bombings, Oppenheimer stood firmly behind the scientific attitude, saying, "It is not possible to be a scientist unless you believe that the knowledge of the world, and the power which this gives, is a thing which is of intrinsic value to humanity, and that you are using it to help in the spread of knowledge and are willing to take the consequences."

Oppenheimer went on to work, with others, on the Acheson-Lilienthal Report, which, as Richard Rhodes says in his recent book *Visions of Technology,* "found a way to prevent a clandestine nuclear arms race without resorting to armed world government"; their suggestion was a form of relinquishment of nuclear weapons work by nation-states to an international agency.

This proposal led to the Baruch Plan, which was submitted to the United Nations in June 1946 but never adopted (perhaps because, as Rhodes suggests, Bernard Baruch had "insisted on burdening the plan with conventional sanctions," thereby inevitably dooming it, even though it would "almost certainly have been rejected by

Stalinist Russia anyway"). Other efforts to promote sensible steps toward internationalizing nuclear power to prevent an arms race ran afoul either of U.S. politics and internal distrust, or distrust by the Soviets. The opportunity to avoid the arms race was lost, and very quickly.

Two years later, in 1948, Oppenheimer seemed to have reached another stage in his thinking, saying, "In some sort of crude sense which no vulgarity, no humor, no overstatement can quite extinguish, the physicists have known sin; and this is a knowledge they cannot lose."

In 1949, the Soviets exploded an atom bomb. By 1955, both the U.S. and the Soviet Union had tested hydrogen bombs suitable for delivery by aircraft. And so the nuclear arms race began.

Nearly 20 years ago, in the documentary *The Day After Trinity*, Freeman Dyson summarized the scientific attitudes that brought us to the nuclear precipice:

"I have felt it myself. The glitter of nuclear weapons. It is irresistible if you come to them as a scientist. To feel it's there in your hands, to release this energy that fuels the stars, to let it do your bidding. To perform these miracles, to lift a million tons of rock into the sky. It is something that gives people an illusion of illimitable power, and it is, in some ways, responsible for all our troubles—this, what you might call technical arrogance, that overcomes people when they see what they can do with their minds."[11]

Now, as then, we are creators of new technologies and stars of the imagined future, driven—this time by great financial rewards and global competition—despite the clear dangers, hardly evaluating what it may be like to try to live in a world that is the realistic outcome of what we are creating and imagining.

---

11 Else

In 1947, *The Bulletin of the Atomic Scientists* began putting a Doomsday Clock on its cover. For more than 50 years, it has shown an estimate of the relative nuclear danger we have faced, reflecting the changing international conditions. The hands on the clock have moved 15 times and today, standing at nine minutes to midnight, reflect continuing and real danger from nuclear weapons. The recent addition of India and Pakistan to the list of nuclear powers has increased the threat of failure of the nonproliferation goal, and this danger was reflected by moving the hands closer to midnight in 1998.

In our time, how much danger do we face, not just from nuclear weapons, but from all of these technologies? How high are the extinction risks?

The philosopher John Leslie has studied this question and concluded that the risk of human extinction is at least 30 percent,[12] while Ray Kurzweil believes we have "a better than even chance of making it through," with the caveat that he has "always been accused of being an optimist." Not only are these estimates not encouraging, but they do not include the probability of many horrid outcomes that lie short of extinction.

Faced with such assessments, some serious people are already suggesting that we simply move beyond Earth as quickly as possible. We would colonize the galaxy using von Neumann probes, which hop from star system to star system, replicating as they go. This step will almost certainly

---

12 This estimate is in Leslie's book *The End of the World: The Science and Ethics of Human Extinction*, where he notes that the probability of extinction is substantially higher if we accept Brandon Carter's Doomsday Argument, which is, briefly, that "we ought to have some reluctance to believe that we are very exceptionally early, for instance in the earliest 0.001 percent, among all humans who will ever have lived. This would be some reason for thinking that humankind will not survive for many more centuries, let alone colonize the galaxy. Carter's doomsday argument doesn't generate any risk estimates just by itself. It is an argument for revising the estimates which we generate when we consider various possible dangers."

be necessary 5 billion years from now (or sooner if our solar system is disastrously impacted by the impending collision of our galaxy with the Andromeda galaxy within the next 3 billion years), but if we take Kurzweil and Moravec at their word it might be necessary by the middle of this century.

What are the moral implications here? If we must move beyond Earth this quickly in order for the species to survive, who accepts the responsibility for the fate of those (most of us, after all) who are left behind? And even if we scatter to the stars, isn't it likely that we may take our problems with us or find, later, that they have followed us? The fate of our species on Earth and our fate in the galaxy seem inextricably linked.

Another idea is to erect a series of shields to defend against each of the dangerous technologies. The Strategic Defense Initiative, proposed by the Reagan administration, was an attempt to design such a shield against the threat of a nuclear attack from the Soviet Union. But as Arthur C. Clarke, who was privy to discussions about the project, observed: "Though it might be possible, at vast expense, to construct local defense systems that would 'only' let through a few percent of ballistic missiles, the much touted idea of a national umbrella was nonsense. Luis Alvarez, perhaps the greatest experimental physicist of this century, remarked to me that the advocates of such schemes were 'very bright guys with no common sense.'"

Clarke continued: "Looking into my often cloudy crystal ball, I suspect that a total defense might indeed be possible in a century or so. But the technology involved would produce, as a by-product, weapons so terrible that no one would bother with anything as primitive as ballistic missiles."[13]

---

13 Clarke, p. 526

In *Engines of Creation,* Eric Drexler proposed that we build an active nanotechnological shield—a form of immune system for the biosphere—to defend against dangerous replicators of all kinds that might escape from laboratories or otherwise be maliciously created. But the shield he proposed would itself be extremely dangerous—nothing could prevent it from developing autoimmune problems and attacking the biosphere itself. [14]

Similar difficulties apply to the construction of shields against robotics and genetic engineering. These technologies are too powerful to be shielded against in the time frame of interest; even if it were possible to implement defensive shields, the side effects of their development would be at least as dangerous as the technologies we are trying to protect against.

These possibilities are all thus either undesirable or unachievable or both. The only realistic alternative I see is relinquishment: to limit development of the technologies that are too dangerous, by limiting our pursuit of certain kinds of knowledge.

Yes, I know, knowledge is good, as is the search for new truths. We have been seeking knowledge since ancient times. Aristotle opened his Metaphysics with the simple statement: "All men by nature desire to know." We have, as a bedrock value in our society, long agreed on the value of open access to information, and recognize the problems that arise with attempts to restrict access to and development of knowledge. In recent times, we have come to revere scientific knowledge.

14 And, as David Forrest suggests in his paper "Regulating Nanotechnology Development," available at www.foresight.org/NanoRev/Forrest1989.html, "If we used strict liability as an alternative to regulation it would be impossible for any developer to internalize the cost of the risk (destruction of the biosphere), so theoretically the activity of developing nanotechnology should never be undertaken." Forrest's analysis leaves us with only government regulation to protect us—not a comforting thought.

But despite the strong historical precedents, if open access to and unlimited development of knowledge henceforth puts us all in clear danger of extinction, then common sense demands that we reexamine even these basic, long-held beliefs.

It was Nietzsche who warned us, at the end of the 19th century, not only that God is dead but that "faith in science, which after all exists undeniably, cannot owe its origin to a calculus of utility; it must have originated *in spite of* the fact that the disutility and dangerousness of the 'will to truth,' of 'truth at any price' is proved to it constantly." It is this further danger that we now fully face—the consequences of our truth-seeking. The truth that science seeks can certainly be considered a dangerous substitute for God if it is likely to lead to our extinction.

If we could agree, as a species, what we wanted, where we were headed, and why, then we would make our future much less dangerous—then we might understand what we can and should relinquish. Otherwise, we can easily imagine an arms race developing over GNR technologies, as it did with the NBC technologies in the 20th century. This is perhaps the greatest risk, for once such a race begins, it's very hard to end it. This time—unlike during the Manhattan Project—we aren't in a war, facing an implacable enemy that is threatening our civilization; we are driven, instead, by our habits, our desires, our economic system, and our competitive need to know.

I believe that we all wish our course could be determined by our collective values, ethics, and morals. If we had gained more collective wisdom over the past few thousand years, then a dialogue to this end would be more practical, and the incredible powers we are about to unleash would not be nearly so troubling.

One would think we might be driven to such a dialogue by our instinct for self-preservation. Individuals clearly have this desire, yet as a species our behavior seems to be not in our favor. In dealing with the nuclear threat, we often spoke dishonestly to ourselves and to each other, thereby greatly increasing the risks. Whether this was politically motivated, or because we chose not to think ahead, or because when faced with such grave threats we acted irrationally out of fear, I do not know, but it does not bode well.

The new Pandora's boxes of genetics, nanotechnology, and robotics are almost open, yet we seem hardly to have noticed. Ideas can't be put back in a box; unlike uranium or plutonium, they don't need to be mined and refined, and they can be freely copied. Once they are out, they are out. Churchill remarked, in a famous left-handed compliment, that the American people and their leaders "invariably do the right thing, after they have examined every other alternative." In this case, however, we must act more presciently, as to do the right thing only at last may be to lose the chance to do it at all.

As Thoreau said, "We do not ride on the railroad; it rides upon us"; and this is what we must fight, in our time. The question is, indeed, Which is to be master? Will we survive our technologies?

We are being propelled into this new century with no plan, no control, no brakes. Have we already gone too far down the path to alter course? I don't believe so, but we aren't trying yet, and the last chance to assert control—the fail-safe point—is rapidly approaching. We have our first pet robots, as well as commercially available genetic engineering techniques, and our nanoscale techniques are advancing rapidly. While the development of these technologies proceeds through a number of steps, it isn't necessarily the case—as happened in the Manhattan Project and the Trinity test—that the last step in proving a technology is large and hard. The breakthrough to wild self-replication in robotics, genetic engineering, or nanotechnology could come suddenly, reprising the surprise we felt when we learned of the cloning of a mammal.

And yet I believe we do have a strong and solid basis for hope. Our attempts to deal with weapons of mass destruction in the last century provide a shining example of relinquishment for us to consider: the unilateral U.S. abandonment, without preconditions, of the development of biological weapons. This relinquishment stemmed from the realization that while it would take an enormous effort to create these terrible weapons, they could from then on easily be duplicated and fall into the hands of rogue nations or terrorist groups.

The clear conclusion was that we would create additional threats to ourselves by pursuing these weapons, and that we would be more secure if we did not pursue them. We have embodied our relinquishment of biological and chemical weapons in the 1972 Biological Weapons Convention (BWC) and the 1993 Chemical Weapons Convention (CWC).[15]

As for the continuing sizable threat from nuclear weapons, which we have lived with now for more than 50 years, the U.S. Senate's recent rejection of the Comprehensive Test Ban Treaty makes it clear relinquishing nuclear weapons will not be politically easy. But we have a unique opportunity, with the end of the Cold War, to avert a multipolar arms race. Building on the BWC and CWC relinquishments, successful abolition of nuclear weapons could help us build toward a habit of relinquishing dangerous technologies. (Actually, by getting rid of all but

15 Meselson

100 nuclear weapons worldwide—roughly the total destructive power of World War II and a considerably easier task—we could eliminate this extinction threat.[16])

Verifying relinquishment will be a difficult problem, but not an unsolvable one. We are fortunate to have already done a lot of relevant work in the context of the BWC and other treaties. Our major task will be to apply this to technologies that are naturally much more commercial than military. The substantial need here is for transparency, as difficulty of verification is directly proportional to the difficulty of distinguishing relinquished from legitimate activities.

I frankly believe that the situation in 1945 was simpler than the one we now face: the nuclear technologies were reasonably separable into commercial and military uses, and monitoring was aided by the nature of atomic tests and the ease with which radioactivity could be measured. Research on military applications could be performed at national laboratories such as Los Alamos, with the results kept secret as long as possible.

The GNR technologies do not divide clearly into commercial and military uses; given their potential in the market, it's hard to imagine pursuing them only in national laboratories. With their widespread commercial pursuit, enforcing relinquishment will require a verification regime similar to that for biological weapons, but on an unprecedented scale. This, inevitably, will raise tensions between our individual privacy and desire for proprietary information, and the need for verification to protect us all. We will undoubtedly encounter strong resistance to this loss of privacy and freedom of action.

Verifying the relinquishment of certain GNR technologies will have to occur in cyberspace as well as at

16 Doty, p. 583

physical facilities. The critical issue will be to make the necessary transparency acceptable in a world of proprietary information, presumably by providing new forms of protection for intellectual property.

Verifying compliance will also require that scientists and engineers adopt a strong code of ethical conduct, resembling the Hippocratic oath, and that they have the courage to whistleblow as necessary, even at high personal cost. This would answer the call—50 years after Hiroshima—by the Nobel laureate Hans Bethe, one of the most senior of the surviving members of the Manhattan Project, that all scientists "cease and desist from work creating, developing, improving, and manufacturing nuclear weapons and other weapons of potential mass destruction."[17] In the 21st century, this requires vigilance and personal responsibility by those who would work on both NBC and GNR technologies to avoid implementing weapons of mass destruction and knowledge-enabled mass destruction.

Thoreau also said that we will be "rich in proportion to the number of things which we can afford to let alone." We each seek to be happy, but it would seem worthwhile to question whether we need to take such a high risk of total destruction to gain yet more knowledge and yet more things; common sense says that there is a limit to our material needs—and that certain knowledge is too dangerous and is best forgone.

Neither should we pursue near immortality without considering the costs, without considering the commensurate increase in the risk of extinction. Immortality, while perhaps the original, is certainly not the only possible utopian dream.

I recently had the good fortune to meet the distinguished author and scholar Jacques Attali, whose book *Lignes*

17 See also Hans Bethe's 1997 letter to President Clinton, at www.fas.org/bethecr.htm.

d'horizons (*Millennium*, in the English translation) helped inspire the Java and Jini approach to the coming age of pervasive computing, as previously described in this magazine. In his new book *Fraternités*, Attali describes how our dreams of utopia have changed over time:

"At the dawn of societies, men saw their passage on Earth as nothing more than a labyrinth of pain, at the end of which stood a door leading, via their death, to the company of gods and to *Eternity*. With the Hebrews and then the Greeks, some men dared free themselves from theological demands and dream of an ideal City where *Liberty* would flourish. Others, noting the evolution of the market society, understood that the liberty of some would entail the alienation of others, and they sought *Equality*."

Jacques helped me understand how these three different utopian goals exist in tension in our society today. He goes on to describe a fourth utopia, *Fraternity,* whose foundation is altruism. Fraternity alone associates individual happiness with the happiness of others, affording the promise of self-sustainment.

This crystallized for me my problem with Kurzweil's dream. A technological approach to Eternity—near immortality through robotics—may not be the most desirable utopia, and its pursuit brings clear dangers. Maybe we should rethink our utopian choices.

Where can we look for a new ethical basis to set our course? I have found the ideas in the book *Ethics for the New Millennium*, by the Dalai Lama, to be very helpful. As is perhaps well known but little heeded, the Dalai Lama argues that the most important thing is for us to conduct our lives with love and compassion for others, and that our societies need to develop a stronger notion of universal responsibility and of our interdependency; he proposes a standard of positive ethical conduct for individuals and societies that seems consonant with Attali's Fraternity utopia.

The Dalai Lama further argues that we must understand what it is that makes people happy, and acknowledge the strong evidence that neither material progress nor the pursuit of the power of knowledge is the key—that there are limits to what science and the scientific pursuit alone can do.

Our Western notion of happiness seems to come from the Greeks, who defined it as "the exercise of vital powers along lines of excellence in a life affording them scope."[18]

Clearly, we need to find meaningful challenges and sufficient scope in our lives if we are to be happy in whatever is to come. But I believe we must find alternative outlets for our creative forces, beyond the culture of perpetual economic growth; this growth has largely been a blessing for several hundred years, but it has not brought us unalloyed happiness, and we must now choose between the pursuit of unrestricted and undirected growth through science and technology and the clear accompanying dangers.

It is now more than a year since my first encounter with Ray Kurzweil and John Searle. I see around me cause for hope in the voices for caution and relinquishment and in those people I have discovered who are as concerned as I am about our current predicament. I feel, too, a deepened sense of personal responsibility—not for the work I have already done, but for the work that I might yet do, at the confluence of the sciences.

But many other people who know about the dangers still seem strangely silent. When pressed, they trot out the "this

18 Hamilton p. 35

is nothing new" riposte—as if awareness of what could happen is response enough. They tell me, There are universities filled with bioethicists who study this stuff all day long. They say, All this has been written about before, and by experts. They complain, Your worries and your arguments are already old hat.

I don't know where these people hide their fear. As an architect of complex systems I enter this arena as a generalist. But should this diminish my concerns? I am aware of how much has been written about, talked about, and lectured about so authoritatively. But does this mean it has reached people? Does this mean we can discount the dangers before us?

Knowing is not a rationale for not acting. Can we doubt that knowledge has become a weapon we wield against ourselves?

The experiences of the atomic scientists clearly show the need to take personal responsibility, the danger that things will move too fast, and the way in which a process can take on a life of its own. We can, as they did, create insurmountable problems in almost no time flat. We must do more thinking up front if we are not to be similarly surprised and shocked by the consequences of our inventions.

My continuing professional work is on improving the reliability of software. Software is a tool, and as a toolbuilder I must struggle with the uses to which the tools I make are put. I have always believed that making software more reliable, given its many uses, will make the world a safer and better place; if I were to come to believe the opposite, then I would be morally obligated to stop this work. I can now imagine such a day may come.

This all leaves me not angry but at least a bit melancholic. Henceforth, for me, progress will be somewhat bittersweet.

———

Do you remember the beautiful penultimate scene in Manhattan where Woody Allen is lying on his couch and talking into a tape recorder? He is writing a short story about people who are creating unnecessary, neurotic problems for themselves, because it keeps them from dealing with more unsolvable, terrifying problems about the universe.

He leads himself to the question, "Why is life worth living?" and to consider what makes it worthwhile for him: Groucho Marx, Willie Mays, the second movement of the Jupiter Symphony, Louis Armstrong's recording of "Potato Head Blues," Swedish movies, Flaubert's Sentimental Education, Marlon Brando, Frank Sinatra, the apples and pears by Cézanne, the crabs at Sam Wo's, and, finally, the showstopper: his love Tracy's face.

Each of us has our precious things, and as we care for them we locate the essence of our humanity. In the end, it is because of our great capacity for caring that I remain optimistic we will confront the dangerous issues now before us.

My immediate hope is to participate in a much larger discussion of the issues raised here, with people from many different backgrounds, in settings not predisposed to fear or favor technology for its own sake.

As a start, I have twice raised many of these issues at events sponsored by the Aspen Institute and have separately proposed that the American Academy of Arts and Sciences take them up as an extension of its work with the Pugwash Conferences. (These have been held since 1957 to discuss arms control, especially of nuclear weapons, and to formulate workable policies.)

It's unfortunate that the Pugwash meetings started only well after the nuclear genie was out of the bottle—roughly 15 years too late. We are also getting a belated start on seriously addressing the issues around 21st-century technologies—the prevention of knowledge-enabled mass destruction—and further delay seems unacceptable.

So I'm still searching; there are many more things to learn. Whether we are to succeed or fail, to survive or fall victim to these technologies, is not yet decided. I'm up late again—it's almost 6 am. I'm trying to imagine some better answers, to break the spell and free them from the stone.

SOURCES

BOOKS

Drexler, Eric, *Engines of Creation* (Anchor, 1987).

———, Chris Peterson, and Gayle Pergamit, *Unbounding the Future: The Nanotechnology Revolution* (Quill, 1993).

Dyson, George, *Darwin Among the Machines* (Perseus Publishing, 1998).

Garrett, Laurie, *The Coming Plague: Newly Emerging Diseases in a World Out of Balance* (Penguin, 1994: 47-52, 414, 419, 452).

Gelernter, David, *Drawing Life: Surviving the Unabomber* (Free Press, 1997: 120).

Hamilton, Edith, *The Greek Way* (W. W. Norton & Co., 1942: 35).

Leslie, John, *The End of the World: The Science and Ethics of Human Extinction* (Routledge, 1996: 1, 3, 145).

Stone, Irving, *The Agony and the Ecstasy* (Doubleday, 1961: 6, 144).

ARTICLES

Clarke, Arthur C., "Presidents, Experts, and Asteroids." *Science,* June 5, 1998.

Doty, Paul, "The Forgotten Menace: Nuclear Weapons Stockpiles Still Represent the Biggest Threat to Civilization." *Nature,* 402, December 9, 1999: 583.

Easterbrook, Gregg, "Food for the Future: Someday, rice will have built-in vitamin A. Unless the Luddites win." *The New York Times* (November 19, 1999).

Hillis, Danny, "Test of Time" in *Wired* 8.03 (March 2000).

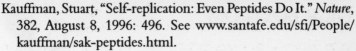

Kauffman, Stuart, "Self-replication: Even Peptides Do It." *Nature*, 382, August 8, 1996: 496. See www.santafe.edu/sfi/People/kauffman/sak-peptides.html.

Lovins, Amory, "A Tale of Two Botanies" in *Wired* 8.04 (April 2000).

Meselson, Matthew, "The Problem of Biological Weapons." Presentation to the 1,818th Stated Meeting of the American Academy of Arts and Sciences, January 13, 1999. (minerva.amacad.org/archive/bulletin4.htm).

WEBSITES

Bethe, Hans, www.fas.org/bethecr.htm (1997).

Else, Jon, *The Day After Trinity: J. Robert Oppenheimer and The Atomic Bomb* (available at www.pyramiddirect.com).

Forrest, David, "Regulating Nanotechnology Development," (available at www.foresight.org/NanoRev/Forrest1989.html).

NICK BOSTROM

ARE

WE

LIVING

IN

Almost everyone who sees The Matrix *considers, at least for a second or two, the uncomfortable possibility that they might in fact be in the Matrix. Yale philosopher Nick Bostrom considers this possibility as well, and concludes that it's far more likely than you might imagine.*

THE MATRIX?

THE SIMULATION ARGUMENT

The Matrix provides us with a bizarre and horrific scenario. Humanity lies comatose in pods, every aspect of reality defined and controlled by malevolent computers.

For most viewers, this scenario is interesting as science fiction, but inconceivably remote from anything that exists today or is likely to exist in the future. But, upon careful consideration, a scenario much like this is much more than conceivable. It is quite likely.

An earlier essay by Ray Kurzweil discusses the trend we are on, towards increasingly powerful computing capabilities. Kurzweil projects that within the next fifty years a virtually unlimited amount of computing power will become available. Let's assume that Kurzweil is correct and humankind will, sooner or later, develop virtually infinite computing capabilities. For purposes of this discussion, it doesn't matter how long it will take. It can take one hundred years, one thousand years, or one million years.

As noted in Kurzweil's essay, unlimited computing power would enhance mankind's capabilities to an incredible degree. This civilization would be "posthuman," capable of awesome technological feats.

Posthuman civilization could take many forms. It could be similar in many ways to our current civilization or it could be radically different. It is, of course, almost impossible to predict how such a civilization would develop. But the one thing we know, by definition, is that posthuman civilization has access to virtually unlimited computing power.

Posthuman civilization may be capable of converting planets and other astronomical resources into enormously powerful computers. It is currently hard to confidently place any upper bound on the computing power that may be available to posthuman civilizations.

1. This essay explains the simulation argument, which argues that *at least one* of the following statements is true: The human species is very likely to become extinct before reaching a "posthuman" stage.
2. Any posthuman civilization is extremely unlikely to run a significant number of simulations of their evolutionary history (or variations thereof).
3. We are almost certainly living in a computer simulation.

Let's consider these three statements in turn. The first statement is straightforward. If we destroy ourselves through nuclear war, biological catastrophe, or nanotech disaster, then the rest of this argument is irrelevant. But let's assume that this statement is false, that we manage to avoid destruction and enter the posthuman age.

The nature of human civilization in the posthuman age is impossible to fully imagine. The various uses to which a virtually infinite supply of computing capacity will be put are equally difficult to imagine. But let's consider one specific use, the creation of complex simulations of human civilizations.

Imagine historians of the future simulating various historical scenarios. These would not be the simplistic simulations of today. With the vast computing power at their disposal, the simulations can be extremely fine-grained—every building, every geographical feature, every individual. And each of these individuals could be given the same level of computing power, complexity, and intelligence as a living human. Like Agent Smith, they would be built out of software, but they would have the mental characteristics of a human. Of course, they might never realize they were software. To create an accurate simulation, the perceptions of the simulated individuals would have to be indistinguishable from those of people living in the real world.

Like the inhabitants of the Matrix, these individuals would be living in an artificial world, believing it was real. Unlike in the Matrix scenario, these individuals would be entirely composed of software.

But would these simulated individuals really be "people"? Would they be intelligent, regardless of how much processing power they had? Would they be conscious?

The reality is no one really knows. But it's common for philosophers of the mind to make the assumption of *substrate-independence*. Basically this means that consciousness may depend on many things—knowledge, intelligence (processing power), mental organization, the details of computational structure, and so on—but one of the things it doesn't necessarily require is biological tissue. It is not an essential property of consciousness that it is implemented on carbon-based biological neural networks inside a cranium; silicon-based processors inside a computer could, in principle, do the trick as well.

For many people familiar with the computing of today, the idea of conscious software seems incredible. But this intuitive disbelief is a product of the relatively pathetic capabilities of today's computers. With ongoing advances in computers and software, computers will increasingly seem more intelligent, more conscious. In fact, given the human tendency to anthropomorphize anything that seems remotely human, people may start to credit computers with consciousness long before this becomes a reality.

Arguments for substrate-independence have been made in the philosophy of mind literature, and I won't attempt to repeat these arguments here. But I will point out that this assumption is sensible. The brain cell is a physical object with certain characteristics. If we come to fully understand these characteristics and learn to replicate them electronically, then surely our electronic brain cell can perform the same functions as an organic one. And if it can be done with a brain cell, then why not with an entire brain? And if that were done, why wouldn't the resulting system be just as conscious as a brain?

The implications are interesting. Given enough computing power, posthumans can create simulations of historical individuals that are fully conscious, that believe themselves to be biological humans living in an earlier age. This brings us to statement number two.

The first statement suggested that we will survive long enough to develop a posthuman civilization. This posthuman civilization would have the capability of developing Matrix-like simulations of reality. Statement two represents the possibility that posthumans would choose not to develop these simulations.

We can imagine that in the "posthuman age" there would be no interest in running historical simulations. This would require significant changes to the motivations of individuals in a posthuman age, for there are certainly many humans today who would like to run ancestor simulations if they could afford to do so. But perhaps many of our human desires will be regarded as silly by anyone who becomes a posthuman. Maybe the scientific value of ancestor simulations to a posthuman civilization will be negligible (which is not too implausible, given its unfathomable intellectual superiority), and maybe posthumans regard recreational activities as merely a very inefficient way of getting pleasure—which can be obtained much more cheaply by direct stimulation of the brain's reward centers. This conclusion implies that posthuman societies will be very different from human societies: they will not contain relatively wealthy independent agents in possession of the full gamut of humanlike desires and free to act on them.

Alternatively, it's possible that individual posthumans may have a desire to run ancestor simulations, but that they are prevented from doing so by posthuman laws. What would lead to these laws? One can speculate that advanced civilizations all develop along a trajectory that leads to the recognition of an ethical prohibition against running ancestor simulations because of the suffering that is inflicted on the inhabitants of the simulation. However, from our present point of view, it is not clear that creating a human race is immoral. On the contrary, we tend to view the existence of our race as constituting a great ethical value. Moreover, convergence on an ethical view of the immorality of running ancestor simulations is not enough. It must be combined with convergence on a civilization-wide social structure that enables activities considered immoral to be effectively banned.

So while it is possible that statement two is true, it would require posthumans to have dramatically different motivations from humans, or they would have to enforce a prohibition on ancestor simulations universally and effectively. Further, this would have to be true for almost every posthuman civilization throughout the universe.[1]

We must therefore consider the possibility that human-level civilizations stand a chance of becoming posthuman and that at least some posthuman civilizations would contain individuals who run ancestor simulations. This brings us to our third statement: we are almost certainly living in a computer simulation. This conclusion follows very naturally.

If posthumans are running ancestor simulations, they are almost certainly being run on a very broad scale. One can easily imagine millions of individuals running thousands of variations on hundreds of themes, each containing billions of simulated individuals. Scientists, hobbyists, artists, and schoolchildren might all be running these simulations. Trillions and trillions of these simulated individuals would exist, all believing that they are real and are living in an earlier generation.

There are approximately six billion biological humans living in 2003. In a posthuman age, there may very well be

---

1 It's a reasonable possibility that civilizations with posthuman resources would have spread beyond our solar system.

trillions of software-based humans living in the year 2003 of their simulated world, all believing they are biological, just as you and I do. The math is simple; the overwhelming majority of these individuals are wrong; they believe they are biological, but they are not. There is no reason to exclude our civilization from this calculation. The odds are overwhelming that we are living in a simulated 2003 and that our physical bodies are a software illusion.

It is worth emphasizing that the simulation argument doesn't purport to show that we are living in a computer simulation. It only shows that at least one of the three statements listed above is true. If one rejects the conclusion that we are in a simulation, one would instead have to accept either that virtually all posthuman civilizations abstain from running ancestor simulations, or that we will likely become extinct before we reach a posthuman age. This could be as a result of a leveling off of current progress in computer science, or a general collapse of civilization. Or, you could acknowledge that scientific progress seems to be accelerating, not leveling off, and you could predict that this acceleration will be the cause of our extinction. One candidate, for instance, is molecular nanotechnology, which in its mature stage would enable the construction of self-replicating nanobots capable of feeding on dirt and organic matter—a kind of mechanical bacteria. Such nanobots, designed for malicious ends, could cause the extinction of all life on our planet. Elsewhere I have tried to catalogue what the main existential risks for humanity are.[2]

If our civilization is, in fact, a simulation, this doesn't imply any necessary limit on our progress. It may be possible for simulated civilizations to become posthuman. They may then run their own ancestor simulations on powerful computers they build in their simulated universe. Such

1 Bostrom

computers would be "virtual machines," a familiar concept in computer science. (Java script-based Web Applets, for instance, run on a virtual machine—a simulated computer—inside your desktop.) Virtual machines can be stacked: it's possible to simulate a machine simulating another machine, and so on, in arbitrarily many steps of iteration. If we do go on to create our own ancestor simulations, this would be strong evidence against statements one and two, and we would therefore have to conclude that we live in a simulation. Moreover, we would have to suspect that the posthumans running our simulation are themselves simulated beings; and their creators, in turn, may also be simulated beings.

Reality may thus contain many levels (this theme has been explored in many science fiction works, notably the film *The Thirteenth Floor*). Even if it is necessary for the hierarchy to bottom out at some stage—the metaphysical status of this claim is somewhat obscure—there may be room for a large number of levels of reality, and the number could be increasing over time. (One consideration that counts against the multilevel hypothesis is that the computational cost for the basement-level simulators would be very great. Simulating even a single posthuman civilization might be prohibitively expensive. If so, then we should expect our simulation to be terminated when we are about to become posthuman.)

Although all the elements of such a system can be naturalistic, even physical, it is possible to draw some loose analogies with religious conceptions of the world. In some ways, the posthumans running a simulation are like gods in relation to the people inhabiting the simulation: the posthumans created the world we see; they are of superior intelligence; they are "omnipotent" in the sense that they can interfere in the workings of our world even in ways that violate its physical laws; and they are "omniscient" in the sense that they can monitor everything that happens. However, all the demigods except those at the fundamental level of reality are subject to sanctions by the more powerful gods living at lower levels.

Further rumination on these themes could climax in a *naturalistic theogony* that would study the structure of this hierarchy, and the constraints imposed on its inhabitants by the possibility that their actions on their own level may affect the treatment they receive from dwellers of deeper levels. For example, if nobody can be sure that they are at the basement-level, then everybody would have to consider the possibility that their actions will be rewarded or punished, based perhaps on moral criteria, by their simulators. An afterlife would be a real possibility, as would reincarnation. Because of this fundamental uncertainty, even the basement civilization may have a reason to behave ethically. The fact that it has such a reason for moral behavior would of course add to everybody else's reason for behaving morally, and so on, in truly virtuous circle. One might get a kind of universal ethical imperative, which it would be in everybody's self-interest to obey, as it were "from nowhere."

In addition to ancestor simulations, one may also consider the possibility of more selective simulations that include only a small group of humans or a single individual. The rest of humanity would then be zombies or "shadow-people"—humans simulated only at a level sufficient for the fully simulated people not to notice anything suspicious. It is not clear how much cheaper shadow-people would be to simulate than real people. It is not even obvious that it is possible for an entity to behave indistinguishably from a real human and yet lack conscious experience. Even if there are such selective simulations, you should not think that you are in one of them unless you think they are much more numerous than complete simulations. There would have to be about a hundred billion times as many "me-simulations" (simulations of the life of only a single mind) as there are ancestor simulations in order for most simulated persons to be in me-simulations.

There is also the possibility of simulators abridging certain parts of the mental lives of simulated beings and giving them false memories of the sort of experiences that they would typically have had during the omitted interval. If so, one can consider the following (far-fetched) solution to the problem of evil: that there is no suffering in the world and all memories of suffering are illusions. Of course, this hypothesis can be seriously entertained only at those times when you are not suffering.

Supposing we live in a simulation, what are the implications for us humans? The foregoing remarks notwithstanding, the implications are not all that radical. Our best guide to how our posthuman creators might have chosen to set up our world is the standard empirical study of the universe we see. The revisions to most parts of our belief networks would be rather slight and subtle—in proportion to our lack of confidence in our ability to understand the ways of posthumans. Properly understood, therefore, the truth of statement three should have no tendency to make us "go crazy" or to prevent us from going about our business and making plans and predictions for tomorrow.

If we learn more about posthuman motivations and resource constraints, maybe as a result of developing towards becoming posthumans ourselves, then the hypothesis that we are simulated would come to have a much richer set of empirical implications. Of course, if the unfortunate reality is that we are simulations of some posthuman civilization, then we are argueably better off than the inhabitants of the Matrix. Rather than being held captive by a malevolent AI in order to power their civilization, we have been created out of software as part of a scientist's research project. Or perhaps created by a posthuman teenage girl for her science homework. Nevertheless we're better off than inhabitants of the Matrix. Aren't we?

SOURCES

ARTICLES

Bostrom, Nick, "Existential Risks: Analyzing Human Extinction Scenarios and Related Hazards," *Journal of Evolution and Technology*, vol. 9 (2002). Available online at *www.jetpress.org*.

THE

MATRIX

GLOSSARY

101—Neo's apartment number, reference to his being "The One." Note that it's written in binary code.

303—the room Trinity occupies at the beginning of the film. She's talking to Cypher, who is not in the Matrix at the time. Trinity means three; Cypher is another word for zero, thus: 303. Neo is shot and killed by Agent Smith in this same room. 303 also represents the three days from Christ's death to his resurrection, though for Neo it's more like three seconds.

1313—in this room at the Hotel Lafayette, Neo first encounters Morpheus and chooses the fateful red pill. Another variation of 1 and 3. Is 13 bad luck?

312-555-0690—312 is an area code in Chicago. *The Matrix* was filmed in Sydney, Australia. The city in the Matrix was anonymous, but the street locations and phone numbers are all based on Chicago, the Wachowskis' home town.

9/18—Andy Wachowski's wife's birthday. The clock in Neo's apartment reads 9:18.

Actor—see Mr. Reagan.

Adams Street Bridge—where Neo first meets Switch, Apoc, and Trinity. This bridge actually exists in Chicago; it's a famous historic structure that straddles the river.

Agents (Smith, Brown, and Jones)—as Morpheus says, "inside the Matrix, they are everyone and they are no one." Their generic last names are evidence of their anonymity. They move freely within the constraints of the Matrix, and their mutable nature makes them difficult to pinpoint. Thus, all persons in the Matrix are a potential threat.

Alice in Wonderland—Neo is a hipper, sexier version of innocent Alice; when he falls down the rabbit hole, he finds bleak reality rather than a magical dream world. Of course, *The Matrix* reverses the *Alice* paradigm; real life is the dream and reality is the Wonderland.

Allegory of the cave—a Platonic metaphor in which humans are described as prisoners chained in a cave, watching an elaborate show of shadow puppetry. The prisoners assume that the shadows are reality, because they can't see the puppets. Before Neo took the red pill, he couldn't see the Matrix for the shadow puppetry it was. By the end of the film he sees the actual green-lettered code flowing through all the objects—the highly advanced "puppetry" controlled by AI.

Analog vs. digital—in a world digitally controlled by Artificial Intelligence, "analog" devices serve as the sole escape for the rebels. The agents seem to be able to change most things in the Matrix, but they leave the telephones (nominally analog devices, but in fact digital, like everything else in the Matrix) alone. They can wall up a room with bricks and manipulate other objects in the Matrix, but must physically destroy these lines of escape.

When asked in an online chat about the telephone's symbolic significance, the Wachowski brothers said that they "liked the analog nature of older technology . . . the suggestion of old original phone hackers."[1]

---

1 www.8ung.at/michamarcus/matrix/inter.htm.

The release of *The Matrix* on DVD signaled a change in technology, from analog to digital. The DVD version (digital) sold many more copies than VHS tapes (analog), an unprecedented occurrence. *The Matrix* DVD remains the bestselling DVD of all time. When DVDs were first introduced to the market, they had difficulty convincing consumers to switch from VHS. *The Matrix*'s popularity (and all the extras included in the DVD) is credited with boosting the sales of DVD players and other DVDs.[2]

Anderson—Anderson is an English surname meaning "son of Andrew." Andrew is derived from the Greek Andreas, which means "man." Thus, Anderson is etymologically "son of man," an epithet that Jesus Christ favored.

Also a possible reference to Chicago-based Anderson Consulting (later renamed Accenture), famous for conformist consultants known as "Anderson Androids." This is not to be confused with sister company Arthur Anderson, which later became embroiled in the Enron debacle.

Apoc—first two syllables of Apocalypse.

Apocalypse—typically portrayed in the form of the four horsemen, fiery locusts from bottomless pits, the mark of the beast and the Antichrist; the apocalypse in the film features total devastation of the planet Earth and man's enslavement by the AI.

Armageddon—a great determining battle between good and evil. In *The Matrix*, The One's appearance signals the beginning of this particular Armageddon, the fight between man and machine.

Artificial Intelligence (AI)—machines capable of thinking and creating beyond what can be programmed into them by humans. Intelligent machines that "think" just like humans do—the distinguishing factor between AI and humanity is the physiological makeup; humans are organic and the AI are mechanical. Some argue that AI is humanity's evolutionary destiny. (See essays by Kurzweil, Lloyd, and Joy.)

Balls to bones—totally, completely.

---

2 www.icr2.com/articles/news/648.html.

Batteries—in *The Matrix*, humans have been reduced to the status of mere batteries. Their brains are hooked into a realistic vibrant dream world; they lie in capsules and feed the machines that control them. (See Coppertop.)

Baudrillard—famous French postmodern theorist. His theories of reality, simulacra, and simulation informed many of the complex themes of the film. In typical French philosophical tradition, Baudrillard has snorted in derision regarding *The Matrix*. He says that no film can fully explore the ideas of *Simulacra and Simulation* and that the attempts to do so in *The Matrix* are misinformed and misguided. (See Felluga and Gordon essays.)

Blue—the film's production team decided to give scenes that occurred in reality a cool blue hue. Bill Pope, the film's director of photography, said that ". . . to distinguish the Matrix from 'reality,' from the *Nebuchadnezzar* and the pods, reality was given a cooler look, a bluer, more normal, less sickly look. The future in the film is cold, the sun is blotted out, there is no real warmth unless it is artificial heat, so that is why they went for the cool side."[3] (See Green.)

Blue pill—the key to a lifetime of ignorant bliss: juicy steaks, happy careers, and petty problems that have nothing to do with the epic battle between man and machine. Take this pill and there's no need to worry about the desolate world of the real.

Bioelectricity—before the humans scorched the sky, AI was solar-powered. After this source of power was extinguished, the industrious machines found a better source: the humans themselves, combined with a "new form of fusion." Humans produce bioelectricity (an electric current produced by living tissue), "more than a 120-volt battery" as Morpheus tells Neo. (See essays by Lloyd and Sawyer.)

"Brain in a vat" hypothesis—a standard philosophical question posed by Hilary Putnam: "How do I know that I'm not just a brain in a vat somewhere, being stimulated by some mad scientist?" *The Matrix* took this question to the next level: "How do I know that I'm not just a body in a disgusting capsule

---

3 www.hollywoodjesus.com/matrix.htm.

somewhere, being stimulated by an evil machine?" (See essays by Boettke and Zynda.)

Bullet-time—when the Wachowskis were shooting *The Matrix*, they didn't yet have the technology to create the bullet-time effect—but they shot the scenes as if they did. Fortunately, several different effects teams worked on the film during postproduction, and were able to perfect the stylized effect that would contribute to the film's success. (*The Matrix* won the 2000 Academy Award for Best Visual Effects.) From Gap ads to *Shrek*, the effect has been used and parodied countless times since the film's release.

Cancer—Agent Smith likened the human race to a cancer that chews away at the planet. In this scene Agent Smith seemingly displays near-human emotions; he expresses disgust and hatred towards humans themselves. There's a sense of urgency—Agent Smith wants the codes from Morpheus so that he can cease fighting the rebels and be freed of the Matrix himself. But where would he go?

A distinguishing factor between AI and humanity is the human scope of emotional capability. But this scene calls that into question. Could AI (and its creations, like the agents) be more human-like than we imagine? (See Lloyd essay.)

Capsule—Neo must take the red one to discover that he is just a body *in* a capsule, feeding the machine.

Chicago—the town where the Wachowski brothers grew up. Though the film was shot in Sydney, all the street names and landmarks are named after places in Chicago. The directors' first feature film *Bound* was set in Chicago, as was *The Matrix* in the initial versions of the script. When they found out they were shooting in Australia, they kept the street names and locations in the shooting script.

Comic Books—*The Matrix* is a comic book come to life. The director of photography framed each shot in such a way that if you pause the film at any given point, the image you see could be directly from a comic or graphic novel. The Wachowskis made a comic-book version of the film to pitch it to the studio and, obviously, it worked.

Construct—the Matrix is one big construction, compliments of AI. A construct is generally accepted as "natural," but it's actually been *constructed*, built or defined by someone/something else—be it society, oppressive patriarchy, or malevolent beings.

Coppertop—a Duracell battery. Or a human being in 2199. Switch calls Neo "coppertop" upon first meeting him, because he's still feeding the machine.

Crops—much of Agent Smith's language has a dehumanizing effect. When he refers to the rows and rows of human prisoners as crops, it's clear that the AI and its workers consider the humans only a convenient source of food and energy.

Cypher—a word for zero. Possibly a derivative of Lucifer (he *does* wear a snakeskin coat). Cypher is the quintessential Judas figure in the film; that he betrayed Morpheus for a T-bone rather than silver is particularly poignant. (See Fontana essay.)

Desert of the real—a concept from Baudrillard's *Simulacra and Simulation*. One who is living in the desert of the real exists on the map rather than the territory; what they believe is real is actually a copy with no original. (See Felluga and Gordon essays.)

Digital pimp—though busy fighting evil, the rebels do have needs. It's ironic that sexual pleasure, in fact pleasure of all types, seems to lie for the rebels solely in the virtual world. Apparently, they're not engaging in sexual behavior in the social space of their world, but rather only in cyberspace. Cypher says that when he looks at the code he only sees "blonde, brunette, redhead . . ." We don't know what Zion looks like yet, but we can assume that currently there are no women in red walking around. (Just look at the clothes the *Neb*'s inhabitants are wearing.)

Director's cut—the Wachowski brothers like their film just as it is. They see no need for producing a director's cut; besides, they're too busy making the sequels.

Doubting Thomas—in the New Testament, the disciple Thomas refuses to believe that Jesus has risen from the grave until he sees the Lord with his own eyes. Likewise, Thomas

Anderson has a difficult time believing the Matrix is real. Once Thomas Anderson doubts no more (it only takes a couple of nasty encounters with Agent Smith and a few meals aboard the *Nebuchadnezzar*), he fully assumes his hacker appellation: Neo.

Dozer—his name recalls old-fashioned, analog machines.

Easter weekend—after being crucified on a Friday, Christ rose from the grave as he'd promised on the following Sunday, surprising Mary and other mourners. Christians celebrate this triumph over death on the Sunday following the fourteenth day of the paschal moon. With all the Christian mythology woven into *The Matrix*, it's no surprise that the film was first released on Easter weekend.

EMP (electromagnetic pulse)—the electrical charge used in defense against sentinels. The Wachowskis did their homework; it's completely feasible that the *Nebuchadnezzar* is equipped with such a weapon.

An electromagnetic pulse is activated when gamma rays collide with air molecules, sending a wide-spread pulse of intense voltage. Electromagnetic weapons are actually in development today; they could be used to wipe out planes, ships, or even destroy power generators, telephone systems, etc. (They're being touted as a kinder weapon of war for their ability to wreck a country's electric power infrastructure and defense units, and keep the casualty rate low.)

The United States first thought of manipulating the earth's electromagnetic field as a weapon when it discovered that high-altitude nuclear bomb detonation produces a far-reaching EMP.

It's logical that the *Nebuchadnezzar* could be equipped with a device much like the ones that countries are secretly developing today (in the 1970s, the Soviets tried to talk the United Nations into monitoring and policing the development of such weapons). Such a weapon could immediately render Squiddy ineffective.

Enlightenment—a state of spiritual or intellectual insight that some individuals seek. What this state actually consists of differs according to who you talk to. The thinkers of the eighteenth-century Enlightenment (like Rousseau and Voltaire) sought knowledge through reason; Buddhists seek Nirvana; Neo sought to discover the true nature of reality. (See Ford essay.)

Franklin and Erie—the scene of Cypher's betrayal, also a real-life intersection found in Chicago.

Gestapo crap—the heavy-handed manner in which the agents threaten Neo while he's in their custody. This encounter was one of a series of clues that informed Neo that the world was not what it seemed.

Green—this color was prominent in the scenes within the Matrix—the director of photography used green filters and carefully chosen types of film stock to get the green look in locations like Thomas Anderson's office. The actual code of the Matrix is green because it reminded the Wachowskis of the "phosphorous green of old PCs."[4] (See Blue.)

Hacker—a computer whiz with a mischievous streak. Hackers can crack codes, break into databases, and beef up their TiVos illegally. The rebels in *The Matrix* are all hackers; they understand the ins and outs of digital technology, which makes them good prospects for fighting within the Matrix.

Heart O' the City Motel—Agent Smith shoots Neo in the chest at this location, presumably damaging his heart.

Highway—an old airfield was turned into a highway on the Almeda set (located on the San Francisco Naval base). This location is rumored to be the site of the most exciting scenes in the coming sequels. Second unit director David Ellis told *Sci-fi Wire* that the car chase scenes are going to blow audiences away. He says, "You have seen some really good freeway chase sequences in your day, but you haven't seen one where guys are leaping from car to car and fighting as they leap and doing all the Matrix stuff in the middle of the car chase as well . . . and Trinity does some pretty amazing motorcycle riding."[5]

Home-grown human—they pride themselves on not being crops for the AI. Because they lack the hardware to plug in to the Matrix, they serve as operators for the rebels or populate Zion. Their existence signifies the resilience and hope of the human race outside of the Matrix.

---

4 www.8ung.at/michamarcus/matrix/inter.htm.

5 www.scifi.com/scifiwire/art-main.html?2002-05/28/14.00.film.

Hong Kong cinema—cinematic convention that finds its origins in Hong Kong. When kung fu first penetrated the Hollywood bubble, America loved it. The fighting action was like nothing they'd ever seen. The Wachowskis included kung fu action scenes in the film, punching them up a notch with bullet-time technology. Hugo Weaving, Keanu Reeves, Carrie-Anne Moss, and Laurence Fishburne all trained for months—it was the first time that regular actors trained to perform difficult kung fu action sequences themselves. (See Yuen Woo-Ping.)

Hotel Lafayette—Neo meets Morpheus here; it's their first encounter. In the script this location is described as "a place of putrefying elegance, a rotting host of maggotry." The rebels stuck to seedy, seldom-inhabited places like this to avoid detection by agents. Because of the low level of activity in these places, there was less "traffic" and they could keep a low profile. Like with a website that is seldom visited, it's harder to track the rebels when they're in areas like this. The agents can't find them here without a digital trace (or tips from Cypher).

"I'm Beginning to See the Light"—Duke Ellington song playing at the Oracle's home.

IRS d-base—Neo is surprised to find that Trinity, the one who hacked into the IRS database, is a woman. There are multiple references to "paying your taxes" as the prototypical Matrix activity. Is it a stretch to conclude that the Wachowskis are not fans of the IRS?

John the Baptist—this Biblical figure preceded the ministry of Christ; John the Baptist proclaimed the Messiah's coming all over Judah, paving the way for Jesus. Morpheus is the futuristic equivalent of this character. His faith in Neo sets into motion the first events of the film, and ultimately guides Neo to the discovery of his Matrix-bending abilities. (See Fontana essay.)

Juris-my-dick-tion—jurisdiction, which the human police seem to think they have. In reality, the AI has all the control and authority.

Labyrinth of cubicles—Thomas A. Anderson works in a matrix of corporate infrastructure. The company is a metaphor for the evil control of AI, the ultimate controlling "corporation."

Along with *The Matrix*, a slew of popular films have deconstructed the experience of working for "the man." *Office Space*, *American Beauty*, and *Fight Club* (among others) questioned the status quo of water-cooler culture. The idea that humans waste their lives sitting in front of screens, surrounded by the drab particle board of cubicles, led the characters in these films to rebel against conformity.

"Know Thyself"—inscription in Latin on a plaque in the Oracle's kitchen. (Inscribed in Greek at the Oracle at Delphi.)

Mark 3 No. 11—the ship's model number and info found on a plaque on the *Nebuchadnezzar*. In the King James version of the Bible: "And unclean spirits, when they saw him, fell down before him, and cried, saying, Thou art the Son of God." The *Nebuchadnezzar* itself seems to be proclaiming that Neo is The One. (See *Nebuchadnezzar*.)

Matrix—"the world that has been pulled over your eyes." (See Schuchardt essay.)

Messiah—a chosen one who comes to kick ass and deliver his people from evil. Christ was expected to come wielding a sword; his "love thy neighbor" approach and eventual martyrdom/resurrection contrasted deeply with God's warlike ways in the Old Testament. Neo's violent rescue of Morpheus is more in line with what Israelites expected from their messiah. (See Fontana essay.)

Meta CorTechs—software development company where Neo works. The Wachowskis escaped a lawsuit by adding the "meta" part to the name; CorTechs is the name of a real software company.

Metaphysics—philosophical speculation and exploration of questions unanswerable by science. Generally the study of metaphysics involves questioning the nature of reality.

Mindjob—Cypher employs this quaint colloquialism to describe his opinion of Neo's prophesied divine destiny.

Mirrored glasses—the agents and the rebels wear hip mirrored sunglasses while in the Matrix. There are several mirrors in *The Matrix*, reminding the audience that Neo has gone "through the looking glass," finding reality rather than Wonderland.

Morpheus—he's John the Baptist, the white rabbit who leads Neo into the antithesis of Wonderland. Morpheus is the god of dreams in Ovid's epic *Metamorphosis*. To morph is to transform something, of which Morpheus does plenty (be it opening Potentials' minds to the truth, to manipulating the Matrix to the best of his ability).

Mr. Reagan—Cypher asks to be someone important, "like an actor," when he returns to the Matrix—this is fitting, as his last name in that world is Reagan.

Nebuchadnezzar—the aging ship that carries a ragtag team of rebels through the bowels of the earth.

The historical king Nebuchadnezzar II reportedly built the hanging gardens of Babylon (one of the Seven Wonders of the World). He also looted and burned the original Jewish temple in Jerusalem. King Nebuchadnezzar is most important in the Bible for his dreams; the prophet Daniel interpreted dreams the king couldn't even remember! These dream interpretations led to a series of prophecies proclaiming the coming of the messiah.

The ship's name is appropriate indeed, as Morpheus has dedicated himself to searching for the Messiah.

Neo—an anagram for "one," a prefix meaning "new," and Thomas A. Anderson's cybername that he adopts permanently after discovering that he actually is The One.

Neuromancer—William K. Gibson's cyberpunk novel that featured the word "matrix" to signify a complex computer network. Many have speculated that *The Matrix* revived the cyperpunk genre.

Night of the Lepus—the horror film showing on the Oracle's TV waiting room. It features white rabbits.

The One—the prophesied savior of mankind.

The Oracle—a sweet old granny-type, the Oracle has a penchant for baking cookies and prophesying the future. Gloria Foster, the actress who played the Oracle, passed away after shooting most of the scenes for *Matrix Reloaded*. The Wachowski brothers had to do a series of hurried rewrites on the script for *Matrix Revolutions* as a result of her death, and speculation is running wild about the appearance of the Oracle in the final film of the trilogy. What form will the Oracle take?

Perfect human world—the first failed Matrix. The machines created a perfect harmonious world, but as Agent Smith said, "entire crops were lost." The problem is that humans cannot conceive of a world without suffering. (See Suffering.)

Rabbit hole—another reference to *Alice in Wonderland*.

Red pill—take this and be plunged into the depths of shocking reality. (See Lloyd essay.)

Reloaded—the Wachowskis and their production team have promised that the first sequel to *The Matrix* would feature effects that will blow the mind, never to be duplicated or topped by any other film (except perhaps *Matrix Revolutions*).

Residual self-image—the mental projection of your electronic self. Whenever someone is jacked into the Matrix or a training video, they see themselves without the plugs and wiring that hook them into the hardware. Their senses tell them that what they're experiencing is real, though they may know that it's just highly advanced virtual reality.

Resurrection—the bedrock of Christian belief, Jesus' resurrection demonstrates that he is the prophesied messiah. Likewise, Neo's resurrection is required for him to become the prophesied "One."

Rhineheart—the "ultimate company man" (as he's described in the shooting script), Neo's boss who lectures Neo on the finer points of conformity.

Sentient programs—they "can move in and out of software still wired to their system"—anyone who hasn't been unplugged is a potential agent. Morpheus illustrates this point effectively during the training program featuring the woman in red, who unexpectedly morphs into Agent Smith.

Sentinel—"Squiddies" are mechanical creatures, the primary threat to humans not hooked into the Matrix. They can only be defeated by an EMP.

Spoon boy—a very Buddhist-looking young boy who practices bending the Matrix with other children in the Oracle's living room. He states that "there is no spoon . . . it is not the spoon that bends. It is yourself."

This is a reflection of the Zen Koan:

Two monks were arguing about the temple flag waving in the wind. One said "the flag moves." The other said "the wind moves." They argued back and forth and could not agree. Hui-neng, the sixth Patriarch, said: "Gentlemen! It is not the flag that moves. It is not the wind that moves. It is your mind that moves." The two monks were struck with awe.

State and Balbo—location of the subway showdown between Neo and Agent Smith. (Also the location of a Chicago subway station.)

Steak dinner—the 2199 version of thirty pieces of silver.

Storyboards—were very important to the final look of the film. This tool is usually used as a form of communication between the director and director of photography—the director's vision is recorded in comic-book-like panels to show the director of photography how to frame each shot.

The Wachowskis commissioned Steve Skroce and Tani Kunitake to draw up the storyboards after studio execs had difficulty visualizing and understanding the screenplay. Pieces of art in and of themselves, they were used as a point of reference constantly during the shooting of *The Matrix*.

Stunt wire—sure it looks like fun, but the actors had to train very hard to do their wire work. The cause of many injuries and bruises, the wire work helped contribute to the unique look of the film. Carrie-Anne Moss broke her leg while shooting the sequels (she also twisted her ankle while shooting the government-building fight scene where she cartwheels across the wall). Keanu Reeves trained for the first film with a neck injury; they all sustained minor injuries during the course of training.

Stylized violence—with the proximity of the release of the film to the Columbine school shootings, *The Matrix* (along with other films and video games) came under fire. The violent nature of the film proved to be problematic for some, though most were still able to appreciate the very particular, unique look the fight and action scenes lent the film. It's tough to defeat evil without anyone getting hurt.

Suffering—another problematic subject addressed in the film. The humans couldn't believe the perfect world the AI first constructed for them, because they could not understand an existence without suffering.

Many philosophers (especially Christians like Kierkegaard and Buber) grappled with this idea in quite the opposite way— how can one conceive of a just God, given human suffering? These thinkers struggled to understand an existence (the one they were experiencing) that included suffering. *The Matrix* posits the suffering as an integral part of human nature.

Switch—one of the rebels. Computers are, conceptually, a set of "switches" alternating between 0 and 1.

Sydney, Australia—*The Matrix* was filmed on location here rather than in Hollywood to save money. Though the Wachowski brothers were given much more money to make the sequels, they chose to go ahead and film the bulk of them in Australia where they had already formed relationships with talented crew members.

Tank—like Dozer, a down-to-earth piece of analog equipment. Played by Marcus Chong, Tank will not appear in the sequels; there were some problems with the contract negotiation.

Tastee Wheat—a comical example of the increasingly complex issues one encounters when dissecting *The Matrix*. When liberated humans reminisce about the food they had in the Matrix, they're not sure that they actually know what it tasted like. They only know what the machines constructed it to taste like. As Mouse says, what if they got it wrong? This is true of most of their memories of that virtual reality. They have no idea what 1999 was really like; they must trust that the machines got it right. This is a simple illustration of Baudrillard's simulacra—what they remember "eating" (Tastee Wheat) could be a copy with no original. (See Lloyd essay.)

Trinity—an androgynous Mary Magdalene, she's the spiritual and faithful member of the group.

The word "trinity" is not actually found in the Bible; it's a word Christians use to describe the three-in-one nature of the Godhead: God, Jesus, and the Holy Spirit. However, it does carry a strong Christian connotation.

Truth—not something to be discerned by the senses. If this is the case, how does Neo know that the hellish world he experiences outside of the Matrix isn't yet another Matrix? If one cannot rely on the senses, how can you *know* anything?

Unplug—disconnect from the Matrix.

Viable exit—a way out of the Matrix.

Virgin birth—in a sense, Neo is the product of a virgin birth, though his mother is a machine rather than a saint.

Virus—Agent Smith likens the human race not to other mammals but to a virus; the organisms multiply and use up resources until they're forced to move on to destroy something else.

Wells and Lake—the intersection Trinity flees to after Cypher discloses her other exit. The Wells and Lake represents salvation from the present danger; the watery names of the streets suggest a baptism of sorts. (Baptism is a ritual performed by many Christians to assure their salvation from sin.)

White rabbit—the mischievous rodent who got Alice into all that trouble.

Yuen Woo-Ping—helped shape the careers of Jackie Chan and Jet Li; he trained the actors and designed the choreography for the fight scenes in *The Matrix*.

Zion—a heavenly city, promised by God to the Israelites. A place of harmony and great beauty, located on the top of a hill in Jerusalem. Zion in *The Matrix* provides quite the contrast. Located near the center of the earth, "where it's still warm," this last human city does contain as much hope as the Biblical one. We get to see it in *Reloaded*.

Zion Mainframe—Agent Smith wants the codes so they can hack it, discover the rebellion's secrets, and then crush the rebels.

CONTRIBUTORS

Peter J. Boettke is an economics professor at George Mason University and the author of several books on the history, collapse, and transition from socialism in the former Soviet Union. His most recent books are *Calculation and Coordination* (Routledge, London, 2001) and *The Economic Way of Thinking* (Prentice Hall, 2002). Before joining the faculty at GMU, Boettke taught at New York University and was a National Fellow at the Hoover Institution on War, Revolution and Peace at Stanford University. Boettke earned his Ph.D. at George Mason University and his B.A. at Grove City College.

Dr. Nick Bostrom is a philosopher at Yale University. He founded the World Transhumanist Association in 1998 (with David Pearce) and is a frequent spokesperson and commentator in the media. Bostrom's research interests are in philosophy of science, probability theory, and the ethical and strategic implications of anticipated technologies (including AI, nanotech, genetics, etc.). He has a background in cosmology, computational neuroscience, mathematical logic, philosophy, artificial intelligence, and stand-up comedy, and is the author of the book *Anthropic Bias: Observation Selection Effects in Science and Philosophy* (Routledge, New York, 2002).

Dino Felluga is an English professor at Purdue University, West Lafayette. His first book, *The Perversity of Poetry: Romantic Ideology and the Popular Male Poet of Genius* is forthcoming from SUNY Press. He is currently working on expanding a website (with accompanying book) that introduces critical theory to students and scholars by way of popular culture: *www.purdue.edu/guidetotheory*.

Paul Fontana graduated from Colby College in 1996 with honors in philosophy. This essay was written while he was studying the New Testament at Harvard Divinity School. He currently lives in New York City.

James L. Ford is a professor of East Asian religions in the department of religion at Wake Forest University, North Carolina. He earned an M.A. in 1996 and Ph.D. in 1998 in East Asian religions from Princeton University. Dr. Ford's primary research centers on medieval Japanese Buddhism and he recently completed a manuscript titled *Boundless Devotion: Jokei (1155–1213) and the Discourse of Kamakura Buddhism*. At present, he is executive secretary for the

Society for the Study of Japanese Religion and serves on the steering committee for the Japanese Religions Group of the American Academy of Religion.

Andrew Gordon is an English professor and director of the Institute for the Psychological Study of the Arts (IPSA) at the University of Florida. He has been a Fulbright lecturer in American literature in Spain, Portugal, and Serbia, and a visiting professor in Hungary and Russia. He teaches contemporary American fiction, Jewish-American fiction, and science-fiction literature and film. His publications include *An American Dreamer: A Psychoanalytic Study of the Fiction of Norman Mailer*; *Psychoanalyses/Feminisms* (coedited with Peter L. Rudnytsky); and *Screen Saviors: Hollywood Fictions of Whiteness* (coauthored with Hernan Vera; the book discusses many films, including the science fiction or fantasy films *Raiders of the Lost Ark*, *Men in Black*, and *The Matrix*). He has written numerous essays on science fiction and science-fiction film, including the films of George Lucas, Steven Spielberg, and Robert Zemeckis, in *Science-Fiction Studies* and other journals.

James Gunn is both a writer and a teacher of science fiction. His first story was published in 1949; since then he has published 99 stories and 38 books, including *The Joy Makers*, *The Listeners*, *Kampus*, *The Dreamers*, and *The Immortals*, which became a 1969 TV film *The Immortal* and a 1970–71 TV series. He taught for forty years at the University of Kansas, where he still teaches a summer course in science fiction as emeritus professor of English. He has served as president of the Science Fiction Writers of America and of the Science Fiction Research Association, and has won the Hugo Award, the Pilgrim Award, and the Eaton Award. Among his academic books are *Alternate Worlds: The Illustrated History of Science Fiction*; *Isaac Asimov: The Foundations of Science Fiction*; *The Science of Science-Fiction Writing*; and the six-volume historical anthology *The Road to Science Fiction*.

Robin Hanson is a professor of economics at George Mason University. In 1998 Robin received his Ph.D. in social science from the California Institute of Technology, and then served as a Robert Wood Johnson Foundation health policy scholar at the University of California at Berkeley. Earlier he received a master's in physics and a master's in the philosophy of science from the University of Chicago, and spent nine years researching artificial intelligence, Bayesian statistics, and hypertext publishing at Lockheed, NASA, and independently. Robin's work has appeared in several publications, including *CATO Journal*, *International Joint Conference on Artificial Intelligence*, *Journal of Evolution and Technology*, *Social Philosophy and Policy*, and *Theory and Decision*.

Bill Joy is a co-founder, Chief Scientist and Corporate Executive Officer of Sun Microsystems and has played a critical role in the development of a number of critical technologies, including Jini and Java. In 1997 he was appointed Co-Chairman of the Presidential Information Technology Advisory Committee. His many contributions were recognized by a cover story in *Fortune Magazine*, which called him the "Edison of the Internet."

Ray Kurzweil, inventor and technologist. Mr. Kurzweil created the first reading machine for the blind and is responsible for many other technology firsts. He has founded and built nine highly successful technology companies and is the best-selling author of *The Age of Spiritual Machines* (Viking, 1999). Mr. Kurzweil has received eleven honorary doctorates and numerous awards, including the 1999 National Medal of Technology, the nation's highest honor in technology, and the $500,000 MIT-Lemelson Prize for Invention and Innovation.

Peter B. Lloyd graduated in mathematics at Cardiff University, Wales, where he stayed on to carry out research in solar engineering. He later worked as a software developer in the ISIS medical research group in the University of Oxford, where he expanded his interest in philosophy by studying under Dr. Michael Lockwood at the Oxford University department for external studies. Since 1994 he has worked as a freelance software developer. He has maintained an active presence in the *Journal of Consciousness Studies Online*, and has self-published two books on the nature of consciousness. He lives in London, England, with his wife, Deborah Marshall-Warren, a leading figure in hypnotherapy.

Robert Sawyer, called "just about the best science fiction writer out there" by *The Denver Rocky Mountain News* and the leader of sci-fi's next-generation pack by Barnes and Noble, frequently writes science fiction about artificial intelligence, most notably in his Aurora Award-winning novel *Golden Fleece* (named the best sci-fi novel of the year by critic Orson Scott Card in *The Magazine of Fantasy & Science Fiction*); *The Terminal Experiment* (winner of the Science Fiction and Fantasy Writers of America's Nebula Award for Best Novel of the Year); the Hugo Award–nominated *Factoring Humanity*; the Hugo Award–nominated *Calculating God* (which hit #1 on the best-seller list published by *Locus*, the trade journal of the sci-fi field); and his just-released thirteenth novel, *Hominids*, which deals with the quantum-mechanical origin of consciousness. According to Reuters, he was the first sci-fi author to have a website; for more information on Rob and his work, visit that extensive site at *www.sfwriter.com*.

Read Mercer Schuchardt is a professor of media studies at Marymount Manhattan College in New York City. He is the contributing editor on media and culture for *Regeneration Quarterly* magazine, founder of CLEAVE: The Counter Agency (*www.cleave.com*) and the publisher of *Metaphilm* (*www.metaphilm.com*), a film interpretation website. In 2003, Spence Publishing will release his first two books, *Metaphilm: Seers of the Silver Screen* and *The Disappearance of Women: Technology, Pornography, and the Obsolescence of Gender*. He and his wife home-school their five children in Jersey City, New Jersey. He can be reached at read@cleave.com.

Lyle Zynda received his Ph.D. in philosophy from Princeton University in 1995. After spending a year teaching at Caltech, he took up his current position in the philosophy department at Indiana University South Bend (IUSB), where he is now associate professor. Dr. Zynda specializes in philosophy of science, philosophy of mind, cognitive science, epistemology, metaphysics, and logic. He has published articles in internationally renowned journals such as *Synthese*, *Philosophy of Science*, and *Philosophical Studies*. He also periodically teaches a course at IUSB called "Philosophy, Science, and Science Fiction."

---

www.summersdale.com